Hungarian National Gallery

The Collections

GUIDE

Hungarian National Gallery

The Collections

GUIDE

VINCE BOOKS

Editors:
Nóra Veszprémi (HNG)
Ferenc Gosztonyi

Responsible editor:
Szilvia Cseh (Vince Books)

Authors:

É. B.	Éva Bajkay	Á. M.	Árpád Mikó
E. B.	Enikő Buzási	E. P.	Edit Plesznivy
G. B.	Gábor Bellák	E. R.	Enikő Róka
K. B.	Katalin Bakos	G. Sz.	Gizella Szatmári
Zs. B.	Zsuzsanna Bakó	Gy. Sz.	György Szücs
Zs. Bo.	Zsuzsanna Boda	J. Sz.	Judit Szeifert
I. D.	István Dévényi	L. Sz.	László Százados
G. E.	Gábor Endrődi	A. Sz. M.	Anna Szinyei Merse
M. G.	Mariann Gergely	G. T.	Gábor Tokai
O. H.	Orsolya Hessky	Gy. T.	Gyöngyi Török
A. J.	Anna Jávor	S. T.	Sándor Tóth
Zs. J.	Zsuzsa Jobbágyi	A. Z.	András Zwickl
A. K.	Anna Kopócsy	F. Zs.	Ferenc Zsákovics
M. K.	Marianna Kolozsváry		

Photo credits:
Zsuzsa Berényi
Zsuzsa Bokor
Tibor Mester

www.vincekiado.hu
The Publishing House is a member of the Association
of Hungarian Book Publishers and Book Distributors founded in 1795.
The director of the Vince Books is responsible for the publication.

Designer: Judit Kállói

Magyar Nemzeti
Galéria

The reproductions were made available by courtesy
of the Hungarian National Gallery.

ISBN 978-963-9731-30-1

Contents

The Architectural History of Buda Castle **7**

History of the Museum **9**

Old Hungarian Collection **11**

Collection of 19th–20th-century Art **55**

Contemporary Collection **169**

Index of Artists' Names **219**

Further Reading **221**

hold. The reconstruction of the buildings damaged during the events of the War of Liberation in 1848/49 was completed in 1856. Extensions implying major reconstructions inside and outside so as to create a royal residence again began after the Compromise with Austria and the coronation of Francis Joseph as king of Hungary (1867). Miklós Ybl planned a new row of buildings looking westward (building F, today the National Széchényi Library). Construction work interrupted by Ybl's death was resumed by Alajos Hauszmann in 1893. He attached a new wing (B) to building C from the north to echo building D. This is joined by building A from the north.

Hauszmann's intention was to unite the series of buildings by a unifying system of roof design. Emphasis was laid on the Danube front of the middle section of the building and the two-storey tall Habsburg Room behind it by the employment of a modest central projection and a dome. In front, a two-armed staircase was built. The facades were adorned with figural groups, symbolic figures and vases. On the court front, he opened an arcade (building D). He designed a "new festive room" (also known as the "great dance hall" or "ball room"), which now houses a section of the 19th-century permanent exhibition. Attached to it on the Danube side is a longitudinal room, the so-called "buffet hall" (where Mihály Munkácsy's and László Paál's paintings are on display today). The extensions by Hauszmann were finished in 1905.

The reliefs and statues that can still be seen on the buildings were added in this period. The pillar on the Danube side of the enclosure at Szent György square supports the Hungarian mythic bird, the saker ("turul") by Gyula Donáth (made in 1903, erected in 1905). In front of the eastern facade of building A, Károly Senyei's fountain statue Children Fishing can be seen (1912). The monument of Eugene of Savoy by József Róna (1900) was originally made for the town of Zenta. Miklós Ligeti's two statues—Csongor and Tünde, characters from a play by the 19th-century romantic poet Mihály Vörösmarty—originally adorning the landing of the Habsburg Staircase now flank the main entrance to the Gallery (building C) placed on separate pedestals. Attached to the northern exterior of the one-time St Sigismund Chapel, Alajos Stróbl's Matthias fountain (1904) conjures up the halcyon days of the palace. The statue entitled Horseherd (or Horse Tamer) by György Vastagh the younger, which is now in front of building B, used to stand outside the southern facade of the riding-hall between 1899 and 1901. The titular statues of the Lion Court were carved by János Fadrusz in 1901–1902. The gate at the south end of this courtyard, the so-called Telegraph Gate leading into the Budapest History Museum is flanked by the sculptural compositions of War and Peace by Károly Senyei (1900).

The royal palace, which gradually became the centre of administration in the early decades of the 20th century, suffered extremely heavy damage during World War II: it was gutted by fire. Restoration began in 1950–1951. In 1975 the Hungarian National Gallery opened its first exhibition in its new home, buildings B, C and D of the Royal Palace rebuilt for exhibiting purposes.

GIZELLA SZATMÁRI

History of the Museum

The Hungarian National Gallery is the largest public museum documenting and presenting the process of the emergence and development of fine arts in Hungary. It has been an autonomous institution since 1957. It moved to its present home, the Royal Palace of Buda, in 1975.

1957 A new museum is founded with the name Hungarian National Gallery to collect and present Hungarian art. The core of its collections is the New Hungarian Picture Gallery of the Museum of Fine Arts, as well as its modern Hungarian sculptures, medals, prints and drawings. At that time, the collection includes some 6000 paintings, 2100 sculptures, 3100 medals, 11,000 drawings and 5000 prints. The Hungarian National Gallery opens in the former Palace of Justice in Kossuth Square (today Museum of Ethnography) on October 5, 1957.

1959 A government resolution names the former Royal Palace of Buda as the new home of the museum.

1975 The Hungarian National Gallery moves to buildings B, C and D of the Royal Palace converted for this end. In October, its exhibitions open temporarily. Its stock is enriched with the collection of the Old Hungarian Department of the Museum of Fine Arts, which now allows the presentation of the entire history of art in Hungary from the 11th century to our day.

1979 The permanent exhibitions of medieval panel painting and wood carving, as well as baroque art are opened.

1982 In the former throne-room of the royal palace, the permanent exhibition of late Gothic altarpieces is opened.

1985 The exhibition of medieval and renaissance stone carvings opens.

1989 The crypt of the Habsburg palatines is opened to the public on the ground floor of building C of the museum.

2005 The exhibiting space of the Hungarian National Gallery is enlarged with building A of the Royal Palace.

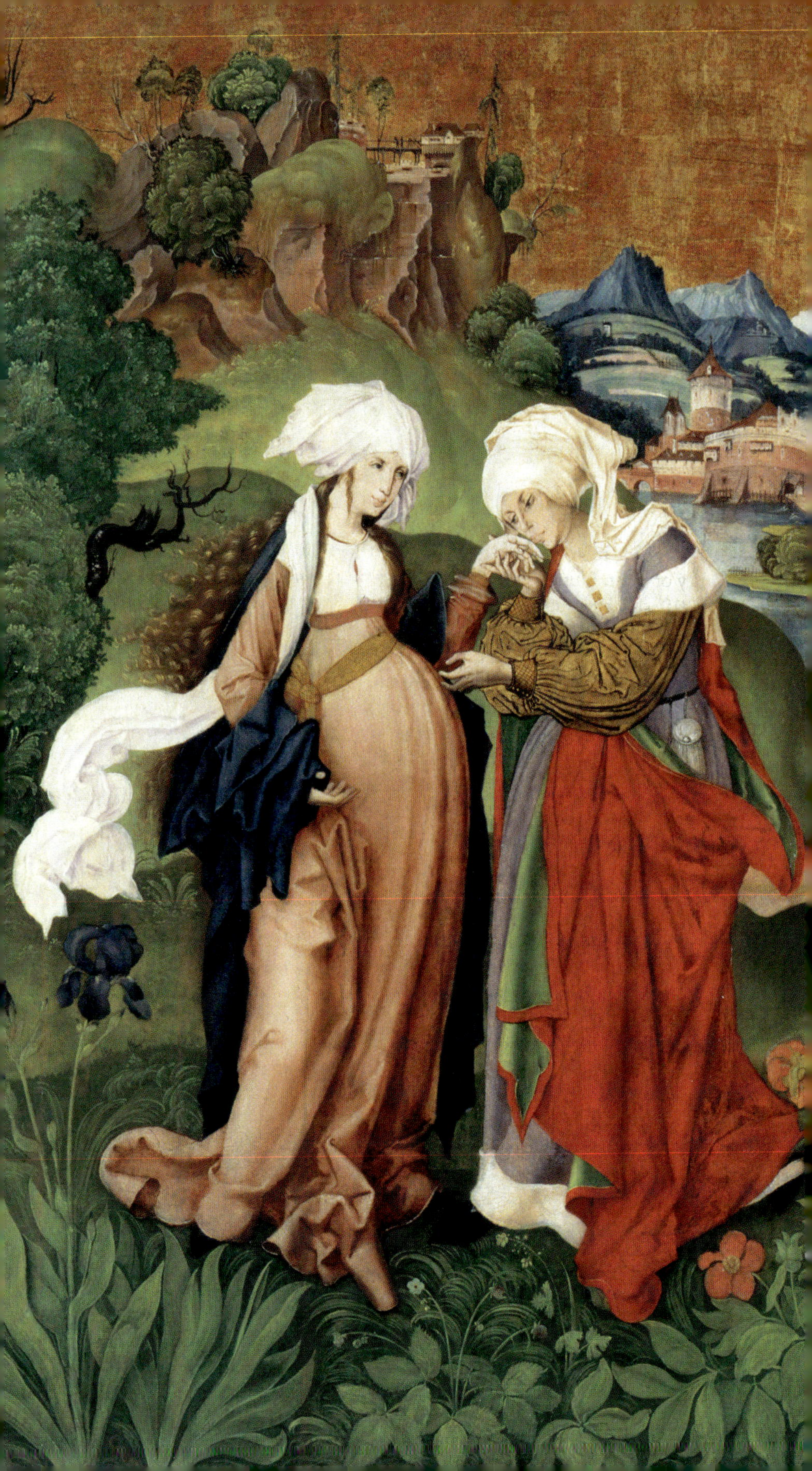

Old Hungarian Collection

The Old Hungarian Collection gathers and exhibits paintings, sculptures, their ensembles, high-quality architectural carvings and tombstones created in Hungary or upon Hungarian commission between the 11th century and 1800–1810, complemented with works created by Hungarian artists abroad. Thus, it interprets the concept of "old Hungarian art" broadly; its history precedes that of the Hungarian National Gallery.

Collecting remains of old Hungarian art began in three national museums: first—in the first half of the 19th century—in the National Museum, later (after 1872) in the Museum of Applied Arts and finally in the Museum of Fine Arts established in 1894. The legendary director of the latter, Elek Petrovics decided to gather the "old Hungarian" material scattered in the three museums at a single place: the Museum of Fine Arts. This took place in the 1930s when nearly every museum underwent some degree of profile purification. However, neither the scientific elaboration nor the exhibition of the collected paintings and sculptures were carried out until the outbreak of World War II.

Most of the artworks were not in exhibitable condition after the war, as many suffered serious damage. In the two rooms to the left of the vestibule modest selections were put on display from time to time. Although the old stock was brought together in a separate department after the war and the director of this collection, Dénes Radocsay published the entire medieval material, the paintings and sculptures were still locked away from the public.

The Old Hungarian Collection was officially included in the stock of the Hungarian National Gallery from the latter's foundation in 1957, but the actual transfer did not take place before the Gallery moved to its new home in the Royal Palace in Buda Castle (1975). Prior to the move, the most important medieval and baroque pieces were put on display in the Palace of Justice in Kossuth Square (the first home of the National Gallery), but its first real exhibition as an independent collection was in the palace, with the high altar of the Virgin from Csíkmenaság under the dome in the middle. This served to demonstrate that, in its new building, the National Gallery was indeed able to present the whole of art in Hungary from the foundation of the state to our day.

After hiding for many decades, the Old Hungarian Collection could at last become public treasure here in the former royal palace. Under the leadership of Miklós Mojzer, a populous department of art historians and restorers teamed up to open one permanent exhibition after the other (on several thousand square meters) after thorough research and restoration work. The first to open was the exhibition of late renaissance and baroque art, followed by the Gothic sculptures and panel pictures. In 1982 the largest collection of winged altarpieces in Central Europe was opened to the public in the former throne room, and in 1985 the medieval and renaissance lapidary was also completed.

For the sake of completeness and authenticity, the Old Hungarian Collection borrows works from other Hungarian museums, church collections and private collectors to complement its basic stock on permanent display. From time to time it stages major exhibitions which are important events in medieval, renaissance and baroque research in Hungary. Since the pre-1800 artistic relations were extremely ramifying, the material of the permanent exhibitions reflects not only painting and sculpture in historical Hungary but also—at least referentially—in entire Central Europe.

Árpád Mikó

Fragment of a tombstone from Aracs

Around 1100

Greyish limestone, 22.5 × 53 × 60 cm

Inv. no.: 55.1014

The stone was excavated next to the ruinous church of Aracs (today Arača, Serbia) in 1896. It has four sides carved in relief (all incomplete), the largest of which is joined at right angles by the other three appearing as a strip. The middle one shows a church with a tower, nave and chancel, on the laterals there are interlaced motifs, to the right framed squares and in these a bird and a saddled horse, to the left a framed double row of circles. The situation of the church and the animals suggests that the larger side was an upper, more or less horizontal surface. In the larger part of its fragment, separated by plaitwork, there is a half-length figure of a priest with a stole closer to the side adorned with the circles, his head towards the church, his bent right arm lifted in blessing, his left holding some object in front of his chest. Beside the figure runs a Latin inscription calling for prayer which can be read from the direction of the circles. Beyond the plait-work, in a more deeply hollowed broken-off field, some vestiges of two heads and a part of another inscription cursing any-one who removes the stone can be seen. The surface slightly tapers away from the end with the church, as appropriate for a gravestone. (Further see Tóth, S.: Az aracsi kő rokonsága [The Relations of the Stone from Aracs]. In: A középkori Dél-Alföld és Szer [The Medieval Southern Lowlands and Szer]. Ed. Kollár, T. Szeged, 2000. 429–447.)

S. T.

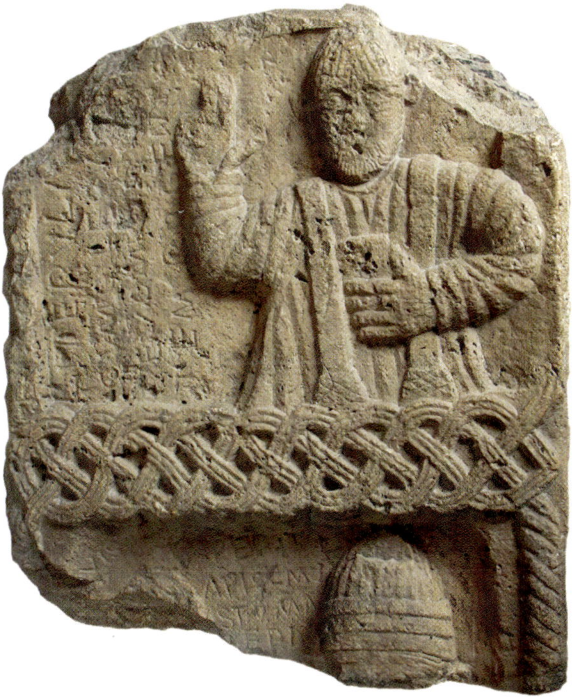

"Abraham and the Three Angels" from Óbuda

Around 1100–1150

Greyish limestone, 79 × 92 × 28.5 cm

Inv. no.: 55.1600

The carving was in the National Museum around 1865. Later Kalocsa was named as its provenance. However, its Óbuda origin is proven by fragments of the same style found there, as well as by several other finds in Buda. This whole group of carvings is associated with the scarcely known first church of the one-time Óbuda provosty. The face of the stone is carved in relief. Its right side is broken, elsewhere it is bordered by planes of jointing, the back is rough. The main part of the relief showed human and angelic figures in a shallow niche bounded by a pair of columns and a flat arch in a rectangular field. On the left there is a part of a vertical field with a bird and two monsters enmeshed in tendrils. Above the surviving column and arch-segment birds sitting on a tree are shown in flatter relief. The column has an Attic base and a composite capital. In the niche two figures with damaged heads and a few fragments of a third figure survived. At the side a hurriedly arriving man and next to him, frontally, a winged figure can be seen. Above his left shoulder a fragment of a wing, in front of his chest a right hand pointing at the arriving figure allude to the next figure. (Further see Levárdy, F.: Abraham et les trois anges. L'iconographie du relief de "Kalocsa". Bulletin du Musée Hongrois des Beaux-Arts, No. 32–33. Budapest, 1968. 31–43.)

S. T.

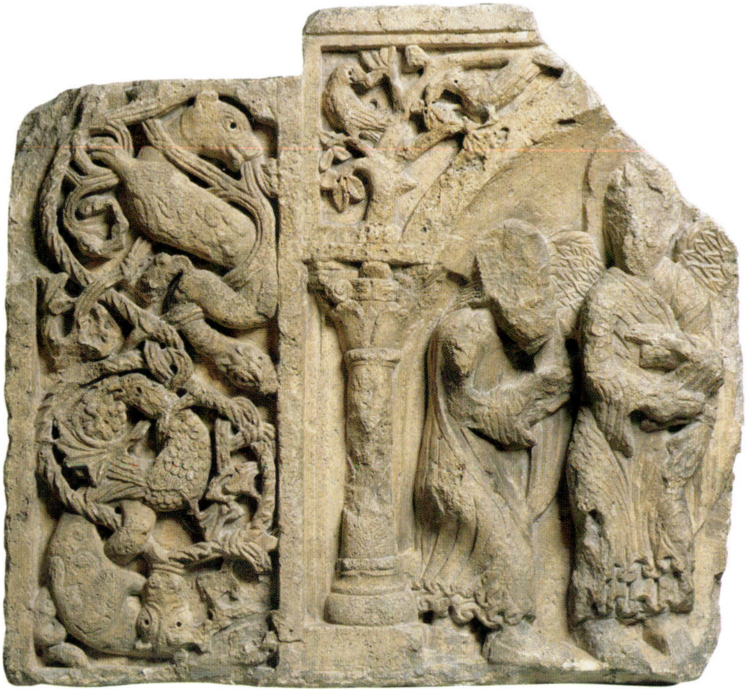

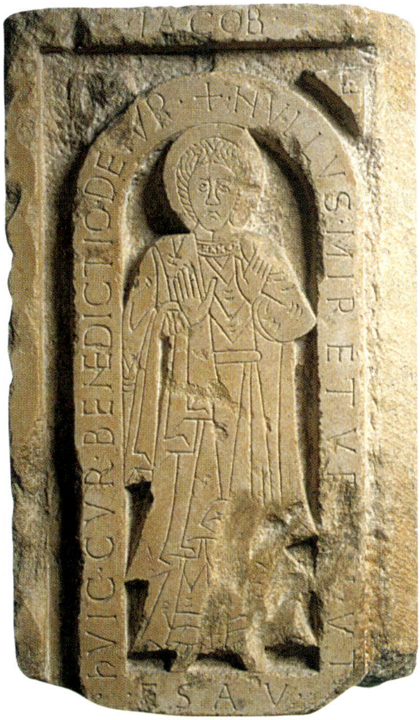

Jacob-stone from Pécs

Around 1170–1190

Yellowish marble, 83.5 × 51.5 × 12 cm

Inv. no.: 55.975

It was unearthed in the episcopal castle in Pécs around 1773. The bottom is broken, the back is worn. On top there is a jointing plane. The two lateral sides and the front are polished. Front right there is a chamfering done later. On the remaining front hollowings of rough ground outline in the polished plane a human figure standing in a semicircular closed frame, a thin border and to the right a spandrel field. Its counterpart is only a slight bulge in the hollowing. Some recessing had adjoined the bottom of the frame carved here and there. The hollowed parts were obviously inlaid with materials of different colours. Below right longtime friction damaged the polished surface. Fine incised lines make up the inner drawing of the figure and—on the frame and the upper border—the letters of an inscription. Above and below the names IACOB and ESAV can be read, the rest says: no one should wonder why this one received the blessing. It alludes to the story of Isaac's sons (1Mos 27,1–29). The surviving figure must be Jacob. Below him probably Esau was shown, and there might have been a figure of Isaac giving blessing on another slab. The stone was probably a facing element for a pillar, maybe for the jamb of a portal. (Further see Pannonia Regia. Művészet a Dunántúlon 1000–1541 [Pannonia Regia. Art in Transdanubia 1000–1541]. Eds. Mikó, Á. – Takács, I. Budapest, 1994. 145–147.: Cat. No. I–74. [Tóth, M.])

S. T.

Head of a King from Kalocsa

Around 1200–1230

Red marble, 17 × 13.5 × 12 cm

Inv. no.: 53.364

The stone came to the National Museum in 1873. Tibor Gerevich thought it was part of "a figure standing on the main portal," perhaps representing King Saint Stephen. (Magyarország románkori emlékei [Romanesque Monuments of Hungary]. Budapest, 1938. 178.) The head, wearing a band crown with crosses, is carved in the round. There are breaks below and on the top. The flat elongated face is framed by a beard marked off sharply from the cheeks. The nose is long, slightly curved and pointed. Under it there is a drooping moustache cut straight above the mouth. The surface is polished in front, but not beyond the line of the great, hardly modelled ears carved only roughly at the back. Behind them the hair cut straight is suggested by coarse vertical grooves, but farthest back these are missing. Only the front arms of its lateral crosses are elaborated and backwards only the lower edge of the band is shown. The roundness of the top of the head is suggested only in front. Below the upper break some kind of rim can be made out. Above the front cross the vestige of a vertical plane is visible. All this suggests that it was an undercarved portion of a relief, as Jolán Balogh opined, who saw in it the head of Christ. (A régi magyar és európai művészet kincsei [Treasures of Old Hungarian and European Art]. Budapest, 2000. 5–6.)

S. T.

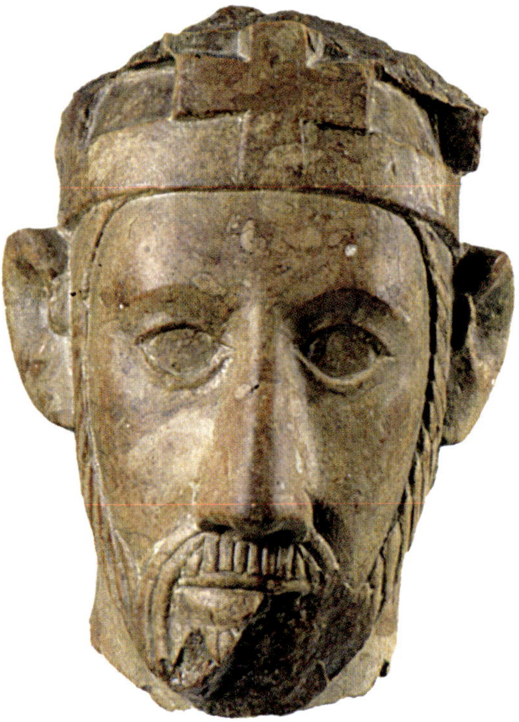

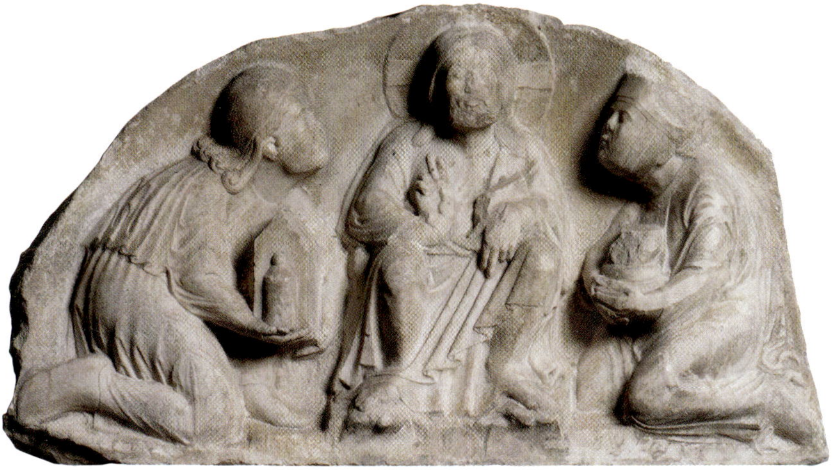

Tympanum from Szentkirály

Around 1230

White marble, 67 × 120 × 25 cm

Inv. no.: 55.976

The relief was once secondary set above the door of the church of the village Szentkirály, annexed later to Szombathely. Removed around 1875, it came from there in 1919 to the Museum of Fine Arts in Budapest. It was made using a Roman carving which is denoted by two plane sections disrupting the arched surface. The ground is concave and scabrous. The figures project massively compared to the edges. In the middle, Christ is sitting in Majesty with a halo bearing a cross on scabrous ground. He is flanked by the—larger—donors turned towards him. The man, on his right knee, holds the model of a church with an apse, the woman, on both knees, perhaps that of a baptismal font. Christ is sitting stooped, his lower arms resting on his thighs, his bare feet supported by a stool with the edge protruding like leaves. His throne is only suggested by a slight bulge under his right elbow. His strangely held right hand makes a blessing gesture, his left, lowered in his lap, holds a book. The faces are broad. Christ's face is damaged in the middle, but his thin moustache and short beard can be made out. His thick hair, parted in the middle and combed flat, falls over his shoulders. The man's long wavy hair with curls at the end falls from under a round cap. The woman's hair is covered by a hat tied under the chin. Both are wearing shoes. The cap and some details of the woman's attire have a scabrous surface. (Further see: Pannonia Regia. Művészet a Dunántúlon 1000–1541 [Pannonia Regia. Art in Transdanubia 1000–1541]. Eds. Mikó, Á. – Takács, I. Budapest, 1994. 183–185.: Cat. No. I–103. [Takács, I.])

S. T.

The First Virgin and Child from Toporc

1340–1350

Lime-wood, with traces of paint, 115.5 cm

Inv. no.: 55.900

The so-called First Madonna from Toporc (today Toporec, Slovakia) has salient importance among the few surviving relics of 14th-century Hungarian wood carving. It was made in the Szepes (Spiš) region. Its stocky figure, kind smile and slightly curving "S" line are reminiscent of the earlier stone Virgins of French cathedrals. The stone Virgin of Fontenay abbey might have been the model of several Austrian Madonnas similar to ours. A stone statue of the Virgin in the Salesian monastery in Vienna dating from the 1320s–1330s closely resembles the statue in the Gallery. The master of the First Toporc Virgin developed an individual variant which greatly influenced sculpture in the Szepes region and neighbouring Little Poland. This is confirmed not only by the Madonna from Ruszkin (Ruskinovce) and the third Virgin from Újszandec (Nowy Sącz, Poland), but also by a whole series of more remotely linked examples. In all of them one finds the main characteristics of the Madonna with Child now in Budapest: the blissful facial expression, the slightly curving S-line of the figures emphasized by the main weight of the body being carried by the left leg, the folds of the garment following the curve of the right leg and the slight inclination of the head to the right. The most remarkable features of the carving are, however the deep and heavy horizontal folds of the drapery of the robe held by the right arm, which are in striking contrast with the lightness of the frilled veil falling over the Virgin's shoulders. The vertical line of the cloak hanging from her right shoulder gives the figure a block-like, closed form. Although this is missing from the French models, it can be seen on the Salesian Madonna in Vienna. The Infant Jesus is shown wearing a long tunic as was traditional in the previous century. The infant was generally not represented naked before the 15th century.

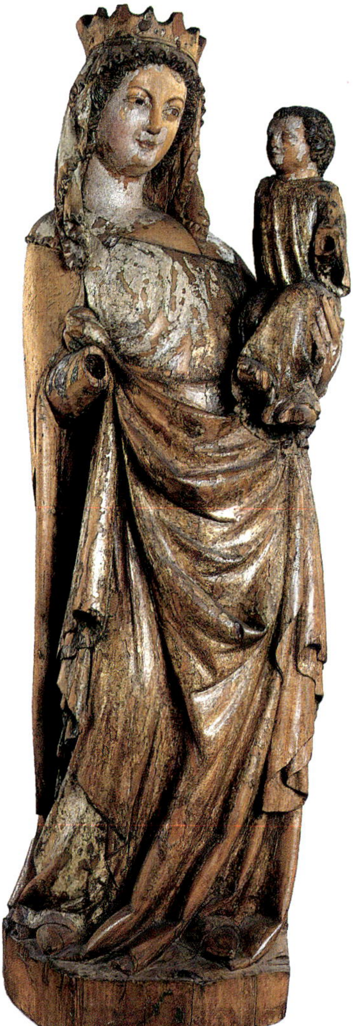

Gy. T.

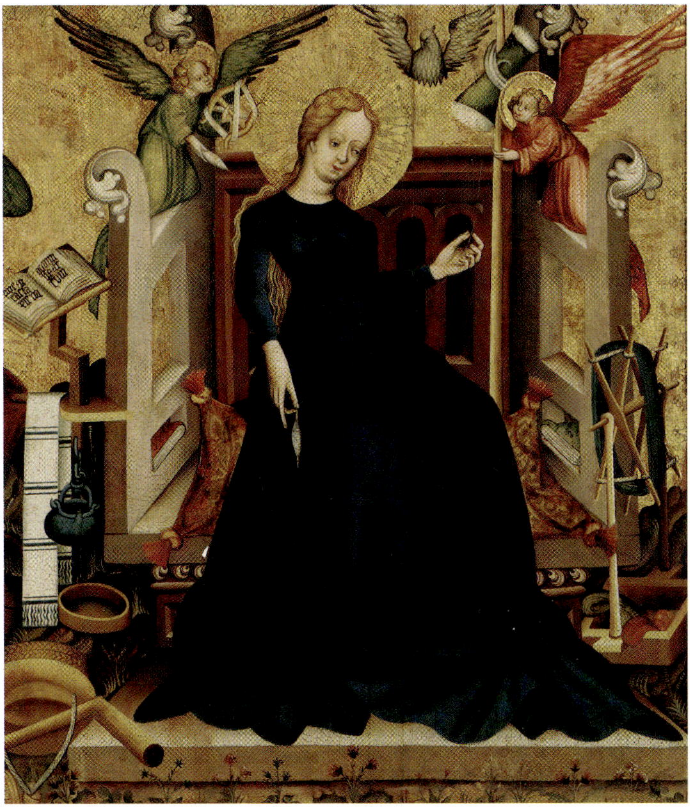

The Pregnant Virgin (Maria Gravida) from Németújvár

(Güssing, Austria)

Around 1410

Tempera on larch-wood, 89 × 78 cm

Inv. no.: 52.656

As the painting comes from the western border area of the country, it is not surprising that its style is related to the Viennese Soft Style. Originally it had belonged to a larger altarpiece of the Virgin with several other scenes, and it had been of horizontal format, but it was truncated on the left. Earlier, the iconography of the picture was determined as a fragment of "the doubts of Joseph", but further refining of this definition became possible when an infrared photograph was taken of the painting in 1993. The photo shows the little Jesus with a cross in a double mandorla under the drapery covering the Virgin's belly. This figure was originally painted on the Virgin's gown, in accord with the under-drawing, but it was painted over in the baroque age. In reply to "the doubts of Joseph", this type of the Annunciation is connected to the cult of the Pregnant Virgin spreading from the late 14th century and leading to the evolution of a separate devotional picture type. The flowers in the foreground, the wash-basin, towel and cauldron on the left are symbols of Mary frequently adopted in German and Austrian painting under the influence of Netherlandish art.

Gy. T.

Saint Catherine (?) from Barka

(Bôrka, Slovakia), 1410–1420
Lime-wood, with traces of gilding, 165 cm
Inv. no.: 99.10. M

The statue is rightly proclaimed to be one of the finest Hungarian works in the International Soft Style. Its counterpart —Saint Dorothy—came into the collection of the Hungarian National Gallery earlier, while Saint Catherine (?) is one of the most important new acquisitions (1999). Although the attributes of the saint are missing, it is likely that she once held the hilt of a sword pointed at the ground in her right hand and a spiked wheel in her left—the symbols of St Catherine of Alexandria's martyrdom. The most typical products of the Soft Style—named after the soft folds of the draperies—were in stone and had a great impact on wood carving. The connection of the statue with Saint Dorothy from Barka became even more obvious after restoration. They share the flat execution of the gown fastened with a clamp over the chest, the wings of the gown falling from the arms resembling organ pipe-like classic folds, and the drapery ends turned softly back from the ground. The modelling of the mouth with a broad upper lip, the dimple under the mouth and the shape of the nose are also shared by the two statues. Although the plasticity and lyrical expression of the faces reflect the influence of the "Beautiful Madonnas" of the age, the two saints from Barka have an unusual individual expressiveness compared to the idealized female saints. The two carvings must have belonged to the shrine of a large winged altarpiece, surrounding the central figure of the Virgin together with another two female members of the "Virgines capitales" and other female saints. Such a monumental altar could not have stood in the small church of Barka. The sculptures were probably transferred as "outdated" pieces from an ecclesiastical centre in the vicinity (e.g. the former high-altar of the St Elizabeth church in Kassa) to the church nearby at the time of the efflorescence of the Gothic.

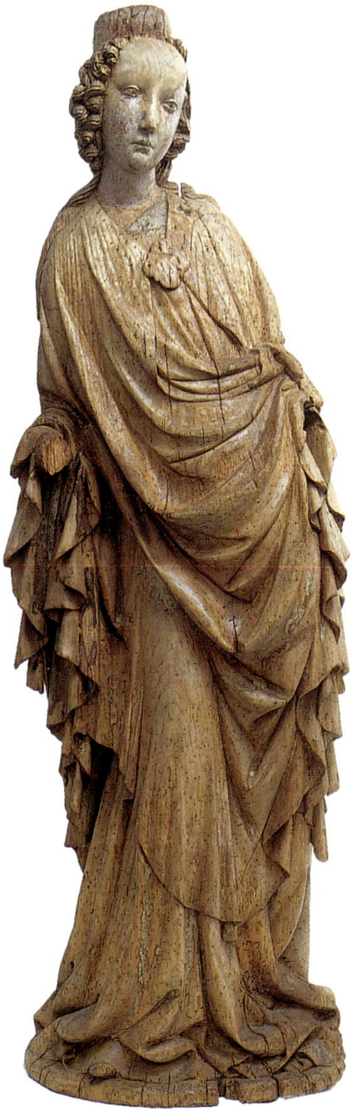

Gy. T.

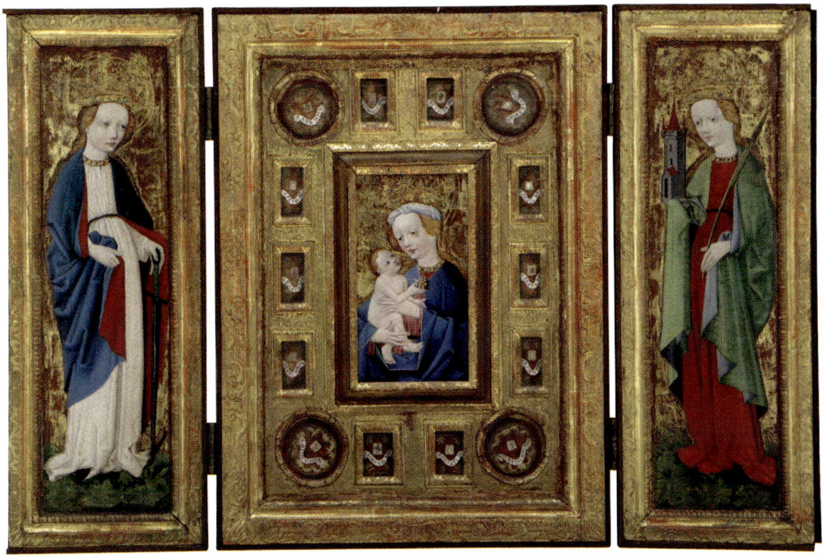

Small reliquary altar with a half-length picture of the Virgin and standing saints, from the Piarist monastery of Trencsén

(Trenčín, Slovakia), around 1440–1450
(frame restored in the 18th century)
Tempera on lime-wood, 47 × 73 cm
with frame
Inv. no.: 53.579.1–5.

The renovation of the frame and the insertion of the relics of eight saints of the baroque age prove the unbroken veneration of the devotional picture of the Virgin throughout the centuries. The parchment inscriptions naming the saints did not only serve the identification of the relics but also had a sacral function. The northern devotional images of the Virgin preserved the original essence of the wonder-working icon, often ensured by the relics, although the icon types were massively reformulated. The half-length picture of the Virgin with the Infant, of Byzantine origin, became particularly popular around the 1400s, well suited to be used as the central image of a triptych. These half-length representations expose the intimate relationship between the Virgin and Child; the latter is often shown touching his mother's face or garment, or trying to snatch at her veil, or, less frequently but as seen in this picture, reaching out for the ornamental clasp which fastens her cloak. The Virgin's crown is raised in relief to imitate encrusted gems—a technique that bears witness to the influence of Bohemian art around 1400, while the twisted kerchief around her head and her downcast eyes point to the impact of more contemporary endeavours characteristic of Netherlandish painting. The sharp folds of the cloak indicate an origin not earlier than the middle of the 15th century. Although this Madonna type became generally prevalent during the age of the International Gothic style, several specimens also framed by relics are known from the latter half of the 15th century, especially among Hungarian and Polish works.

Gy. T.

Saint Jerome and Saint Gregory from Kassa

(Košice, Slovakia), around 1477
Lime-wood, painted, 79 and 78.5 cm
Inv. nos: 7183, 55.880

The realistic rendering of the bony, wizened faces, baggy eyes of the fathers of the church Saints Jerome and Gregory and the intellectual superiority radiating through the shattered physique of the old men, as well as the compositions animated by the deeply undercarved drapery folds make these statues important Hungarian specimens of the realistic trend in sculpture connected with the name of Nicolas Gerhaerts van Leyden. The trend appeared very early—in 1477—in the St Elizabeth high altar in Kassa and probably arrived to Kassa from the easternmost venue of the master's activity, Wiener Neustadt, via Buda. The type of the lion hoisting itself up on St Jerome's cloak is also of Netherlandish origin, appearing on the Strassbourg pulpit and several monuments in Germany. It is highly likely that the huge statues in the shrine of the Kassa high altar were framed by figures of the four doctors of the church, now replaced by 19th-century substitutes. The two figures in our collection might have belonged to that altar.

Gy. T.

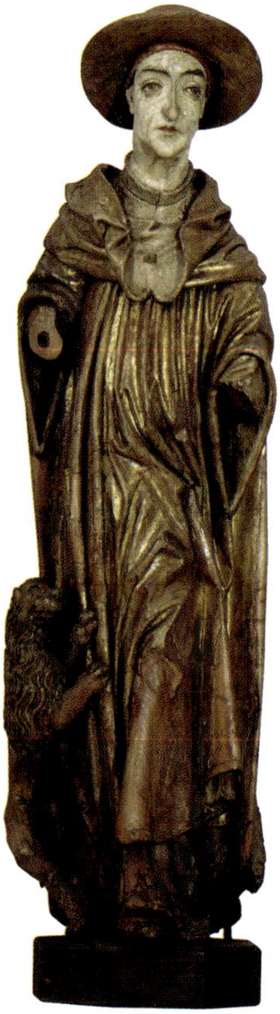

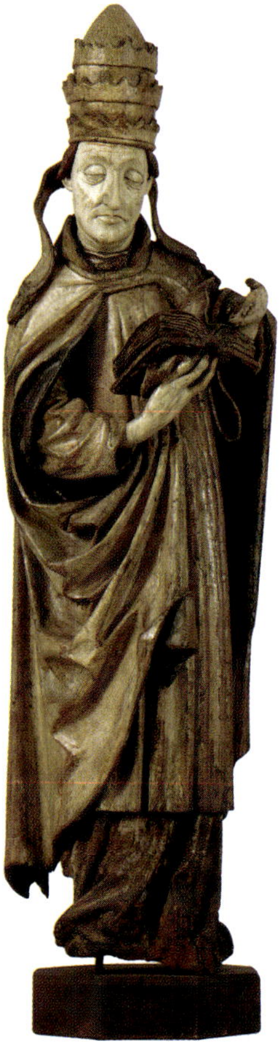

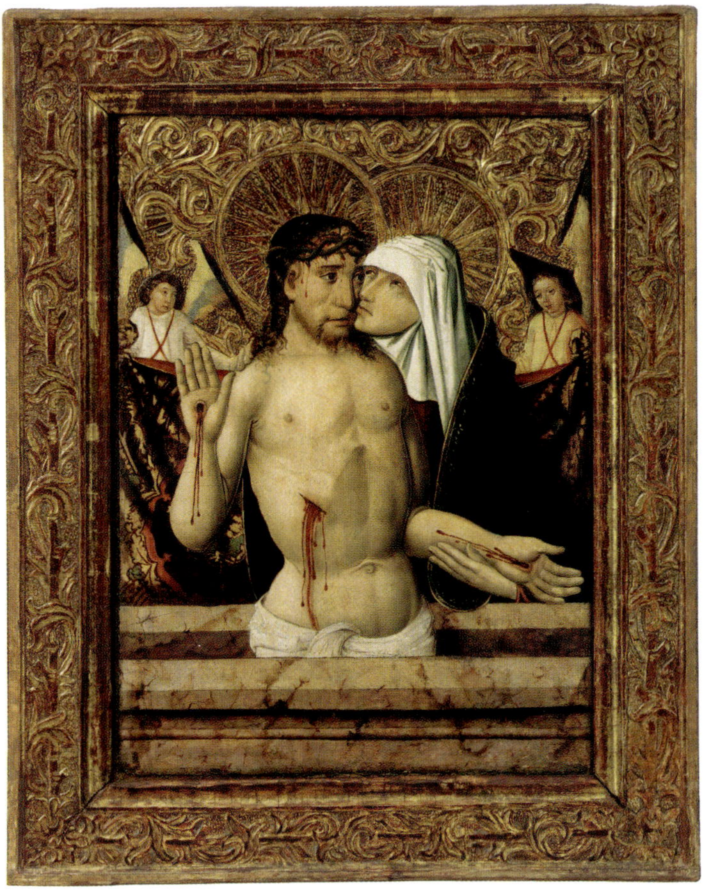

Man of Sorrows from Kassa

(Košice, Slovakia), 1470–1480
Tempera on pine-wood, 63 × 52 cm
with original frame
Inv. no.: 55.911

The representation of the Man of Sorrows (Imago Pietatis) is an autonomous picture intended for devotional purposes and completely detached from the events of the Passion. The intention, as in the Pietà, was to elicit sympathy for the sufferings of Christ among the faithful of the Middle Ages. The two angels in the background are reminiscent of "angel Pietà" scenes, while the elaborate raised and gilded gesso of the frame and background is similar to those seen on devotional pictures of the Virgin (Liptónádasd [Trstenô], Kassa). This picture type was popular throughout Europe in the 15th century. The panels most closely related to it are of Polish origin and come from Iwanowice, Biecz, Zbylitowska Góra and Ószandec (Stary Sącz, Poland). The style was influenced by the realism of the Passion scenes and the stiff folds of the draperies in the high altar of Kassa painted in the 1470s.

Gy. T.

Calvary
Exterior of the right wing of the high altar of St Nicholas from Jánosrét

(Lúčky pri Kremnici, Slovakia), the 1480s
Tempera on panel, 154 × 98 cm
Inv. no.: 55.903.20

The style of the scenes on the exterior of the wings of the St Nicholas high altar (Calvary, Agony in the Garden) reveals that the Master of Jánosrét was an outstanding figure in the art of the northern mining towns in the last third of the 15th century, incorporating the new tendencies of Netherlandish art in his œuvre created in the age of King Matthias Corvinus. This is clearly evident in the detailed landscape filling the entire background—this was not usual at the time—and in some compositional features filtered through German art. The motif of Mary Magdalen embracing the Cross, used by Eyck and Rogier, was transmitted to the Master of Jánosrét by one of the engravings of Master ES, while the figures of the Virgin and St John on the left of the cross and of the centurion on the right bear witness to the influence and accurate imitation of Schongauer's engraving. The harmonious interrelation of the figures and the landscape, the suggestion of aerial perspective and the careful painterly rendering of the whole composition suggest a master of great artistic merit.

Gy. T.

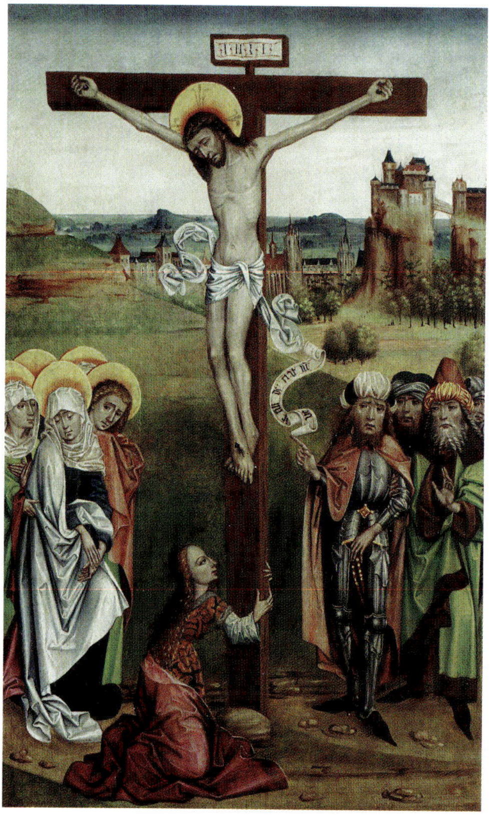

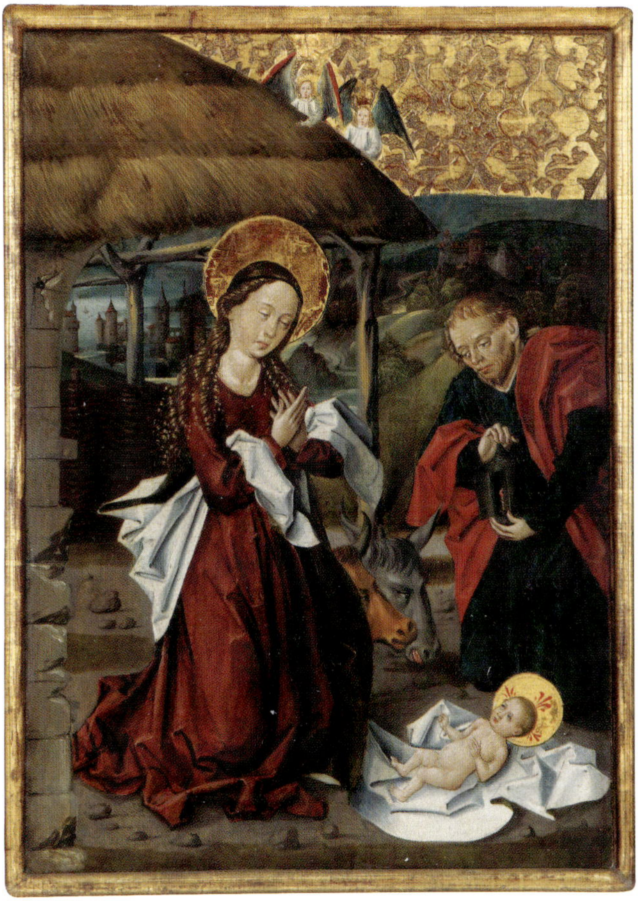

The Nativity on an altarwing from Szepeshely

(Spišska Kapitula, Slovakia), around 1500
Tempera on pine-wood, 86 × 63 cm
Inv. no.: 55.917.2

The Szepes (Spiš) region was one of the most significant centres of art in Northern Hungary, from where far more winged altarpieces survive than from anywhere else. The church of the ecclesiastical centre, Szepeshely, was adorned with several altars. One is the altar of the Coronation of the Virgin (1499), the twelve panel paintings of which are outstanding representatives of the artistic endeavours under Netherlandish influence in the region and had a stimulating impact on contemporary altar painting. Proof is also provided by the two altar wings which used to belong to an altar of the Virgin with statues in the middle. The Nativity panel was the lower picture on the inner side of the left altarwing. St Joseph's realistically depicted face, the deeply shaded, hard folds of the drapery and especially the nocturnal landscape with the sea, and the meticulously painted trees suggest that the painter was trained in the workshop of the creator of the Coronation of the Virgin altarpiece.

Gy. T.

Saint Stephen and Saint Ladislas, provenance unknown

Around 1500

Lime-wood, 114 and 106.5 cm, resp.

Inv. nos: 55.894, 55.895

In addition to the graceful stance and the varied design of the drapery folds, it is the virtuosic rendering of the hair, beard and physiognomy of the figures of the two canonized Hungarian kings that promote them to the echelon of the Old Collection. The interplay of the vigorous musculature and the thick web of wrinkles in the physiognomy of elderly Saint Stephen is both expressive and anatomically premeditated, while it is the gentle undulation of the smooth facial skin of younger St Ladislas that creates his lively expression. A comparison of the two also reveals what a rich arsenal of means of expression was at the disposal of the sculptor. Earlier the provenance of the statues was presumed to be Mateóc (Matejovce, Slovakia) in the Szepes (Spiš) region. Although that was disproved, the two figures probably originate from that area. There is namely a whole row of other works found in the rural churches of the Szepes region and neighbouring counties which were made by the same sculptor, who received his apellation after these figures. Yet the sculptor can also be traced to a farther place, Besztercebánya (Banská Bystrica). He was probably a member of the (presumably) temporary work organization of versatile stylistic profile which produced the Agony in the Garden group carved in stone for the parish church of Besztercebánya, the console figures for the St Barbara chapel there and the altarpieces in neighbouring Zólyomszászfalva (Sásová).

G. E.

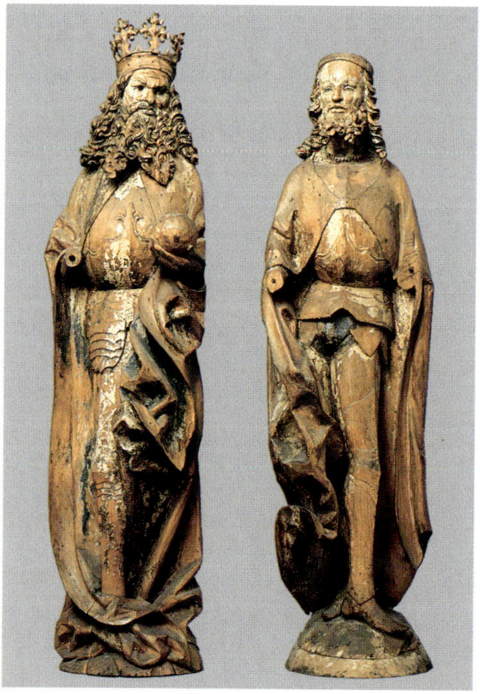

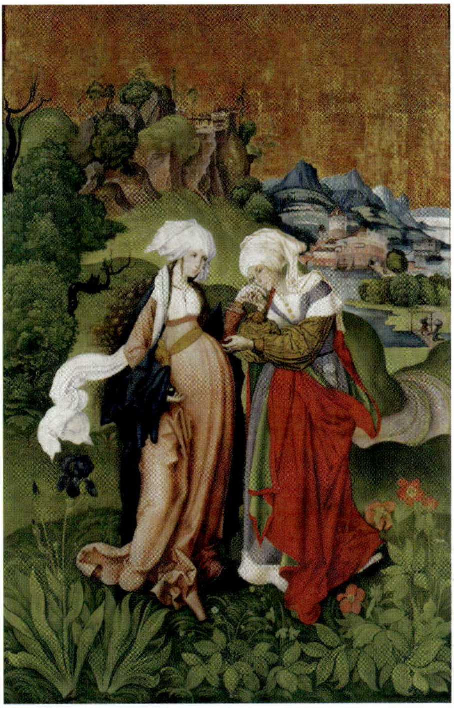

Master M S: The Visitation, from Selmecbánya

(Banská Štiavnica, Slovakia), 1506
Tempera on panel, gilding, 140 × 94.5 cm
Inv. no.: 2151

This is probably the best known panel painting from medieval Hungary. The two female saints are standing in the foreground of a wide open landscape. The representation does not adhere closely to the text of the Gospel: it is not Zacharias' house where the Virgin, pregnant with Jesus, meets Elizabeth who is expecting Saint John the Baptist, but in the open where all the elements of Nature glorify the Lord, following the words of the Magnificat. The idyll is, however, illusory: the barren rocks, the trees with twisted trunks are subtle references to the passion, while the flowers and fruit in the foreground are symbols directly referring to it. The parts of the large winged altarpiece which this painting once belonged to are all scattered. Four scenes of the Passion—the Mount of Olives, Christ Carrying the Cross, the Crucifixion and the Resurrection—are in the Christian Museum in Esztergom; these scenes give out the entire lower row of pictures on the closed altarpiece. The Nativity of the upper row is in the parish church of Hontszentantal (Sväty Antol, Slovakia), the Adoration of the Magi is in the Musée des Beaux-Arts in Lille. The whereabouts of the Annunciation is unknown. The badly worn signature of the master—M and S with a master sign between them—as well as the year 1506 are visible on the rim of Christ's sepulchre in the Resurrection scene. Miklós Mojzer has identified the artist as Marten Schwarcz, the painter of Veit Stoss' high altar in Cracow.

Á. M.

Former high altar of the church of the Descent of the Holy Ghost in Csíkszentlélek

(Leliceni, Romania), 1510

Tempera on pine-wood, 316 × 306 cm

Inv. no.: 53.370.1–11.

The central panel of the high altar dedicated to a subject that fits the name of the church features the Virgin in the circle of the twelve apostles in front of a huge brocade curtain. The upper part is framed by gilded tracery below which, in the node of radiant lightrays, the Holy Spirit appears in the shape of a dove against a cloud. The deep reverence for the Virgin in the area is owing to the Franciscans in Csíksomlyó (Şumuleu). The Franciscan theme can also be found in the Csíkszentlélek altarpiece: St Francis' stigmatization is given a salient role among the pictures of standing saints on the inner sides of the wings of the altar. On the praedella, one finds the donor's coat of arms with the date of the setting up of the altar as well as a banderole reading "Insignia Filiorum Czako, 1510" on the left, and the ruler Vladislav II's coat of arms and the inscription "Insignia Domini Regis Ungariae" on the right. The donors of the altar were thus members of the noble Czakó family. János Czakó who is mentioned by diplomas as the inspector of the iron furnaces in Csík is presumed by some researchers to have been one of them.

Gy. T.

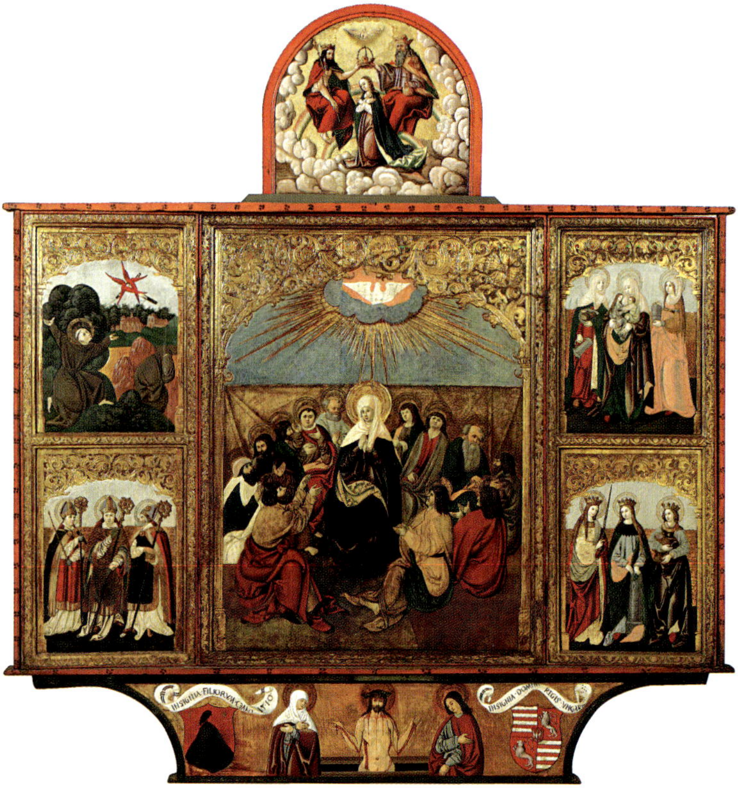

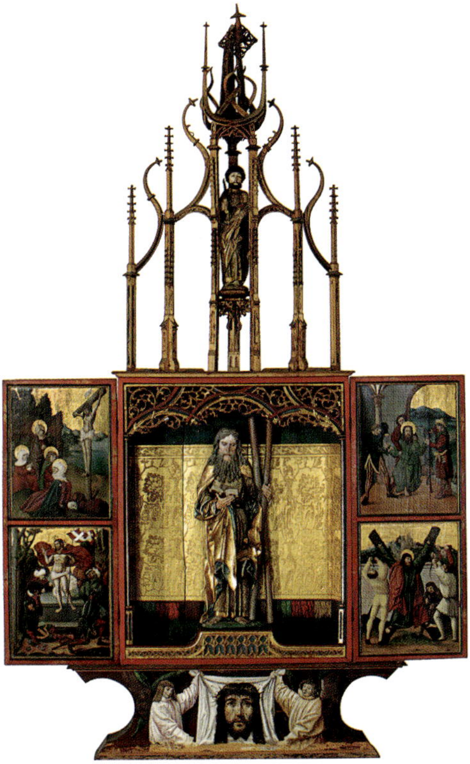

The St Andrew altarpiece from Liptószentandrás

(Liptovský Ondrej, Slovakia), 1512
Wood, painted, gilded, 420 cm
Inv. no.: 53.569.1–12.

The altarpiece stood on the high altar of a small village church in Liptó (Liptov) county. It is exceptional because it was made farther away, probably in Besztercebánya (Banská Bystrica). Its closest analogy is the former altarpiece of the Virgin's chapel in the parish church of Pónik (Poniky). The two retables were made in the same year, as witnessed by the inscriptions put in identical script and text ("ANNO DOMINI 1512 IAR") and on the same location, namely on the crossbars separating the two scenes on both wings. The central pinnacle of the superstructure bends forward in an S line, presumably to fit the curve of the sanctuary vault. While there is no similar motif in the region, the Astwerk closing the shrine above recurs in several works of the same circle, besides the altar of Pónik. The merits of the sculptor of the altarpiece are most apparent in the St Andrew figure of the shrine: in the sensitive rendering of the skin and the ruffles of the cloak folds at some places. This figure and that of St Bartholomew in the superstructure suggest the same stylistic links as the joinery. That also applies to the scenes on the wings painted with lush landscape settings. They depict two scenes from the Passion and two from St Andrew's life. Far higher artistic quality is present in the predella showing two angels holding Veronica's veil, which is comparable with the chief works of this circle, the wing panels of the St Barbara altarpiece in Besztercebánya.

G. E.

Altarpiece of the Annunciation from Kisszeben

(Sabinov, Slovakia), the 1520s
Wood, painted, gilded, 675.5 cm
Inv. no.: 52.576. 1–26.

The eight scenes visible when the altar wings are closed represent events of the Virgin's life from the Visitation to the Assumption in compositions that faithfully adapt to Dürer's woodcut series. It is not self-evident why the Annunciation scene was selected to be carved for the shrine. The feast of the Annunciation on March 25th is the only feast of the Virgin that is almost always in Lent. This meant that, contrarily to general practice, the most sumptuously decorated, richly gilded parts of the altarpiece were exposed to the congregation in Kisszeben at that time. When the altar is open, only carved figures can be seen whose style belongs to the circle of Master Paul, the maker of the high altar in St James' church in Lőcse (Levoča), who was employed widely in the whole of Northeastern Hungary in the early 16th century. Comparing the high altar of Lőcse (erected in 1508) or other early works of Master Paul (e.g. the St Nicholas altarpiece from Nagyszalók [Vel'ký Slavkov] in our collection) with the Kisszeben sculptures, considerable differences can also be found. The faces of the latter are more angular and plane, the eyes are small and set far apart, the draperies have less plasticity and rather clothe the bodies in a fine web of lines. All this and further details such as the trefoil head of the shrine filled with renaissance leaf ornaments bring it closest to the high altar of St Martin's church in Héthárs (Lipany).There is no consensus among researchers whether these works are to be attributed to an independent workshop or to the late period of Master Paul. As a recently found inscription reveals, the altarpiece in Héthárs was completed in 1526, which supports the latter presumption and offers a starting point for the dating of the Kisszeben altarpiece.

G. E.

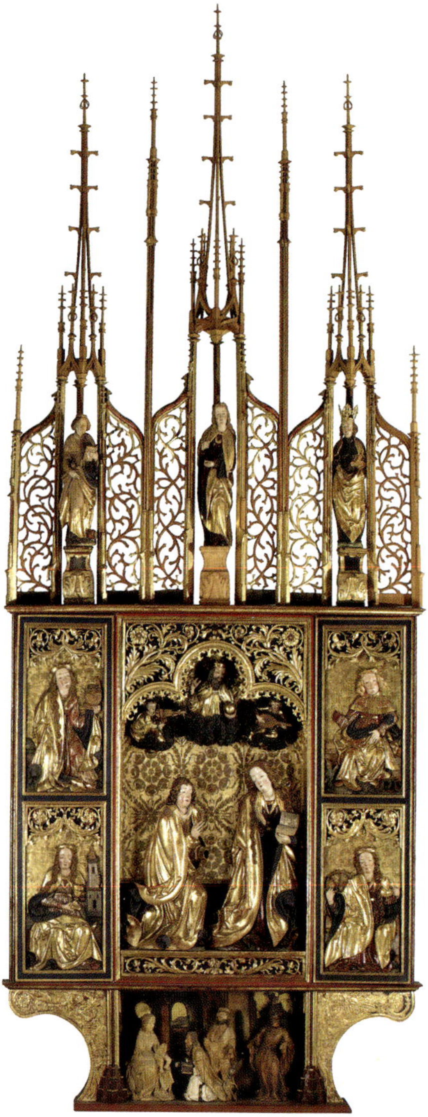

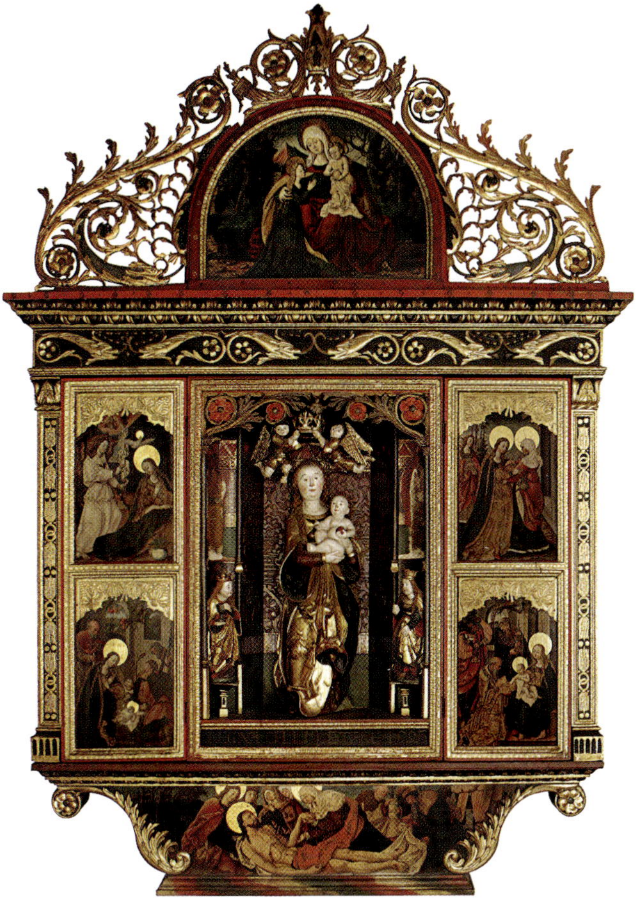

High altar of the Virgin from Csíkmenaság

(Armăşeni, Romania), 1523(?)
Lime-wood carvings, painting in tempera on pine-wood, gilded, 456 × 328 cm
Inv. no.: 53.540. 1–20.

The structure, pillars and cornice of the altarpiece, the painted picture in the superstructure in place of the gothic carved tracery as well as the style of the carved ornaments and painting make this work one of the finest examples of renaissance altar art in Hungary. Entangled into the branches flanking the semicircular painting in the crown are a dolphin and a cornucopia and the cornice running the whole length of the altarpiece features pairs of dolphins facing each other. Based on Dürer's famous woodcut cycle (1511), the paintings on the inner sides of the wings show four main events in the life of the Virgin. The landscape with huge trees and mountain peaks behind the scene of the Virgin and Child with St Anne in the gable suggests direct observation of nature. Behind the Lamentation scene on the praedella the rendering of the trees provides the emotional atmosphere of the scene, in keeping with the style of the Danubian school of painting.

Gy. T.

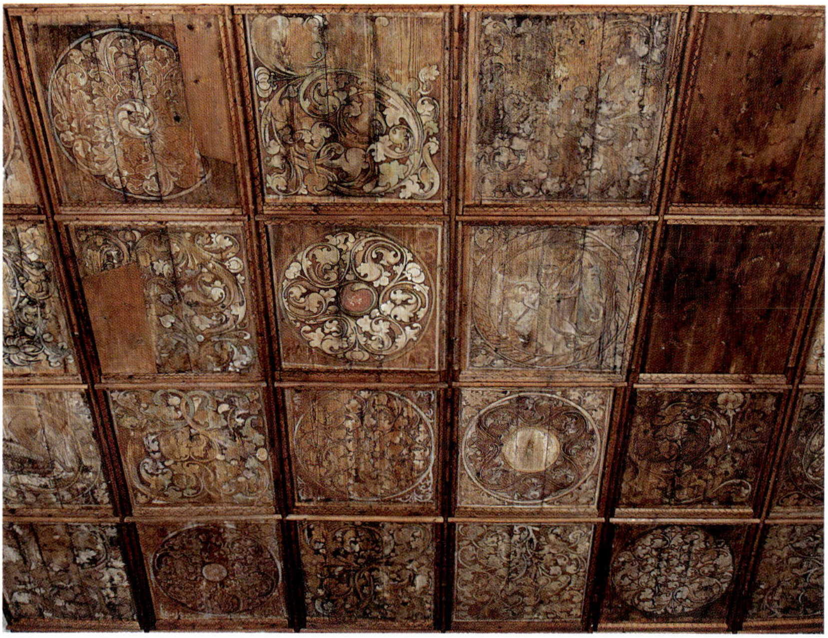

Painted wooden ceiling from Gogánváralja

(Gogan-Varolea, Romania), 1501/1503–1519
Tempera on pine-wood; 6 × 8 fields originally on 24 panels (one lost), one panel measuring about 90 × 180 cm, partly with original framing bars
Inv. no.: 55.966

This is the earliest known renaissance coffered wooden ceiling from medieval Hungary, transferred to the museum from the middle of Transylvania, the area along the Târnava Mică. It consists of 48 square fields, with a sketchy line of leaves on the frames. Two kinds of composition alternate more or less regularly in the fields. One is a foliage motif (with figures hidden in it) filling the entire field, the other has a round field—sometimes a wreath—in the square featuring coats of arms or figures. Examples for the latter type are the symbols of the four evangelists which can be seen at the four corners of the ceiling and the scenes of the Annunciation, the Vir dolorum etc., elsewhere. Although the layout of the ceiling divided into regular coffers adapts to renaissance models, the decisive majority of the pictorial elements are Gothic in style. Such is, first of all, the intricate tangle of omnipresent green foliage probably inspired by engravings, or the fleeting, ethereal figure of the angel of Matthew. Painted wooden ceilings on the verge between the Gothic and the renaissance were prevalent in entire Central Europe at that time, many surviving in Southern Poland, and some in Transylvania (e.g. Ádámos [Adămuş], 1526, also in the HNG's exhibition). The donor of the ceiling is identified by research as Miklós Bethlen of Bethlen, the landowner of the village. The coats of arms include that of the Bethlen family, that of the country and some other—not always conclusively identified—shields.

Á. M.

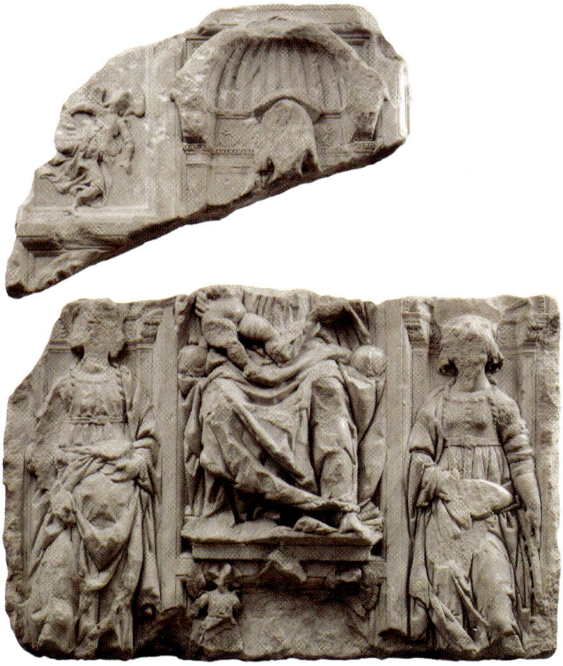

Giovanni Dalmata

(Trogir, c. 1440 – Trogir, before 1514)

Fragment of a relief depicting the Virgin, from Diósgyőr

1485–1490

White marble, lower part: 79 × 123 × 19 cm, upper part: 61 × 91 × 21cm

Lower part inv. no.: 55.981, upper part owned by the Castle Museum of Diósgyőr

This relief is one of the highlights of early renaissance sculpture in Hungary. The two fragments, which do not fit to each other anywhere, are from a retable in whose central shrine the Virgin was shown sitting with the Infant in her lap, flanked in shorter niches by two female saints, St Lucy and St Catherine of Alexandria. Above the lateral niches the Annunciation scene was depicted divided into two; of this, only the figure of the archangel Gabriel in fluttering drapery survives. The high-quality relief is badly fragmented: the faces were crushed, the lower part carved to a rectangle. The two fragments undoubtedly derive from one and the same altarpiece, although while the lower part was removed from a wall of the Pauline church in Diósgyőr, the upper part was found in the castle. The castle always belonged to the regnant queen, so the fragment of the episcopal coat of arms needs to be explained. The original frame of the relief which probably contained further coats of arms is, however, unknown. Research attributes the relief to Giovanni Dalmata (Ivan Duknovich) on the basis of the stylistic marks. He was born in Trogir and worked for the papal court in Rome for a longer period of time. He probably came to Buda in the second half of the 1480s. King Matthias rewarded him for his services with nobility and landed property (1488).

Á. M.

Christ Taking Leave of His Mother, fragment of an epitaph, from Nyitra

(Nitra, Slovakia), 1520–1530
Limestone, 117 × 103 × 11.5 cm
Inv. no.: 55.1594

Christ is standing on the right, Mary is falling on her knees in front of him; behind her, two women are watching the scene with the subtle silhouettes of the houses of Jerusalem (or Bethania) in the background. The right side of the relief is fragmentary; the adjacent part with three apostle figures survived in the Franciscan church in Nyitra, thus, the figures of Christ and his mother were originally in the centre of the composition. The Franciscans of Nyitra also preserve another relief showing the Resurrection, the style of which is related to this work. Both scenes are typical subjects of epitaphs, so the two reliefs might have belonged together in a single grand-scale ensemble, originally in an ornate stone frame adorned with coats of arms and inscriptions. Since no fragment of the frame is known, there is no knowing for whom (and where) one of the highest quality epitaphs of the 1520s–1530s was created. The style and quality of the relief suggest that it was imported, perhaps from an area beyond Vienna (from where epitaphs in northern renaissance style later usually came to the territory of the Kingdom of Hungary); its closest iconographic analogy is in the Deutschordenskirche in Vienna, but is somewhat poorer in quality. This fragment from Nyitra is an early example of the renaissance stone epitaphs becoming frequent in Hungary in the last third of the 16th century.

Á. M.

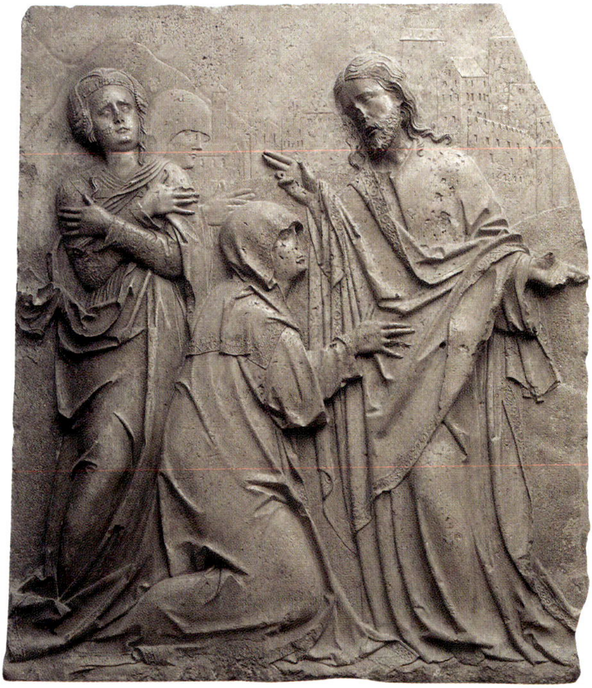

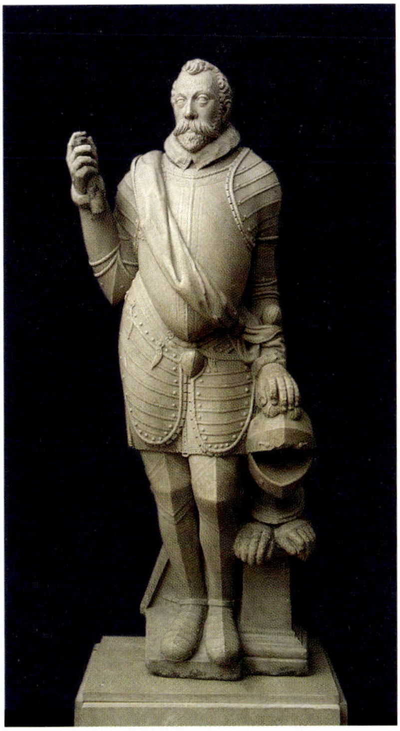

Statue from the tomb of Hans Rueber von Püchsendorf, Captain-General of Upper Hungary (†1584)

White marble, 185 cm

Inv. no.: 55.1953

The life-size figure in armour stands in contrapposto; he holds a commander's staff in his right hand and rests his left on his helmet on a short stand. The marble statue once belonged to a representative upright memorial. As the surviving specimens of the type suggest, it was a large framed construction with the statue of the deceased in a niche in the middle. There were coats of arms, inscribed tablets (sometimes allegorical figures) in the framing structure. This late renaissance sepulchral type arrived in Hungary from the West, with several examples from the first half of the 17th century (Miklós Pálffy, captain-general of Komárom, Érsekújvár [Nové Zámky, Slovakia] and Esztergom, †1600; János Draskovich, Lord Chief Treasurer and banus of Croatia, †1613, both in the cathedral in Bratislava. The first example was Rueber's tomb; the unusual choice can be explained by the high rank of the deceased and his close affiliation with the Habsburg court. The statue is a high-quality specimen of its kind; probably the whole memorial represented a similar level of quality. Its elements arrived in Kassa (Košice) one by one where the whole was merely assembled. Originally it was in the Cromer chapel of St Elizabeth's parish church (later the sacristy of the chapter). In 1733, however, the monument of the protestant captain-general was dissembled, as it was in the way of a new altar. The elements of the framing architecture were scattered, only the central figure is known.

Á. M.

Ottavio Zanuoli (?)
(? –1607)
Maria Christierna, wife of Zsigmond Báthory, prince of Transylvania
1595
Tempera on copperplate, 17.7 × 12.5 cm
Inv. no.: 86.4M

Princess Maria Christierna of Austria married the Transylvanian prince Zsigmond Báthory in 1595. The marriage sealing the anti-Ottoman alliance between Emperor Rudolf and Báthory ended in divorce in 1599. The fiancée is depicted as she looked like and was dressed at the engagement in Graz. The portrait of the bride was painted by Ottavio Zanuoli, a painter active in the archduke's court, in two copies, the other one, a large, full-length picture remained in the family's possession (now in Schloss Ambras), and this small intimate rendering was probably given to the fiancé. Báthory was not personally there at the engagement, but he was represented by István Bocskai, who was entrusted to sign the wedding contract. Maria Christierna is wearing the M-shaped pendant jewel which had earlier belonged to her mother Mary of Bavaria, and her dress is identical with the one her elder sister Anna wears in her portrait as the fiancée of Sigismund III, king of Poland, in 1591/92 (Vienna, Kunsthistorisches Museum). The artist of Italian origin was employed by Maria Christierna's father, archduke Charles as a portrait painter at that time, but his name is also registered later as an architect in the Graz court.

E. B.

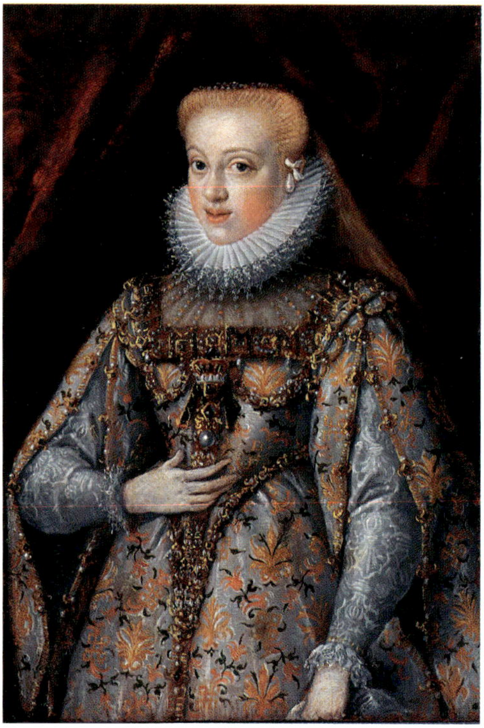

Justus Sustermans

(Antwerp, 1597 – Florence, 1681)

and his workshop

Ferdinand III, King of Hungary

1626

Oil on canvas, 201 × 126 cm

Inv. no.: 92.20M

In November 1625 the 18-year-old Habsburg heir was crowned king of Hungary in Sopron as Ferdinand III. The reports of the participating envoys reveal that the interior of the Franciscan church was decorated in heraldic red, white and green colours. The prospective ruler was also dressed for the ceremony in this vein: in the Hungarian noblemen's attire as seen in the portrait. The picture is the young king's first official portrait and a document of the coronation. This is confirmed by the authentic depiction of the Hungarian Holy Crown, which was very rare at that time. Such a minute depiction, correct even in its colours, is only possible through observation. As an object deprived of "publicity", the crown was only visible during coronations, so the painter could only have observed it during the crowning ceremony. Flemish Justus Sustermans, the court painter of the Medici in Florence, to whom the portrait is attributed by analogy of his contemporaneous works, had visited the Vienna court earlier too, performing commissions for the imperial family. Ferdinand III's representative portrait, which was probably painted in more than one copy, went into the ownership of the noted Spanish art collector of the age, marquis Laganés, Don Diego de Messia. Laganés, a connoisseur and collector of portraits, was busy arranging the marriage of Ferdinand III and infanta Maria to be held in Spring 1626.

E. B.

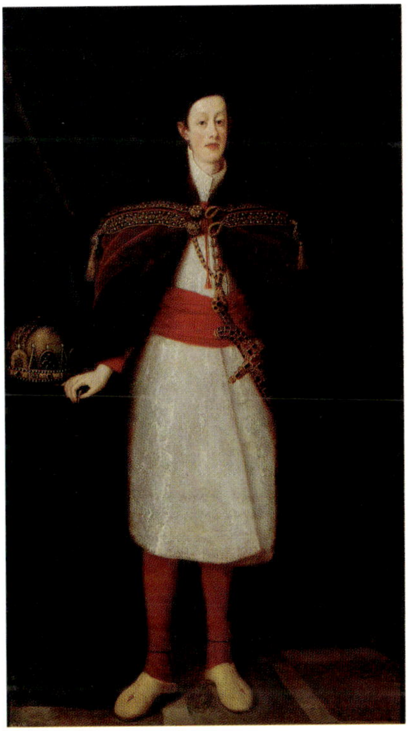

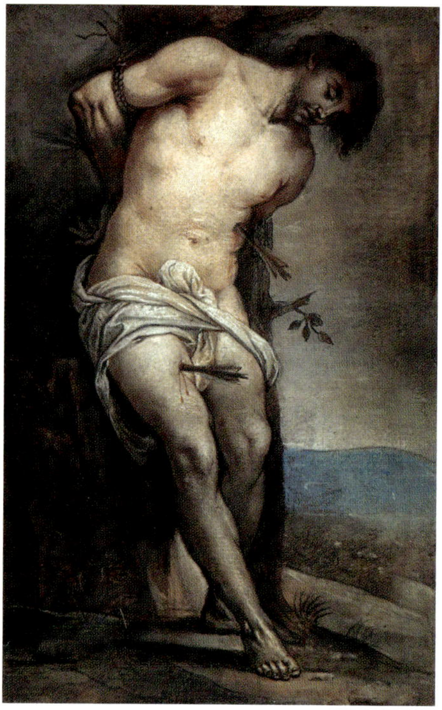

Jan Thomas

(Ieper/Ypres, 1617 – Vienna, 1678)

Saint Sebastian

1669

Chalk on paper, 38 × 25.2 cm

Inv. no.: 2005.1M

As far as we know today, this St Sebastian composition is the only sketch for an altar picture surviving from 17th-century Hungary. The painting was commissioned by Lord Chief Justice Ferenc Nádasdy for the Augustinian church in Léka (Lockenhaus, Austria), and Jan Thomas, whom Nádasdy engaged several times, proposed this exquisite, finely drawn sketch. Its function was to present the painter's idea and to get the donor's consent and inquire about the required modifications, which were effected later, as a comparison with the large variant in oil reveals: as against the bent head of the saint in the drawing, the final variant shows him with lifted head and individualized facial features. Originally, Nádasdy probably intended the painting and its counterpart, St Catherine, as altar pictures, but perhaps because the chief justice was charged with treason and executed in 1671, this plan was not realized and today both paintings hang on the wall of the sanctuary. The patron of the Augustinians at Léka and builder of the church and monastery was Nádasdy, who wished to be buried in the church with his family. The two oil paintings and the sketch were most probably made in the year of the consecration, in 1669. Thomas, who was of Flemish origin, worked in the Viennese court from 1661, from 1662 as the court painter of emperor Leopold I. Literature regards him as one of Rubens' last pupils, which is corroborated by the paintings of reserved elegance in the Léka church.

E. B.

Painter from Western Hungary

Last third of the 17th century

St Elizabeth and a Beggar

Around 1675–1680

Oil on canvas, 198 × 110 cm

Inv. no.: 81.8. M

Together with its counterpart showing St Emeric (son of the first Hungarian king, St Stephen), the picture presumably belonged to the one-time furnishing of the Franciscan monastery in Győr until the end of the 18th century when Joseph II suppressed the order. When the church and monastery of the Franciscans were rebuilt after a fire in 1654, several aristocrats gave donations for its reconstruction and refurnishing including Pál Esterházy, later palatine and imperial prince. The earliest possible date of the paintings showing the two Hungarian saints is the latter half of the 1670s when the renewal of the monastery was completed. In some details the pictures are conspicuously identical with some pieces in the ancestors' gallery of the Esterházy family in Fraknó painted around that time: on account of resemblances in modelling and execution they must be by the hand of one of Pál Esterházy's court painters. St Elizabeth of the Árpád dynasty (the first dynasty of Hungarian kings, 1000–1301) is shown in historicizing regal attire with a robe as marquise of Thuringia, to satisfy the contemporary idea of "historical authenticity". Esterházy as a patron devoted distinguished attention to the Franciscans, supporting not only the convent in Győr but also the order's church in Kismarton (Eisenstadt), which he chose as the burial place for himself and his family.

E. B.

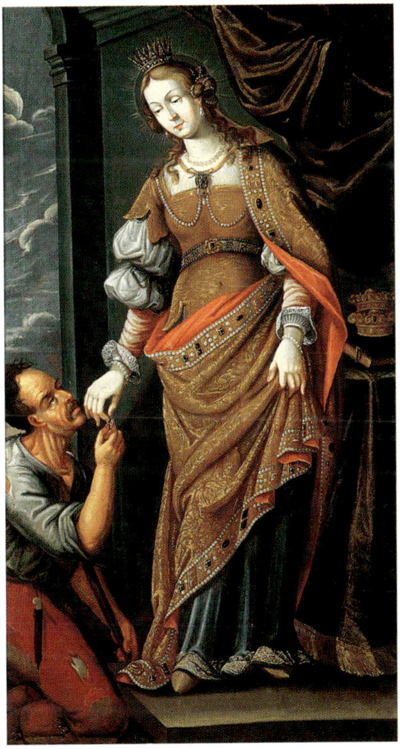

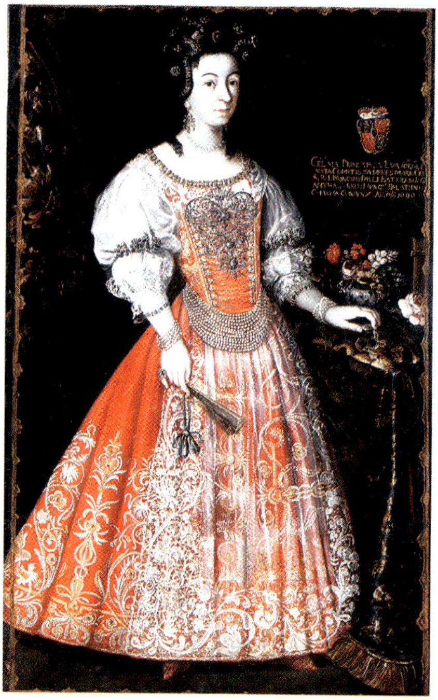

Painter from Western Hungary
End of the 17th century
Éva Thököly, wife of Prince Pál Esterházy
1690
Oil on canvas, 191.5 × 120.5 cm
Inv. no.: 97.2. M

The representative portrait showing palatine prince Pál Esterházy's second wife Éva Thököly used to belong to the ancestors' gallery of the family's branch of counts and was still hanging on the wall of the "ancestors' hall" in the Esterházy mansion in Pápa in the early 20th century. This series of Esterházy ancestors presented in a representative ensemble the family members of the counts' and princes' lines who lived in the 17th–18th centuries. It also included the portrait of Éva Thököly's sister Kata, wife of the one-time lord of the mansion count Ferenc Esterházy (Hungarian National Museum). It is presumed that the sisters' portraits were painted by a single artist working in the court of prince Esterházy. Although it was not earlier than the late 19th century that the portraits of the "ancestors' hall" were arranged into a coherent ensemble with an historicizing attitude, aristocratic ancestors' galleries were continuously made from the mid-17th century to proclaim the notable past and social significance of the family. As the ancestors' gallery items were actually status portraits, their aim was not to convey the personality of the model but to express rank and social position. The tools of expression all satisfy this purpose: the dignified pose, ornate attire and special jewels, the setting also suggesting rank with the adequate furniture and objects. The inclusion of the family coat of arms and of inscriptions with particular data is part of the representation.

E. B.

Jakab Bogdány

(Eperjes [Prešov, Slovakia], before 1660 – London, 1724)

Still Life with Parrots and a White Cockatoo

Oil on canvas, 98 × 128.5 cm
Inv. no.: 3681

The painter left his native town at a young age, first for Vienna and then for Amsterdam where sources mention him in 1684. He might have pursued his studies there. At any rate, the centre of middle-class genres, especially still-lifes, was a perfect school for a starting artist. At first he painted flower and fruit pieces, which proved to be a lifelong experience: the effect of the Dutch example remained discernible in this group of his works throughout his life. Bogdány moved to London in 1688, and his technical expertise soon earned him fame among the English aristocrats. His most important clients were the royal family themselves. As a sign of his artistic and social recognition, he was granted citizenship in 1700 and purchased an estate near London. He began to paint compositions of animals, mainly exotic birds, to be placed above doors or mantlepieces; most of these pictures can still be found in their original places in rural English private collections. These paintings by Bogdány are actually elegant genre pictures with exotic birds as actors against a background of elegant parks and classic buildings. He could study and accurately depict the colourful rare birds in the Windsor Park aviary of one of his main clients, Admiral George Churchill.

E. B.

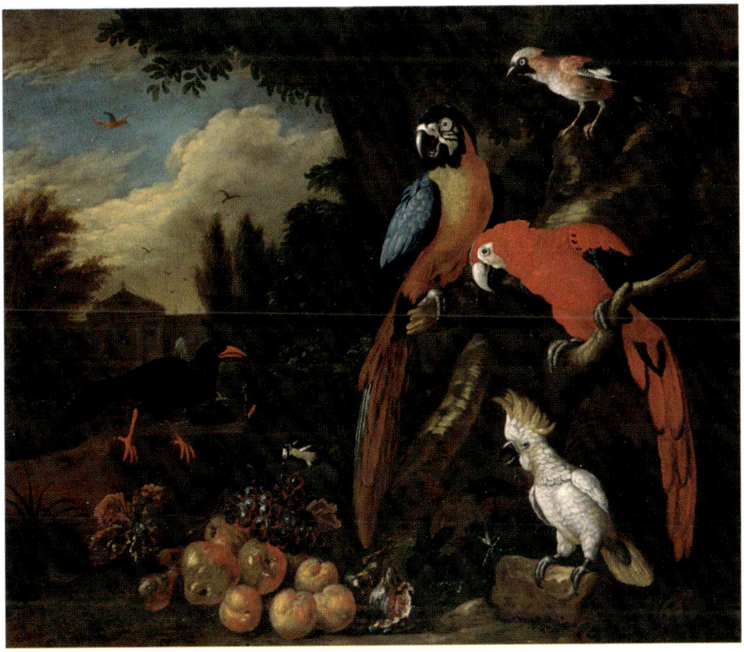

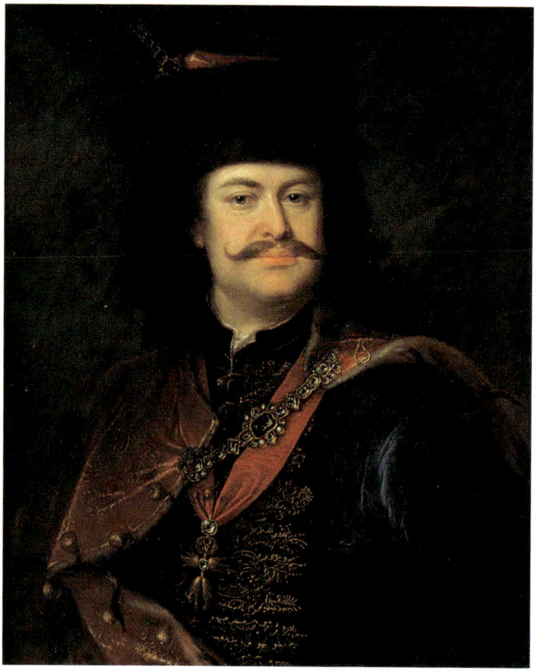

Ádám Mányoki
(Szokolya, 1673 – Dresden, 1757)
Ferenc Rákóczi II
1712
Oil on canvas, 75.5 × 67.5 cm
Inv. no.: 6001

It is not only the person of Ferenc Rákóczi II, prince of Transylvania and leader of an uprising against Habsburg rule (1703–1711), but also the unity of unaffected dignity and intimateness not found anywhere else in Mányoki's œuvre that makes this painting an emblematic work of Hungarian baroque portraiture. The picture is a private portrait of the prince, now living in exile, showing him as a private person in Hungarian noblemen's outfit, without the paraphernalia of the princely rank, with the order of the Golden Fleece he received in 1708. Mányoki, who had lived and worked in German-speaking areas since his childhood, arrived to Hungary from Berlin in August 1707 to serve Rákóczi as his court painter. In addition to painting Rákóczi's portraits, he was also entrusted with confidential missions, printing and disseminating propaganda materials during his trips abroad. He set out on such a mission in the autumn of 1709 to the Netherlands and a few months later to Berlin, from where he did not return to Hungary after the suppression of the uprising but went to the venue of Rákóczi's exile in Poland, Gdańsk. He painted his last portrait of the prince there in October 1712, before Rákóczi left for France. The painting was presumably painted for August the Strong, king of Poland and elector of Saxony and sent as a present by Rákóczi to Dresden. The inventory of 1728 already mentions it as an item in the Saxon ruler's collection. In 1925 Marcell Nemes acquired it and donated it to the Museum of Fine Arts.

E. B.

Ádám Mányoki

(Szokolya, 1673 – Dresden, 1757)

Count Georg Wilhelm Werthern

1719

Oil on canvas, 82 × 69 cm

Inv. no.: 54.327

Mányoki's painting style and compositional solutions were decisively influenced by the great French example, Nicolas Largillière's painting throughout his life. The overwhelming elegance and mundane appearance of the Paris painter's portraits of the haute bourgeoisie recur in Mányoki's works tamed and combined with an unaffected touch, while the technical quality of the paintings remains just as high. Count Werthern's portrait is also the adoption or reformulation of a composition by Largillière. It dates from Mányoki's best period when as freshly appointed court painter in Dresden he was depicting the notabilities of the Saxon court and the rich burghers of Leipzig one after the other with self-confidence and virtuosity. It was a brief period of success and acknowledgement, since his efforts were soon overshadowed by representatives of the new taste requiring decorativeness, rococo ease and diversity. Not much later, he returned to Hungary for a few years. Count Georg Wilhelm von Werthern, a cultivated man with a university education, was the secret councillor of the Trier court, and chief marshal, then chamberlain and later cabinet minister of the elector August the Strong. The portrait, emanating dignity and serenity, was first owned by the counts Festetich, then by the counts Zichy in Vienna. In the early 20th century it came to Budapest, to be included in the Jenő Zichy Museum of the Municipality.

E. B.

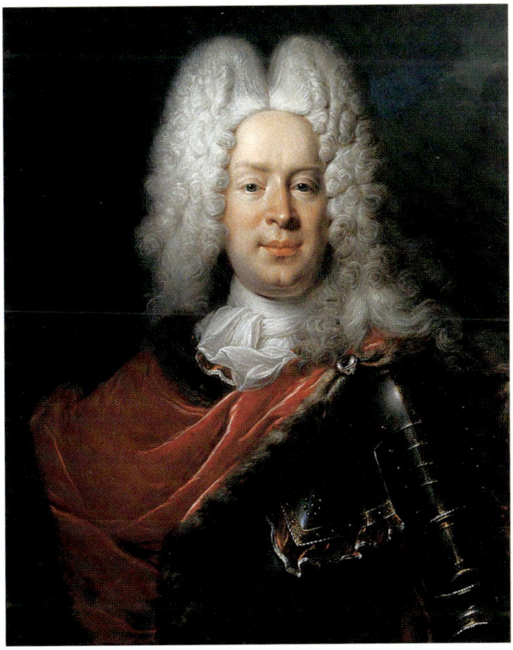

Franz Anton Maulbertsch
(Langenargen, 1724 – Vienna, 1796)

Death of Saint Joseph
Around 1767

Oil on canvas, 324 × 159 cm

Inv. no.: L.5.121

The most outstanding Central European painter of his age, Franz Anton Maulbertsch created a considerable portion of his work in Hungary. He painted innumerable frescoes and altar pictures on Hungarian commission from the early murals in the parish church of Sümeg (1757–1758) to the unfinished decoration of Szombathely cathedral, which provide ample ground to review the change in his style from capricious rococo through visionary painting to classicizing late baroque. The St Joseph altar picture probably made for the Trinitarians in Buda is an excellent piece of his late "visionary" period. In a dark, dim interior St Joseph is lying in bed, lifting his eye to the heavenly Father at the moment of his death. Christ is standing by his bed as the mediator. The figure of Mary, whose gracefulness is so typical of Maulbertsch' art, is not looking at Joseph but at the little angels playing with carpenter's tools and holding lilies in the foreground. The celestial Holy Trinity and the earthly Holy Family are both present in the picture. The scene is arranged parallel with the picture plane, the illumined surfaces clearly and softly rising out of the warm brown dimness of the room. On the basis of style-critical considerations research dates the painting to the second half of the 1760s when Maulbertsch' visionary painting had already been somewhat moderated. A picture for a side altar in the Carmelite church in Székesfehérvár is of identical theme and composition but richer in detail than the picture in the Gallery.

Zs. Bo.

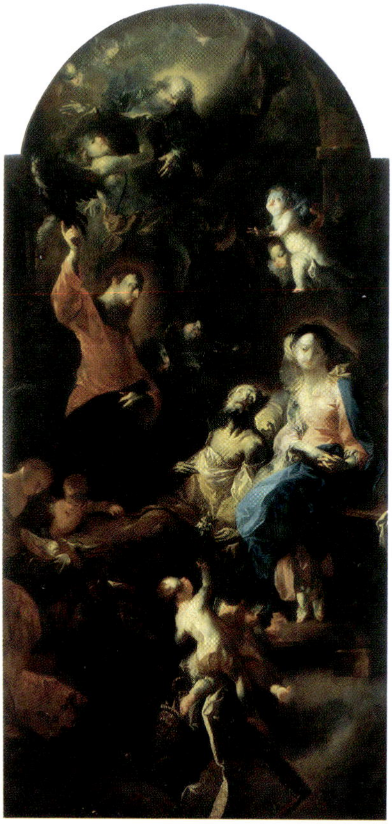

Jakob Christoph Schletterer

(Wenns, Tirol, 1699 – Vienna, 1774)

Immaculata

Around 1754

Alabaster, 38.5 cm

Inv. no.: 86.13M

The alabaster figurine adapts to the popular type of the Immaculate Virgin that evolved during the catholic revival: the Virgin at prayer is standing on the globe and the moon crescent while she is treading on the head of the serpent symbolizing evil. The slender female figure modelled in a slight S curve, the compact silhouette determined by the cloak, the charming face and the picturesque details including the putto hiding under the drapery derive from the Viennese variant of the arsenal of late baroque Venetian sculpture. The most notable representative of this trend in the imperial city was Lorenzo Mattielli, while the leading master of the classical style was Georg Raphael Donner. Both influenced the oeuvre of Tyrolese Jakob Christoph Schletterer, who passed down his increasingly classicistic, sophisticated style to the subsequent generations during his long tutorship at the Academy.

Schletterer mostly made altar sculptures and reliefs for monastic churches in Lower Austria, but sepulchral monuments are also known by his hand. His documented works in Hungary—the Virgin column in Sopron made after Andrea Altomonte's plans in 1745, the garden statues at Darufalva (Drassburg, Austria) from 1758—suggest that he probably delivered other works to Transdanubia, too. The signed, white marble Immaculata removed from the Esterházy castle in Tata to the local museum is a more animated, rococo variant of this statuette. The work in the Gallery is from the Cistercian abbey in Zirc; it was also created in the 1750s.

A. J.

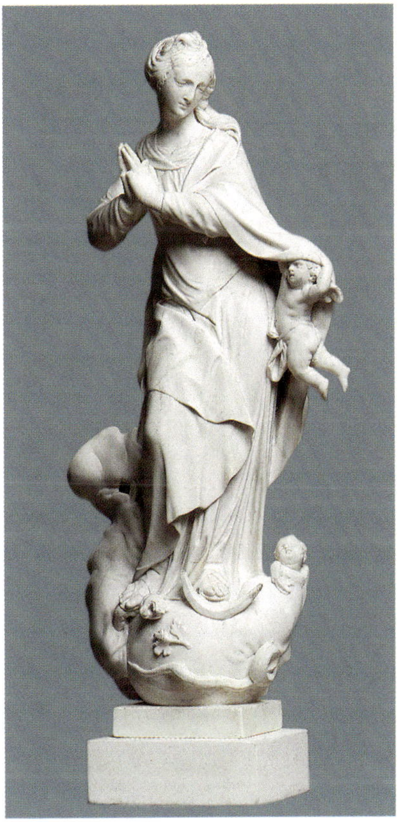

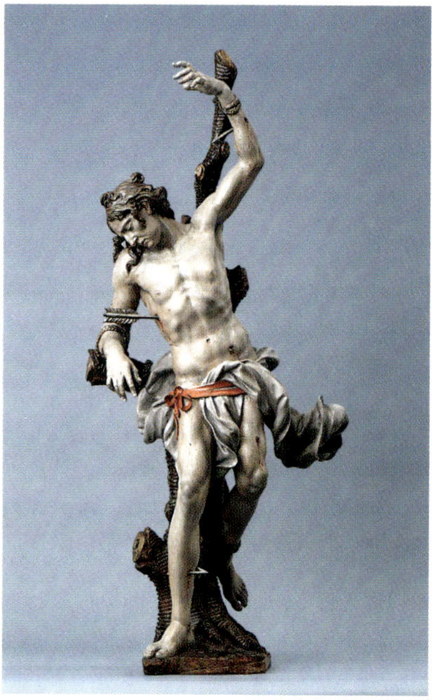

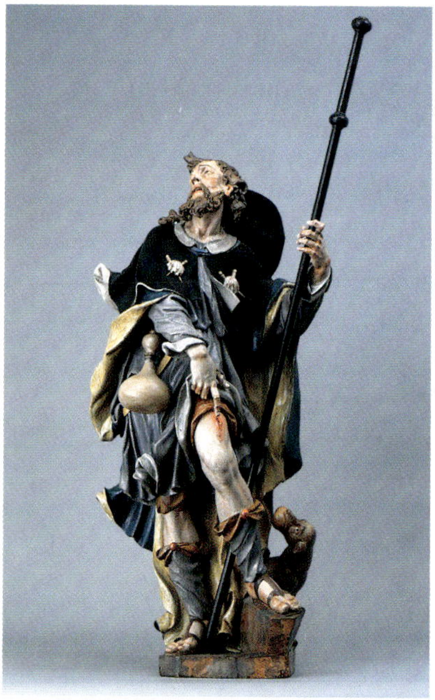

Philipp Jakob Straub
(Württenberg, 1706 – Graz, 1774)
Saint Roch and Saint Sebastian from Egervár
1757
Wood, painted, 121 and 119 cm, resp.
Inv. nos: 4964 and 4963

Philipp Jakob Straub was born in a Württenberg family of sculptors, moved to Vienna with his brother Johann Baptist Straub (later court sculptor in Munich) in 1727, and studied at the Academy of Fine Arts there in 1730–1733. In 1733 he settled in Graz where he worked for the church, the aristocracy and the middle class alike, both in wood and stone. On style-critical grounds, research attributes to him an extensive oeuvre in Styria where he introduced the influence of Bavarian rococo sculpture and the practice of the stone sculpture of the Vienna court. The splendid rococo statues of the two saints came to the museum from the parish church of Egervár in Zala county. The patron of the church, count Ignác Széchényi ordered a large tabernacle with carved figures for the high altar made around 1730 in 1757. The statues of the saints—protectors from the plague—express pain and suffering. St Roch, clad in pilgrim's clothes, turns his eyes to heaven, his lips parting for a cry of pain as he points to the wound on his foot. Next to him a dog appears who brought him bread when he was suffering of the plague. Bound to a tree and wounded by arrows, the young martyr St Sebastian is resigned to his fate. His head rests on his shoulder, the tears dripping slowly from his closed eyes. St Roch's fluttering garments provide the contrast of light and shade, while light glides softly on the sensuously beautiful body of Sebastian. The statues are promoted into the vanguard of rococo sculpture in Hungary by the outstanding quality of modelling, the subtle and reserved colouring and the empathic rendering of emotions.

Zs. Bo.

Dionysius Ignatius Stanetti

(Beneschau/Dolni Benešov, 1710 – Körmöcbánya [Kremnica, Slovakia] 1767)

Saint Florian

1764

Lime-wood, gilded, 248 cm

Inv. no.: 52.799

The wooden statue of St Florian, just as its counterpart St Donatus—both one and a half times life-size—came to the National Museum in Budapest on permanent loan from the town of Körmöcbánya in 1892. There is documentary data to confirm that it had belonged to the furnishing of the parish church of Our Lady on which Stanetti worked in 1763–1764. Owing to a landslide the building had to be pulled down in 1880 and its furnishing was scattered. Most of the statues are now in Slovakian museums. The gilded statues of SS Donatus and Florian were set up as an independent pair of statues in the nave. The two saints from the age of imperial Rome were revered as protectors from lightning, hailstorms and fire since the Middle Ages. They are shown as sturdy athletic men with reserved gestures, their heroic poses borrowed from stone sculpture. Donatus is wearing a wreath of leaves on his head and holding a bundle of lightning by his chest; the sheaf of wheat originally in his left hand is lost. Helmeted St Florian has a burning house at his feet, a pail in his right hand, but the flag from his left hand is lost. Their sculptor, Dionysius Stanetti was the descendant of a noted Silesian dynasty of sculptors. He moved to Hungary in the 1740s, married in Körmöcbánya and was a burgher of the town until his death. Apart from the late baroque furnishing of churches in the neighbourhood, he also created monumental public memorials: the Holy Trinity columns in Selmecbánya (Banska Štiavnica) and Körmöcbánya.

A. J.

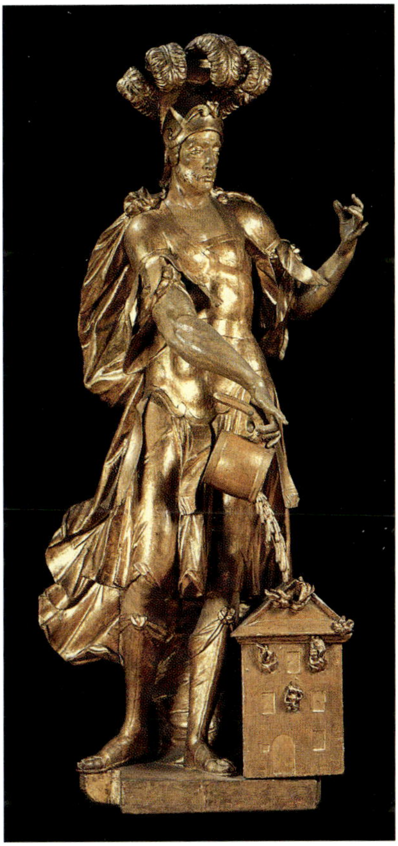

Johann Lucas Kracker

(Vienna, 1719 – Eger, 1779)

Saint Catherine of Alexandria Disputing with the Philosophers

1775

Oil on canvas, 76.5 × 40.5 cm

Inv. no.: 80.3M

Johann Lucas Kracker was born into a Viennese family of sculptors. After his academic studies, his career began in Ljubljana, then continued in Znojmo where he founded a family. From the 1750s he regularly worked in Hungary, first of all for the Premonstratensians in Jászó (Jasov, Slovakia). His chef d'œuvre is the monumental ceiling fresco in the nave of St Nicholas' church in Prague, Malá Straná (1760/61). After "commuting" to Moravia and Lower Austria for over a decade, he settled for good in Eger in 1768. His patron was bishop Károly Eszterházy, who showered him with work. The most notable of the commissions was the fresco in the library of the Lyceum of Eger (The Council of Trent) painted with his assistant Joseph Zach in 1778. A latter-day masterpiece is the signed picture of St Catherine for the high altar of the parish church of Egerbakta, the sketch in oil for which found its way to a museum. The religious dispute of the young Christian woman who lived in the early 4th century adjusts to a Viennese model, Michelangelo Unterberger's composition The Twelve-Year-Old Christ in the Temple. The style of the sketch is rugged, restless, the figures are elongated with small heads. The vibrant colours of the bozzetto are predominated by golden yellow, while in the final large variant both the forms and the colours are calmed down. As victorious Ecclesia, Catherine, who converted fifty sages and the empress in a religious debate, proclaimed the truth of the Church shaken by the Enlightenment.

A. J.

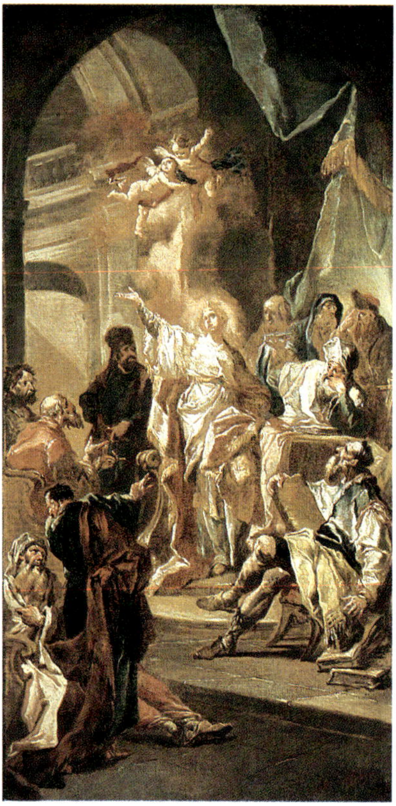

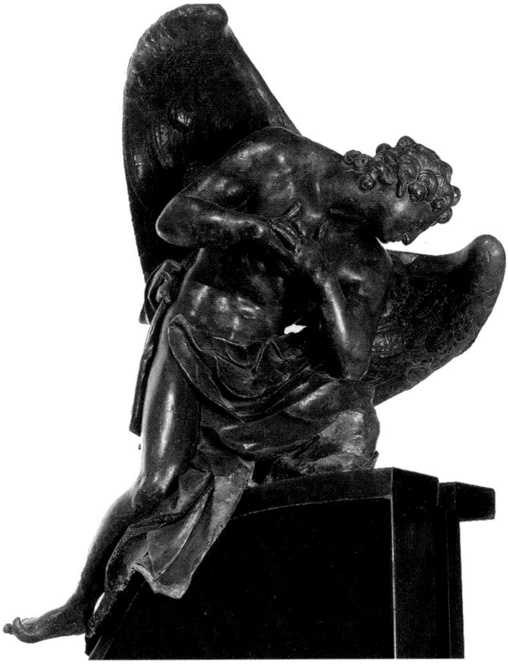

Georg Raphael Donner

(Esslingen, 1693 – Vienna, 1741)

Adoring angels from the high altar of Pozsony (Bratislava) cathedral

1733–1735

Lead, 200 cm

Inv. nos: 76.4M and 76.5M

Georg Raphael Donner was the most prominent and influential artist in Central European sculpture in the first half of the 18th century. He developed his individual neo-classical style at a distance from baroque traditions, relying on antiquity and 16th-century Italian sculpture. Between 1729–1739 he was employed by the prince primate Imre Esterházy in Pozsony, and made the high altar of the cathedral (1733–1735) on his commission. This significant work is characterized by perfect harmony of sculpture and architecture, idea and form. The crowned canopy of the altar was carried by enormous free-standing fluted columns. The central figural group featured St Martin on the back of a rearing horse sharing his cloak with Christ appearing as a beggar lying on the ground. St Martin is wearing a Hungarian noblemen's outfit and the facial features of the archbishop. Two huge kneeling angels whose adoration is directed at the concealed Redeemer join the scene on either side. Despite minor differences in movement, hand gesture and arrangement of drapery, the angels are practically symmetrical; dignified celestial creatures, although their finely modelled strong bodies are very real. Their pose expresses intimate and perfect veneration. The beauties of the modelling are enhanced by the subtle grey hue and silken lustre of lead. The altar was taken to pieces in the 1860s when the cathedral was rebuilt in neo-Gothic style. The main group, the equestrian statue, is in the side aisle of the cathedral of Bratislava.

Zs. Bo.

Karl Philipp Schallhas

(Pozsony, 1769 – Vienna, 1797)

Seaside Landscape

1796

Oil on canvas, 59 × 85 cm

Inv. no.: 98.5M

Born in Pozsony, Karl Schallhas studied at the Academy in Vienna in 1783–1786 tutored by Johann Christian Brand, the professor of landscape painting. From 1790 he was a member of the Academy, from 1795 as corrector at the department of landscape painting. His rising career was terminated by his untimely death. With the exception of four miniature portraits, only landscapes—oil paintings and graphic works—are known by his hand. He published his drawings made during his Austrian trips as series of engravings. His oeuvre is most deeply influenced by Johann Christian Brand. He adopted the traditions of Netherlandish landscape painting and alloyed them with the approach of the Enlightenment to nature. The motifs of nature are always harmoniously arranged in his pictures, people and animals composed in a natural harmony. His gentle, slightly melancholic landscapes and his pictures involving some more animated elements of romantic landscapism are both characterized by specially subtle colour hues and a soft and relaxed painterly quality. This seaside landscape (signed "C. Schallhas 1796") is one of the most outstanding works of the artist, the only known seascape in his œuvre. On the left a rising shore is seen, on the right the storm is approaching, a strong wind whips up and discolours the sea to a bottle green and sends tall waves to the shore. The ships struggle with the wind leaning to one side, the people on the shore hold on to their hats tight. Despite the dramatism of the heaving sea and the whirling grey clouds the painting suggests balanced calmness and some distance.

Zs. Bo.

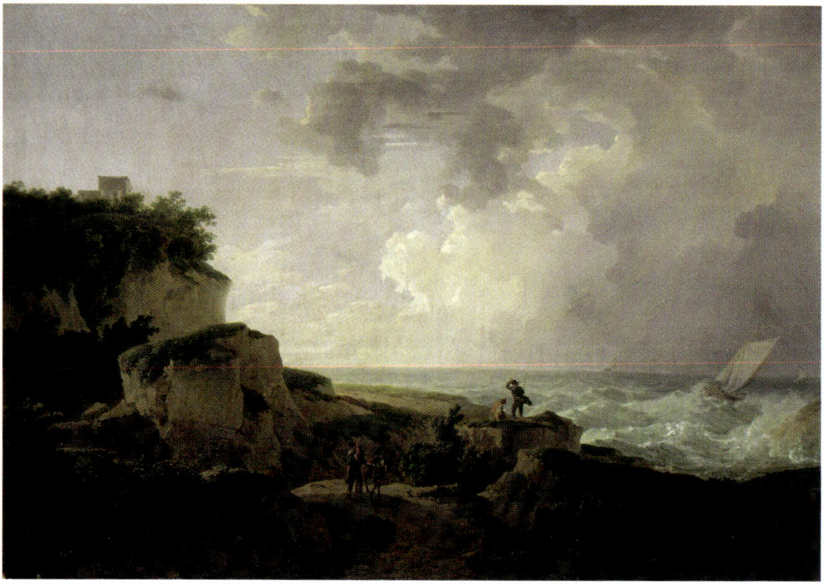

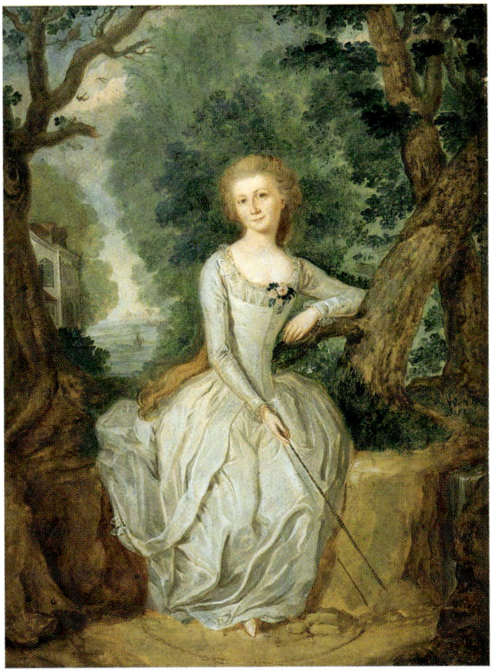

Johann Martin Stock

(Nagyszeben [Sibiu, Romania], 1742 – Nagyszeben, 1800)

Female Portrait

1793

Oil on copperplate, 48 × 37 cm

Inv. no.: 6477

The Transylvanian painter of Saxon descent first studied at the Academy of Fine Arts in Vienna from 1763 and later at the Academy of Engraving. Some years later he settled in Pozsony, then he was engaged by the Esterházy family and worked at Eszterháza. He often visited Vienna where Albert, duke of Saxon-Teschen also took note of his works. He went in for copperplate etching at that time, planning to publish a series presenting the inhabitants of Hungary and Transylvania, but only a few pages of it were completed. In Vienna he came into contact with the governor of Transylvania, Sámuel Brukenthal, the owner of one of the most important picture galleries in the city: he began to employ the painter regularly to help with purchases and restoration apart from painting portraits. In 1786, when the governor retired, Stock moved back to Nagyszeben. He became Brukenthal's employee, painting portraits in addition to caring for his picture gallery. Most of his portraits are from the subsequent years, painted of his employer's family, the noblemen and burghers of Transylvanian (Saxon) towns, officials, army officers. The format being busts or half-length portraits, they are objective works painted with a middle-class awareness. The best works are female portraits placed in natural scenery as is the presented cabinet picture. They reveal the influence of contemporary English portraiture which must have reached Stock via its influence on the works of some leading portraitists of Viennese neo-classicism.

E. B.

István Dorffmaister

(Vienna, 1729/1741 – Sopron, 1797)

The Battle of Mohács

1795–1796

Oil on canvas, 344 × 254 cm

Inv. no.: 55.387

Originally the painting adorned the reception hall of the abbot in the Cistercian monastery of Szentgotthárd as one of a representative series of six panneaux. The six paintings perpetuated important events in the history of the Szentgotthárd abbey as well as two moments of Hungarian history—the battles of Mohács and Szentgotthárd—which were believed to have had direct influence on the fate of the abbey. The large canvases covered the walls of the room like wall-hangings and the uncovered sections of the wall carried landscapes completing the historical compositions. The series and the ceiling decoration were painted by István Dorffmaister on the commission of abbot Marian Reutter. The program was provided by the scholarly Cistercian monk Theophil Heimb's history of the Szentgotthárd abbey published in 1764. The book contains detailed accounts of the both battles (after Miklós Istvánffy), which the painter faithfully translated into visual images. In the foreground of the Mohács painting King Louis II's armoured figure is seen sinking with his horse into the mud of the stream. In the middle Ottomans and Hungarians are engaged in battle and in the background, right under the horizon, the blue ribbon of the Danube and the hills of the countryside are seen enveloped in haze. The picture suggestively conveys the battle and the personal tragedy of the young king, just as the written source does. Born and trained in Vienna, István Dorffmaister settled in Sopron in 1762 and worked as fresco and altar picture painter in Transdanubia until his death. This late work is his second job for Szentgotthárd: in 1784 he also painted the battle of Szentgotthárd on the vault of the church.

Zs. Bo.

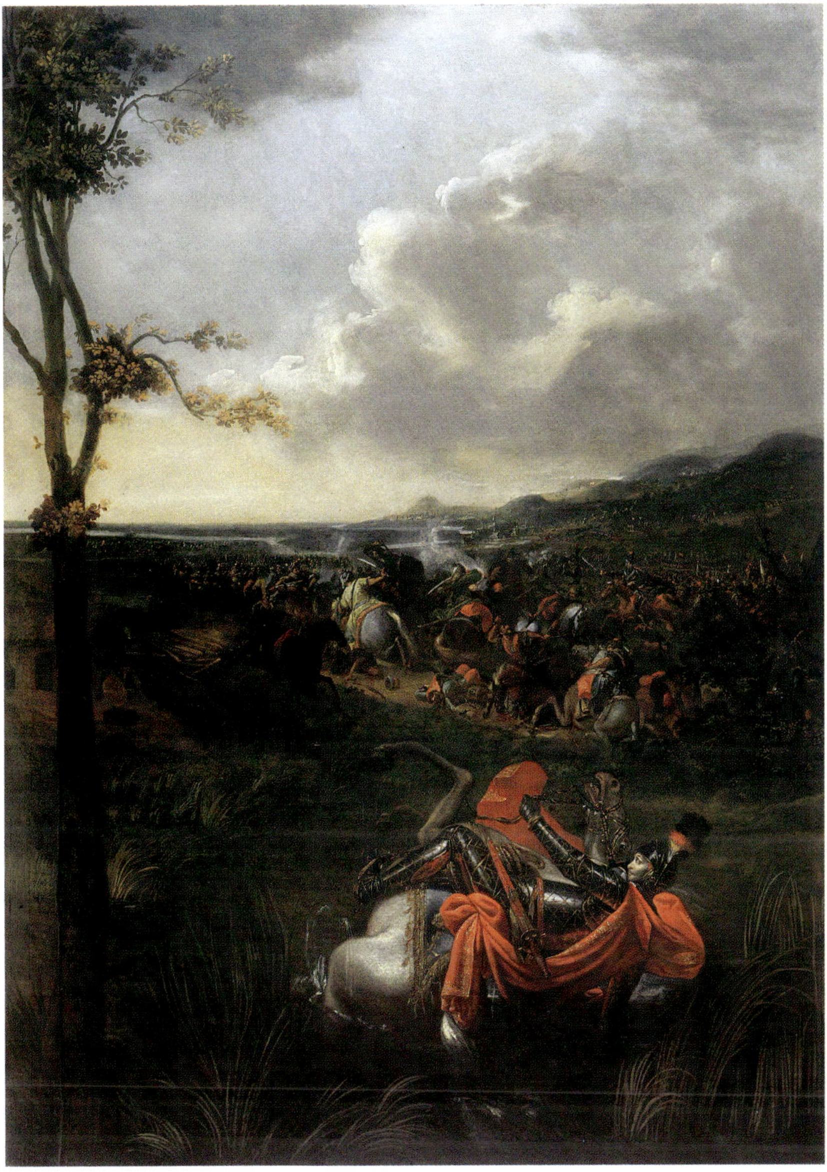

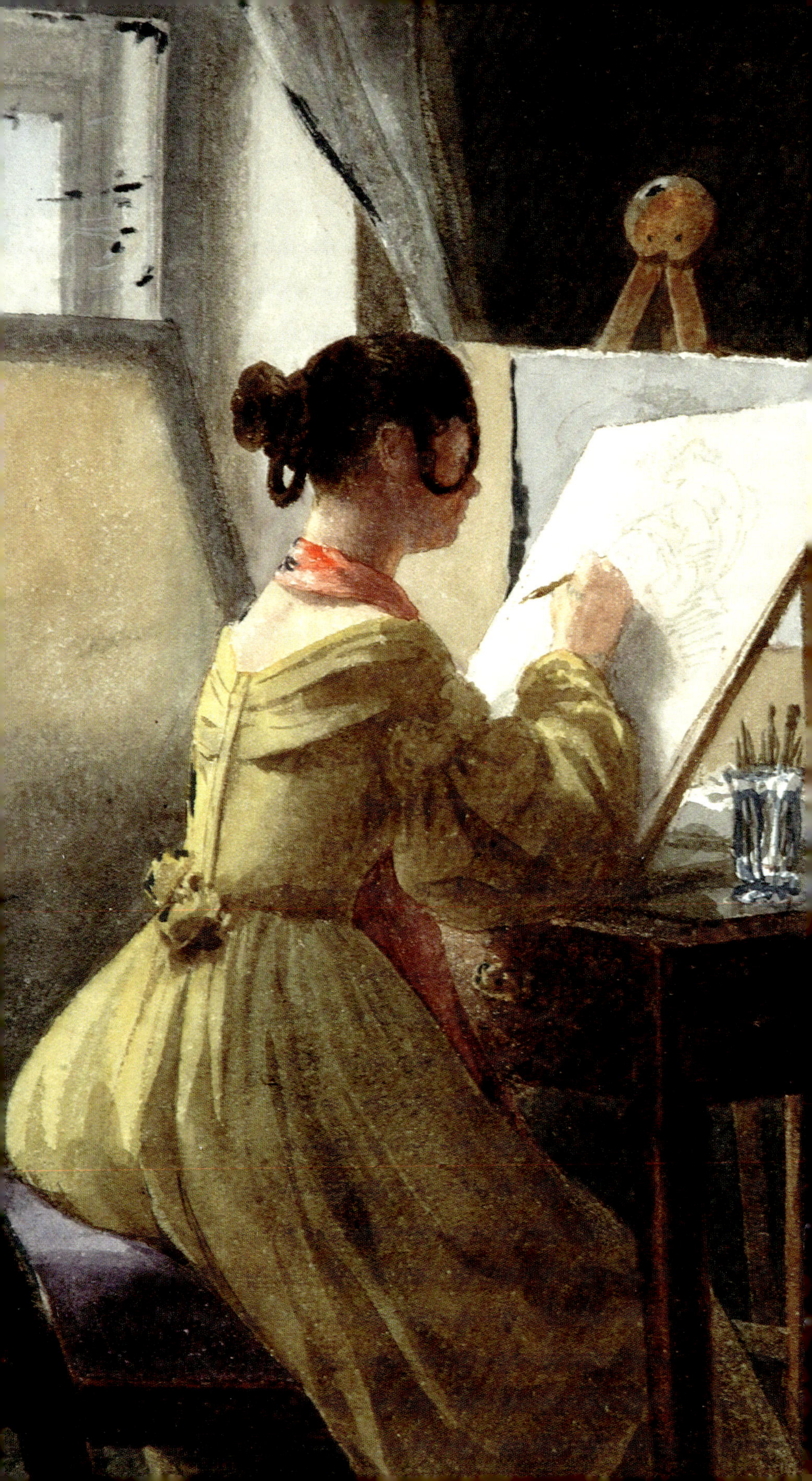

Collection of 19th–20th-century Art

This main department of the Hungarian National Gallery, comprising collections of paintings, prints and drawings, sculptures and medals, has the most voluminous stock in the Museum, which keeps growing through purchases and donations. Its emergence is closely interconnected with the history of the institution, as prior to its foundation in 1957 the Hungarian works belonged to other museums (Hungarian National Museum, Museum of Fine Arts, Municipal Picture Gallery). These data are registered in the old inventory books and in the descriptive cards, which are the sources for the history of a work or the whole collection spanning the period between 1800 and 1945.

Probing into the past, curious museologists and researching art historians may discover lots of intriguing facts. The archbishop of Eger and poet János Pyrker donated his collection of 196 items to the Hungarian National Museum in 1836, therewith laying the foundations of the museum's picture gallery. At that time, the collection included a single Hungarian work: Károly Markó the Elder's From the Pearls of the Sacred Past, which depicts a scene from a cycle of biblical poems written by Pyrker. Collecting was promoted by several civil organizations as well; the rural scene of Ágost Canzi's Grape Harvest near Vác (1859) was a donation by the Art Society of Pest, for example. In 1906, the fine arts stock of the museum was merged with that of the National Picture Gallery housed by the Hungarian Academy of Sciences since 1870, within the institutional frames of the Museum of Fine Arts. The purchase in 1903 of a fine collection of Miklós Barabás' portraits and Italian and Pest-Buda landscapes in watercolour was an outstanding acquisition at that time. From 1912 the Museum of Fine Arts handled the Hungarian stock separately, decisive items of which were several works by Mihály Munkácsy, László Paál, Károly Lotz, Bertalan Székely and Pál Szinyei Merse.

In 1928 the New Hungarian Gallery was formed from this gradually growing collection, and it was shown at a permanent exhibition in the building of the Old Palace of Arts (today Hungarian Academy of Fine Arts) until 1935.

The municipality of Budapest kept purchasing art objects continuously from 1880 but it was as late as 1933 that the Municipal Gallery was established for the presentation of these works including such monumental ones as Gyula Benczúr's emblematic The Recapture of Buda Castle in 1686 (1896) as well as sculpture by the most noted sculptors Alajos Stróbl, Miklós Izsó, János Fadrusz, Ferenc Medgyessy.

Housed at first (from 1957) in the former Palace of Justice and from the mid-1970s in the Castle of Buda, the Hungarian National Gallery's department of painting—still called New Hungarian Gallery—kept enlarging its stock especially with 20th-century works. As a result, large selections by now classic artists such as Tivadar Csontváry Kosztka, Károly Ferenczy, Béni Fereczy, József Rippl-Rónai, János Vaszary, Dezső Bokros Birman, József Egry, István Szőnyi, Gyula Derkovits and others have been collected and exhibited. In the permanent exhibition arranged around art colonies and artistic groups works often exhibited abroad such as one of the highlights of Hungarian art nouveau János Vaszary's Golden Age (1898), Béla Czóbel's Sitting Man (1906) mediating the effects of French Fauvism, or works by Lajos Tihanyi, Lajos Kassák, Sándor Bortnyik abreast of the international avant-garde can be seen. If the subtly refined marble statue of István Ferenczy, Young Shepherdess (The Beginning of Fine Art, 1820–1822) and the idyllic landscape Visegrád (1826–1830) by Károly Markó the Elder mark the symbolic beginning of the 19th–20th-century exhibition, then the weighty and dramatic works by Jenő Barcsay, Imre Ámos and Lajos Vajda made in the 1940s close the period duly and lead over to the art of the second half of the 20th century.

Zsuzsanna Bakó

János Donát
(1744–1830)
Orpheus Begging Hades and Persephone to Return Eurydice
1819
Oil on canvas, 134 × 151.5 cm
Inv. no.: 92.12 T

János Donát, a painter of German lineage settled in Pest in 1812 upon the invitation of the writer Ferenc Kazinczy, after nearly twenty years in Vienna during which he had acquired a considerable name there. Until his death in 1830 he painted the portraits of several prominent figures of Hungarian public life. Though the bulk of his rich oeuvre consists of portraits, he also painted several religious compositions, nudes and mythological subjects. Orpheus was painted in Pest in 1819 commissioned by an unknown person. It was modelled on Heinrich Füger's work of a similar theme. The picture tells a popular story of Greek mythology: Orpheus would like to reclaim his wife Eurydice who was mortally bitten by a serpent. The gods of the Underworld promise to comply on the condition that he would not turn back on the way leading out into the world. Orpheus, however, can't keep his promise and thus loses his beloved wife for ever. The picture shows the moment when Orpheus plays his lute to Hades and his wife who are charmed by his music and therefore agree to fulfil Orpheus's request. Multifigural compositions are rare in Donát's oeuvre, maybe that is why there is some rigidity in the picture and a slight clumsiness of drawing. Still, the work has an important role in early 19th-century art in Hungary as it marks the end of the two centuries long predominance of baroque and the ascendancy of neo-classicism in all genres of art.

Zs. B.

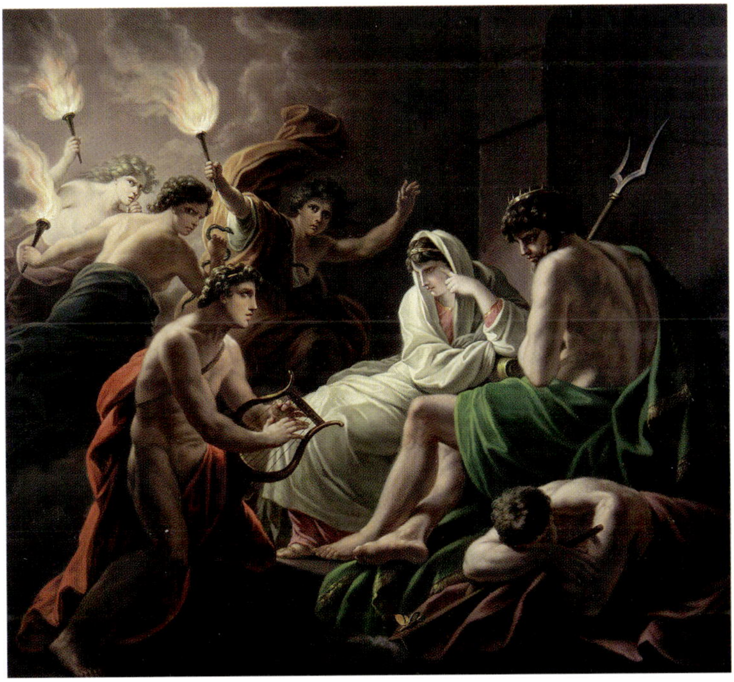

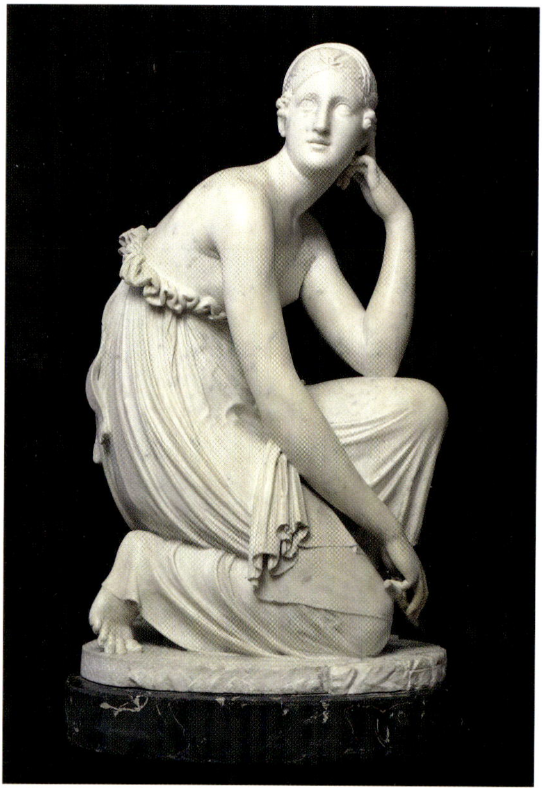

István Ferenczy
(1792–1856)
Young Shepherdess (The Beginning of Fine Art)
1820–1822
Marble, 57 × 40 × 94 cm
Inv. no.: 3662

István Ferenczy wrote to his parents from Rome on May 26, 1821: "by next spring I should like to complete a marble figure that implies the beginning of Kunst, notably: a young shepherdess scratching the shadow of her lover into the soil." This act—as tradition says—marks the beginning of the "fine arts": the girl is the first instinctive artist, listening to the dictates of her emotions when depicting another person. Ferenczy sent home the work dedicated to his patron palatine Joseph and it was put on display in a room on the ground floor of the royal castle and later transferred to the National Museum. It was a great success inspiring poems in praise of the artist and his work. In his epigram Ferenc Kazinczy called the work Graphidion—meaning "kindly little drawer". The sculptor acquired the knowledge leading to the programme of the Young Shepherdess from his studies of the art of classical antiquity. The statue emanates classic timelessness. "What beauties there are here!" Kazinczy writes. "The upper part is uncovered so that nothing of the charms of the girl be hidden, while the lower part—quite intelligently—is veiled by fine drapery and its folds."

G. Sz.

Károly Markó the Elder
(1791–1860)
Visegrád
1826–1830
Oil on canvas, 58.5 × 83.5 cm
Inv. no.: 3097

Hungarian art historical literature regards Visegrád as the first representative piece of independent Hungarian landscape painting in the modern age. The picture shows a time-honoured venue of Hungarian history with the ruined castle of Visegrád—an impressive ensemble in its demise—as well as Castle Hill and the gentle curve of the Danube. The staffage figures that were used as props for the traditional rethorical interpretation of a landscape are missing, so the scenery is to be interpreted by itself and not as the background to some human or mythological event. This autonomous interpretation is made possible by the unambiguous historical implication of the sight. In Visegrád we see Hungarian history with its greatness and tempests. The natural point of view close to the ground and to the sight draws the spectator into the composition. The relatively intact mass of the Salamon tower with the Danube and the mountains on the other side are in the lower third of the picture plane. Castle Hill crowned with the ruins of the palace towers over them. This structuring of the elements of the picture reflects a hierarchy in which the ruin is superior to what is intact, the historical remains have advantage over the natural formations. Eventually, all this is arranged into a suprahistorical unity by the sky taking up nearly half the picture space and repeating the landscape motifs asymmetrically. In the composition of Visegrád a romantic national programme and artistic universalism are united in a harmony which the subsequent historical landscapes more advanced towards romantic subjectivism could no longer reproduce.

G. B.

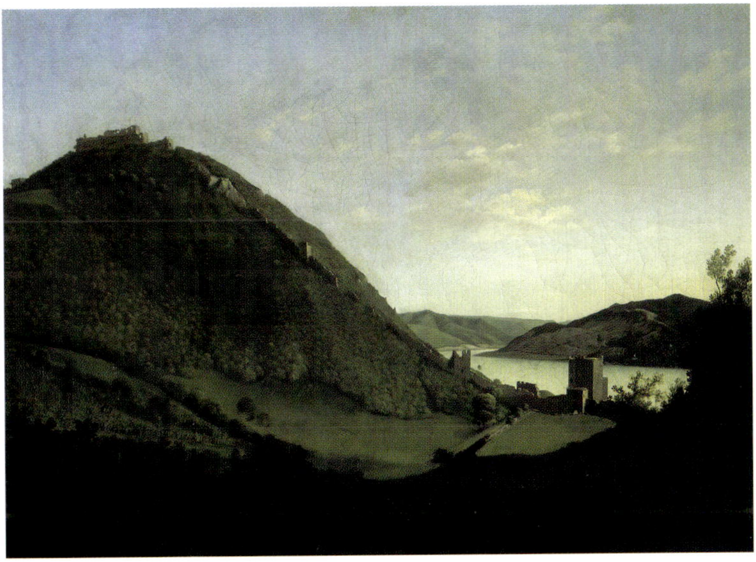

Gábor Melegh
(1801–1832)
Franz Schubert
1827
Oil on panel, 61.5 × 48.5 cm
Inv. no.: 5285

Gábor Melegh was a talented Hungarian painter of the biedermeier who earned a fame with slightly sentimental, subtly painted portraits during his short life. He studied at the Academy of Fine Arts in Vienna in 1817–1823 and graduated with honours. He made good friends with some fellow artists including painters Moritz von Schwind and Leopold Kupelwieser, among whose friends was Franz Schubert. Correspondence and recollections confirm the relationship. Kupelwieser painted a portrait of Schubert, which helped identify the long unknown model of Gábor Melegh's painting. Melegh's portrait depicts the composer in a cozy setting, on a porch with the dog Drago known from Kupelwieser's picture. The meticulously careful rendering of the clothing and environment of the sitter was a typical feature of Viennese biedermeier, the romanticism of the middle-class. It characterizes other portraits of Gábor Melegh, too. The light and bright colours, slightly linear painting, the complete harmony of sitter and setting endow the painting—the artist's most outstanding work—with a serene and convival atmosphere.

Zs. B.

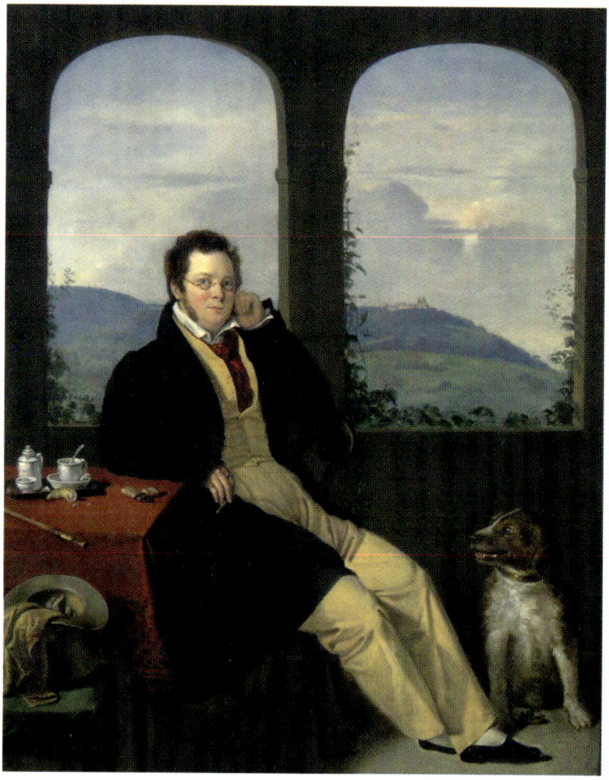

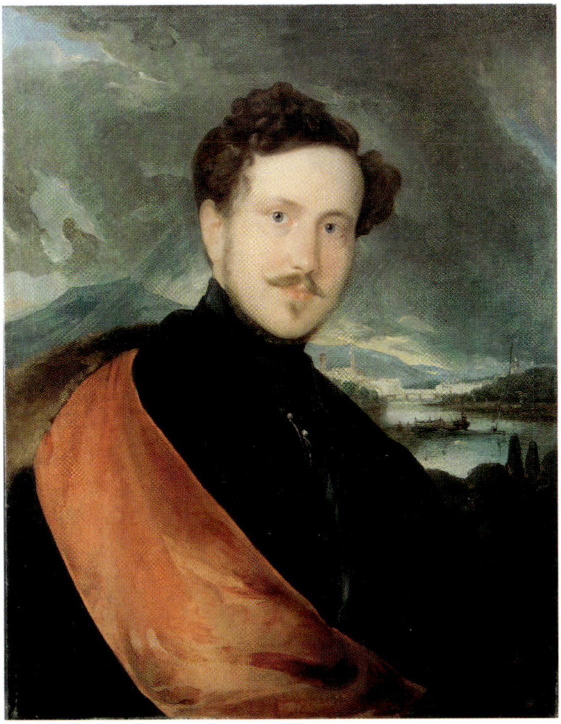

Sándor Kozina
(1808–1873)
Self-portrait
1832
Oil on canvas, 73 × 58 cm
Inv. no.: 6097

Known chiefly for his portraits, Kozina is a representative of early Hungarian romantic painting. During his academic years in Vienna palatine Joseph took note of his painting Deluge and offered him a grant of 400 forints a year for 4 years so that he could improve his artistic skills. In 1829 Kozina went to Italy. The diary notes of his friend and patron Bertalan Szemere reveal that he visited several towns including Florence, Naples and Venice and sojourned longer in Rome. He probably returned to Florence several times, as his Self-portrait of 1832 proves. This romantic self-portrait is of half-length, concentrating on personality traits, character, emotional-psychic states of mind rather than the externalities, a type of portrait that became popular in the mid-century. Yet in Kozina's portrait the background also has significance. It does not merely indicate the venue where the picture was painted like a topographic guide. The swirl of dark clouds and the radiant strip of the blue sky in the distance suggest the passing of the storm. The rays of the setting sun sharply illumine the famous buildings of Florence, the Duomo and the tower of the Campanile as well as the old bridge, and glitter on the Arno. The landscape is not just a sign or empty setting but the emotional background of the portrait, the venue of the painter's life in an important phase of his career.

Zs. B.

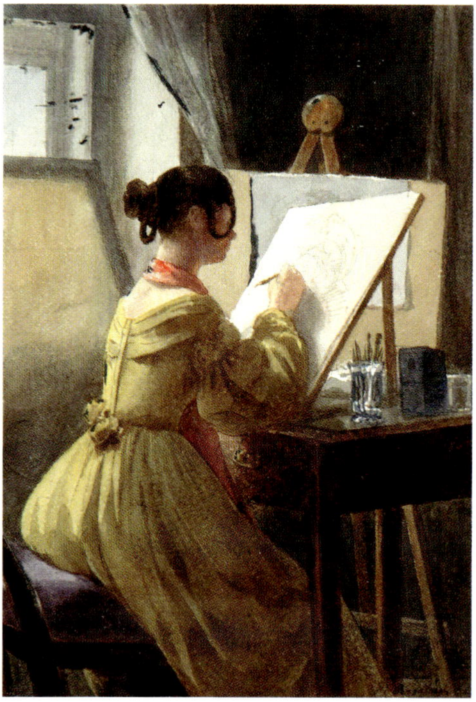

Miklós Barabás
(1810–1898)
In the Studio
(Countess Róza Teleki)
1838
Watercolour on paper, 248 × 175 mm
Inv. no.: 1903–115

Miklós Barabás' graphic output constitutes an extensive part of his oeuvre. He worked on paper in the most diverse genres all through his long life. During his Italian journey in 1834–35 he became the best Hungarian aquarellist of his age by adopting the watercolour technique of contemporary English painters. The brushwork and colour scheme of his watercolours are relaxed, and he solved easily any artistic problem in landscapes and genre scenes alike. After his Italian tour the finest graphic sheets of his œuvre were created until the mid-1840s including this peculiar portrait concealed as a genre picture. Róza Teleki was the painter's pupil in Kolozsvár in the year when the sheet was painted. The watercolour might have been inspired by the moment: the model is depicted quite unusually, almost with her back to the spectator, working by the easel, so the artist was not so much driven to capture the facial features as to convey a mood. The tiny composition is reminiscent of the traditional 17th-century Netherlandish genre pictures—a woman in an interior in front of a window—with also marks of Viennese biedermeier which is mainly present in the props of the scene, furniture, clothing, but without a trace of sentimentalism. The painter does not display any ties to the painterly solutions of his age: he captured the sight in a snapshot suggesting profound absorption in the soft contrasts of light and dark patches.

O. H.

Count Iván Forray

(1817–1852)

Rider

Around 1840

Watercolour on paper, 187 × 238 mm

Inv. no.: F.88.13

Iván Forray studied law in Pest, and did not pursue art studies. In the mid-19th century he earned a fame as an Africa traveller, to which he also owed his title as count, received in 1847. He toured Egypt and Syria and several West European countries including Italy and Malta. His travel notes and sketches made during the trips were published in an ornate album in 1859 after his death as one of the most significant works among many travelogues written upon aristocratic commission. In the period of the upswing of landscape painting and drawing in the mid-19th century, parallel with the spread of the fashion in the upper circles to travel widely, the artists became the perpetuators of these peregrinations. Forray united in his person the travelling, inquisitve nobleman and the artist capturing the experiences. His oeuvre is still awaiting art historical assessment. The presented watercolour cannot be connected to a specific trip but raises the problem of representing equestrian movement probed into by so many European and Hungarian artists some time later. The picture reveals the artist's keen sense of observation down to minute detail and his exact sense of proportions typical of good draftsmen.

O. H.

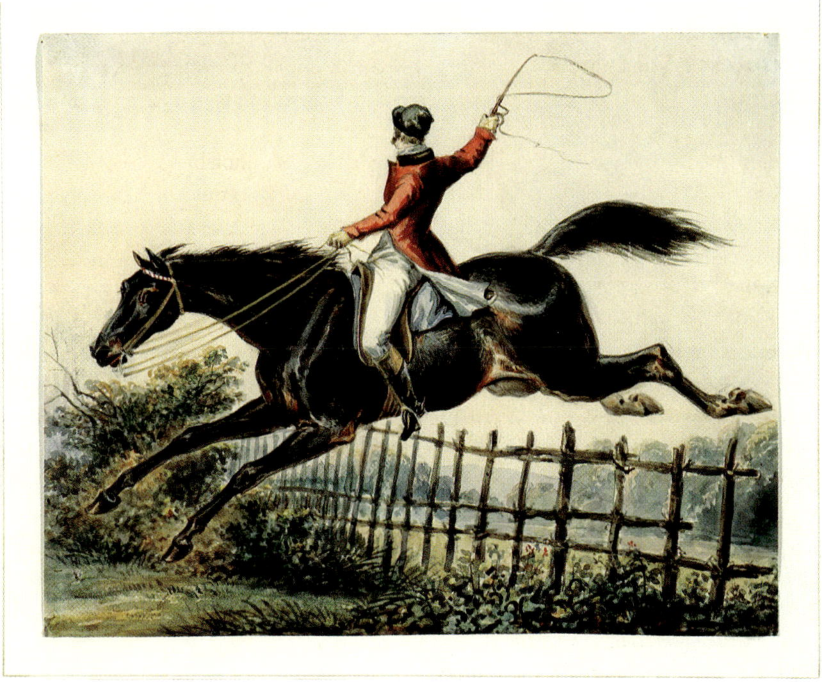

Károly Markó the Elder
(1791–1860)
Landscape sketch with a group of people under a cliff
The 1840s
Bistre, ink and wash on paper,
198 × 306 mm
Inv. no.: 1955-5625

After Károly Markó the Elder moved to Italy in the early 1830s, his individual style—of which his studies and sketches composed an integral part—grew fully fledged. The relatively large number of surviving sheets are studies that lend important hues to our knowledge of the oeuvre and working method of this 19th-century master of ideal landscapes. He constructed his paintings of ideal landscapes on the basis of on-the-spot sketches, first-hand experiences collected during his wanderings and acquaintance with new scenery. Markó shared the joy of directly experiencing nature with the landscapists of his age who laid the foundations of 19th-century landscape painting by withdrawing to nature and working there. The hermetically closed world of his oils is the polar opposite to his bistre sheets sometimes tinted with watercolour that confirm the master's direct contact with nature and his instinctive mastery of drawing and composition. Darker patches of agitated bistre lines, hatched masses and blank spots alternate in a sheet, without a trace of laboured meticulosity—quite contrarily, the sweeping gestures are impressive. At the same time, the figures to be included in the foreground are also indicated with a few light touches, yet anticipating the completed oil painting in its archaism.

O. H.

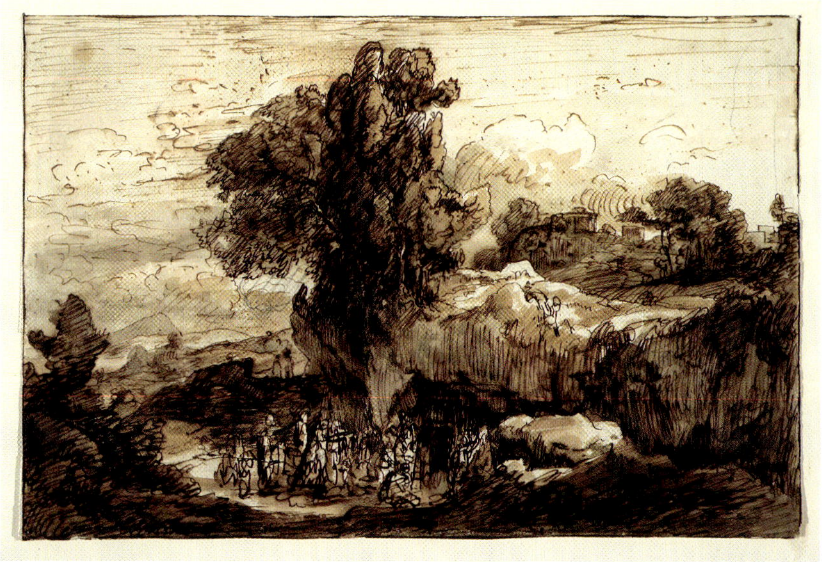

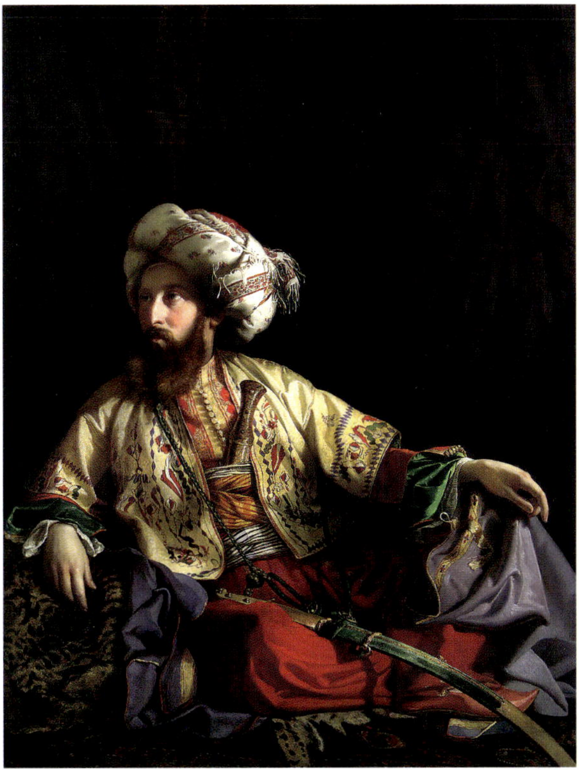

József Borsos
(1821–1883)
Emir of Lebanon
1843
Oil on canvas, 154 × 119 cm
Inv. no.: 2003.3

The Emir of Lebanon is actually count Edmund Zichy (1811–1894) who spent most of his life in Vienna as a passionate art collector and a leading figure in the art life of Vienna and Pest. He was one of the founders of the Museum of Applied Arts in Vienna and a member of Vienna's Künstlerhaus. The "prince" of Viennese painters, Hans Makart painted one of his few male portraits of him. Living in Vienna in the 1840s and earning a name as a portraitist, József Borsos painted Zichy's portrait when he had returned from an oriental trip in 1842, presumably in the attire the count had worn during his visit to Soliman Pasha, a commander of the Egyptian forces stationed in Syria. The portrait is in line with the growing popularity of orientalism in architecture and with the cult of the East that was fed not only by researches into Hungarian prehistory but also by the similarities of eastern and the Hungarian noblemen's traditional way of living. The characteristic Hungarian features of philosophizing and taking time were often compared by Hungarian writers to Lebanon and the tradition of thousand-year-old cedar trees. Thus Zichy's portrait is not only a fine specimen of the portraiture of the period but also the conveyor of a specific national programme.

G. B.

Károly Alexy
(1816–1880)
King Matthias
1844
Bronze, 36 × 30 × 75 cm
Inv. no.: 56.75-N

Alexy studied in Vienna in the first half of the 1840s. His small equestrian statue of Queen Victoria was a success and earned him an intriguing commission: he had to make a sixteen-piece series of the noted army commanders of the Habsburg Empire. At home, the reform diets and movements urged for political-social changes, the idea of the country's independence and the need for a national king were more and more strongly voiced. All this directed the attention to the great figures of the national past: a monument to commemorate King Matthias became timely. Nationawide fund-raising began, István Ferenczy made the plans but his ideas divided the public who thought they were too ambitious. It was probably the general atmosphere that encouraged Alexy to plan a series of Hungarian heroes and kings, with King Matthias modelled first. The small standing bronze figure shows the renaissance ruler, the patron of sciences and arts. His head is adorned with the laurel wreath of a victorious commander instead of the crown. He rests his hand on a traceried Gothic edifice all three sides of which are adorned with allegorical figures. The latter convey a sort of "plastic laudation": Historia, Minerva and Fortuna extol Matthias' life-work and personality. Alexy's work was received warmly at the Pozsony diet of 1844 and in the art exhibition in Pest, bronze copies were cast of the piece, but his idea of the cycle could not be realized.

G. Sz.

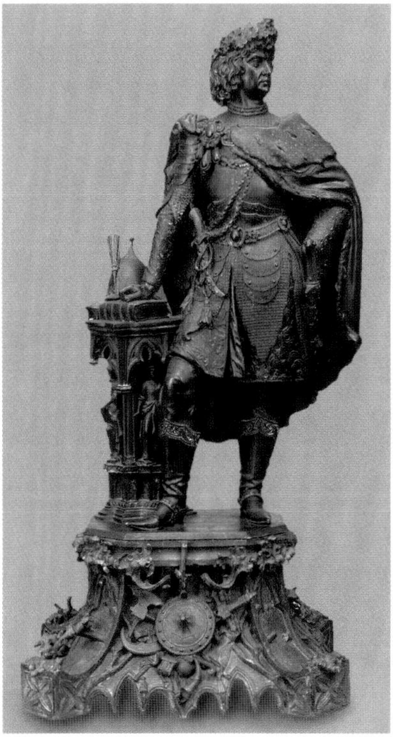

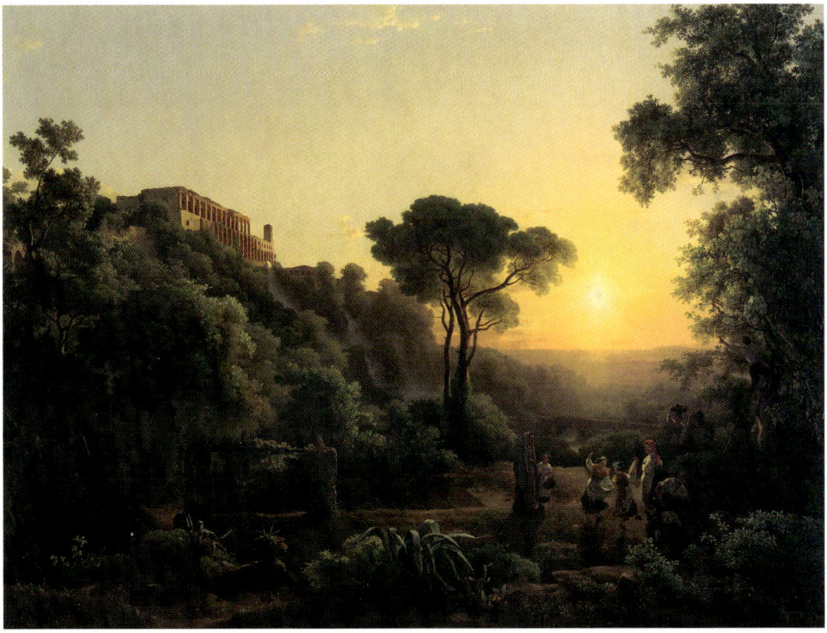

Károly Markó the Elder
(1791–1860)
Landscape with a Vintage Scene near Tivoli
1846
Oil on canvas, 116 × 153.5 cm
Inv. no.: 76.32

Károly Markó the Elder's landscape painting fed by 17th-century neo-classicism played a decisive role in Hungary in the struggles to have Hungarian art acknowledged. The first collectors of Markó's works were the Academy of Sciences, the National Museum and the main patrons of national culture who realized in Markó's oeuvre the birth of a long-desired national art of universal artistic values. This painting was commissioned by Count István Károlyi, who donated a considerable amount of money for the foundation of the Academy of Sciences. Károlyi had several Markó pictures in his mansion at Fót, and the building of the Fót church is also to his credit. In 1843 Markó asked for some advance money for the picture which he painted on the spot in Tivoli near Rome. Tivoli, Tibur in antiquity, was a popular destination of 19th-century painters and artists on account of Hadrian's summer villa, Maecenas' villa, the renaissance Villa d'Este and the nearly 100 m tall waterfall on the river Aniene. The most conspicuous motif in Markó's representative old-age paintings is the disc of the setting sun created with broad, thick brushstrokes. This was the first painting in which Markó used this motif, in 1846. In these large-sized late paintings the setting sun just opposite the spectator has an emphatic, distinguished role. Since it is known that Markó moved out of Pisa on account of his deteriorating eyesight in 1843, this new sun painting was perhaps a self-healing sun therapy for the artist.

G. B.

Károly Brocky

(1807–1855)

Female Head (Modesty)

Around 1848

Pastel on paper, 437 × 331 mm

Inv. no.: 1955-5538

Károly Brocky was one of the several 19th-century Hungarian painters whose graphic work is enormous and cannot be overlooked if one wishes to have an all-round picture of the artist's endeavours. In his large graphic output, various studies are overrepresented, but there are several autonomous graphic works and copies of old masters as well. After his studies in Vienna (1825–1832), Brocky toured nearly all Europe, but his early paintings of a sentimental tone reflect the influence of Viennese biedermeier. The experiences of his travels began to be incorporated in his paintings in the second half of the 1840s after he settled in London. He was highly popular with the English aristocracy for his romantic, slightly erotic nude paintings on mythological themes, using mostly elements of 16th–17th-century Italian painting. Similar in tone is the head study presumably made for a larger composition which appears as the allegory of Modesty. The slightly coloured picture reveals the extreme subtleness of details and the effort to convey as complex a message as possible with the most crystallized tools.

O. H.

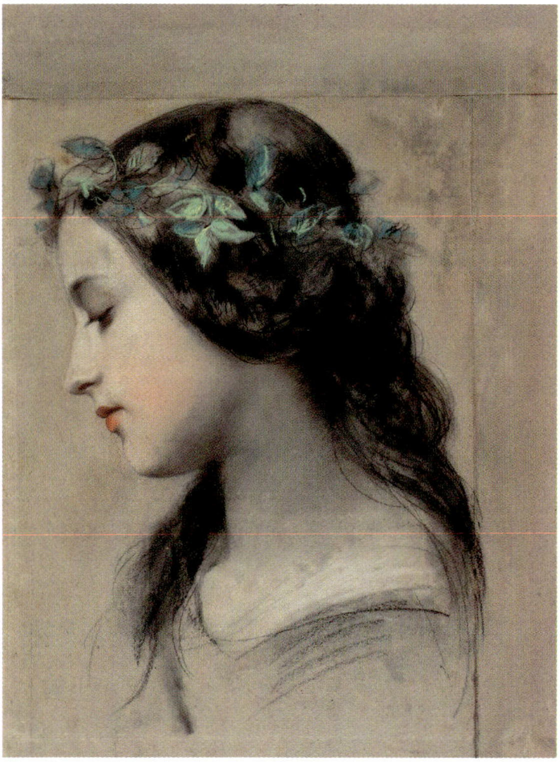

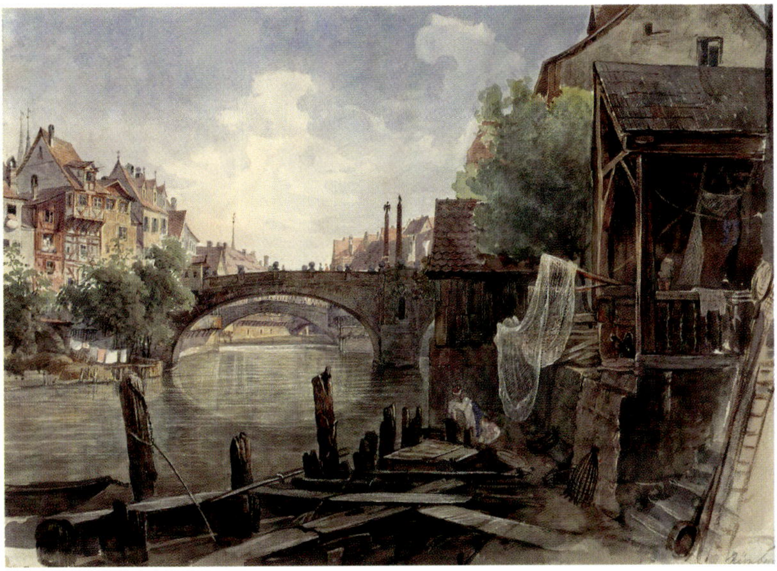

Károly Lajos Libay

(1816–1888)

Nuremberg

1849

Watercolour on paper, 248 × 350 mm

Inv. no.: 1898-205

Károly Lajos Libay is one of the central figures of 19th-century Hungarian landscapism owing not so much to his oil paintings but the immense stock of his drawings preserved in the collection of the Hungarian National Gallery. This collection of more than a hundred and fifty pencil drawings, watercolours and prints perpetuated the artist's landscape impressions during his travels. Owing to the popularity of earlier etchings of similar themes townscapes, veduti—a genre with a great cult in Vienna—had their efflorescence there again in the first half of the 19th century. One of most outstanding practitioners was Thomas Ender who put a deep imprint on Libay. At the Vienna academy, the Hungarian artist learnt from Ender the practice of studying nature and the technique of painting watercolours in the open, a technique that requires considerable bravura. The landscapists of those years were still halfway between the idealization of neo-classicism and the realistic rendering of nature appearing from the first quarter of the century, but their descriptive, topographic drawings and veduti were closer to realism. Libay was practically always on the road, travelling for his own sake or on his patron's commission: his oeuvre is like an enormous travel album. He toured Austria, Italy, Germany, Switzerland, Egypt; his trips can be accurately retraced in his watercolours. Apart from his outstanding technical mastery, he had a special sensitivity for choosing the motifs that could be the finest themes of his watercolours and drawings. He visited Bavaria in 1849, probably attending the Academy at Munich, too. The topographic watercolours of the Munich landscapists are characterized by an extremely light brushwork and minute detailing at places—characteristics shared with this work by Libay.

O. H.

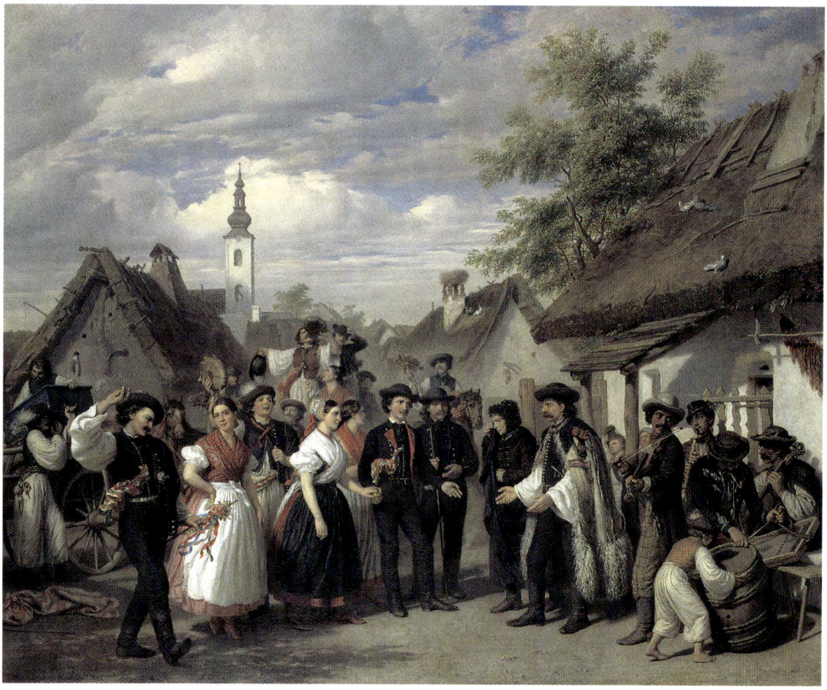

Miklós Barabás
(1810–1898)
Arrival of the Daughter-in-law (Arrival of the Bride)
1856
Oil on canvas, 127 × 157 cm
Inv. no.: 2762

Miklós Barabás was one of the most outstanding Hungarian artists in the first half of the 19th century. He owed his great popularity to his portraits and genre scenes in classicizing romantic style. Though the bulk of his oeuvre consists of portraits, he had a great role in spreading rural genre scenes in Hungary. Barabás was commissioned by the Art Society of Pest in 1855 to paint a multifigural rural genre scene. The theme was chosen by himself. The choice was prompted by the popularity of depicting weddings in Hungarian painting, e.g. by Károly Sterio and János Jankó. The model for The Arrival of the Daughter-in-law is Ferdinand Waldmüller's Wedding at Perchtoldsdorf. Just like Waldmüller's, Barabás' composition is like a scene on a stage. Theatrality is enhanced by the rigidity of gestures, the clumsy dancing movement, the naiveté of the artist's approach. The national colours appear on the nosegay pinned to the suit of the best man dancing on the left of the picture and on the ribbons fluttering from the stick in his hand, as well as on the clothes of the bride and bridegroom next to her. Despite all its awkwardness the picture had great success as is confirmed by the lithograph made by Amédée Charpentier, which was distributed as a present among the members of the Art Society and thus considerably increased the number of shareholders.

Zs. B.

Viktor Madarász
(1830–1917)
The Mourning of László Hunyadi
1859
Oil on canvas, 243 × 311.5 cm
Inv. no.: 2800

Viktor Madarász was one of the greatest Hungarian exponents of romantic history painting. His pictures conjure up the past, especially questions related to national independence, and aim to stir passionate emotions. Most of his works were painted during the nearly 20 years he spent in Paris and reflect the influence of French romantic painting. László Hunyadi, the son of the great defeater of the Ottomans János Hunyadi, was ordered to be killed by Vladislav V. Young Hunyadi was popular among the Hungarians, hence he was a rival to the young, inexperienced king who served foreign interests. The Hunyadi theme was very popular in the history painting of the century; László Hunyadi's farewell, his dying was depicted by many and in many different ways. Madarász' painting captures a very special moment, the deathwatch. Next to the body covered by a white shroud is his mother Erzsébet Szilágyi and his bride Mária Gara, their movements and facial expressions conveying profound grief. The light filtering through the chapel window and the dim light of the candles reinforce the feeling of sadness and mourning in the spectator. On account of the dramatic rendering the picture became a symbol of national mourning over the suppression of the war of liberation of 1848–1849. Madarász received one of the gold medals at the Paris Salon in 1860 for this painting.

Zs. B.

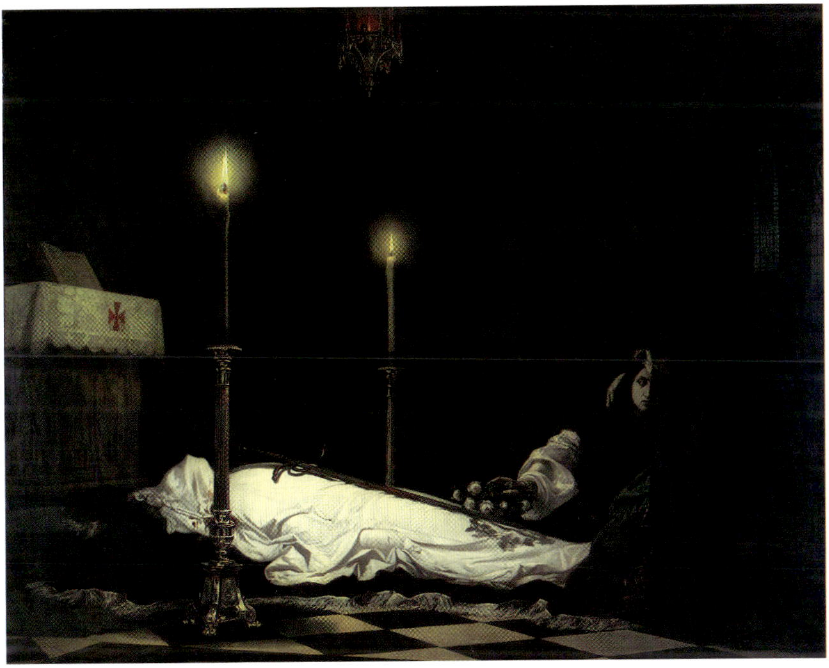

Ágost Canzi
(1808–1866)
Grape Harvest near Vác (Vintage Gaiety at Vác)
1859
Oil on canvas, 116 x 173.5 cm
Inv. no.: 2709

Painter and lithographer of German origin Ágost Canzi (originally called Martin Kanz) settled in Hungary in 1846 and regularly exhibited his portraits and genre pictures at the exhibitions of the Art Society of Pest. Grape Harvest near Vác is one of his most important and popular works. Wine harvests were often accompanied with singing and merry-making during the work, and when Gypsy musicians appeared, the harvester interrupted the work for a vintage dance. Canzi's picture captures the moment when the harvesters take the wreath tied of the finest bunches of grapes to the owner's house singing and dancing on the way. The procession is led by the Gypsy musicians to whose music several people are dancing, though their movements are somewhat awkward. The success of the picture owes in part to the growing importance of the question of national independence, the strengthening of a national awareness related to the war of liberation of 1848–1849.
In the genre-pieces this mainly appeared in the choice of subjects: the typical dances, customs of the Hungarians were depicted with growing frequency. In these works the national colours are often featured on the clothes and national badges are also included. In Canzi's painting the national flag is in mid-ground.

Zs. B.

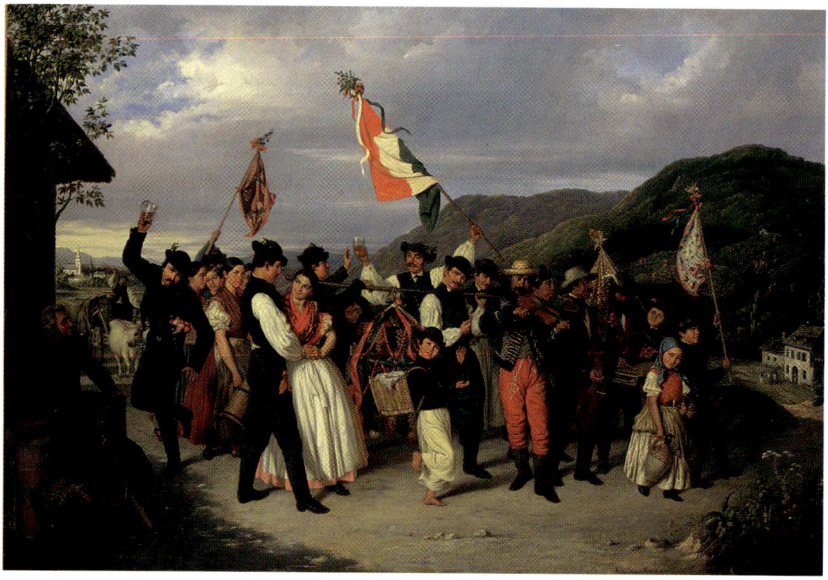

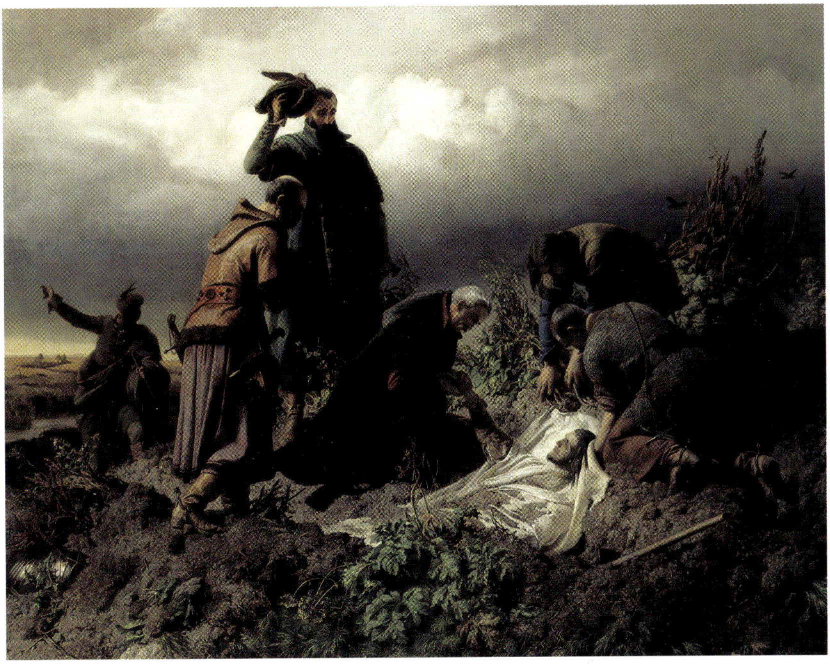

Bertalan Székely
(1835–1910)
The Discovery of the Corpse of King Louis II
1860
Oil on canvas, 140 x 181.5 cm
Inv. no.: 2870

Bertalan Székely was one of the most prominent artists of history painting in Hungary, a representative of its patriotic trend based on the traditions of 1848. The symbolism of his history paintings always refers to the time of painting, mostly analyzing the questions of lost national independence. He was particularly fond of depicting the anti-Ottoman fights for liberation, as these themes had a multi-layered symbolism: apart from the sacrifice for the motherland, they implied the protection of Christianity and the expression of more general human sentiments. This painting elaborates a tragic event of the battle of Mohács, the digging out of the body of king Louis II who was wounded in the battle and drowned in the flooding Csele stream. Laying great weight on authenticity, Székely—staying in Munich at the time—depicted the scene on the basis of a letter by Ferenc Sárffy, captain of the castle of Győr, who took part in the battle. The composition, the movements and faces of the figures, the treatment of light and colours all serve the more effective conveyance of complex emotions with the tools of romanticism. The intricate symbolism of the painting refers to the suppression of the war of liberation in 1848–1849, to the national mourning and to profound human feelings. Owing to the perfect unity of form and content the picture mediates at very high artistic level the feeling of grief caused by the lost battle and by death in a melancholic mood enveloping the spectator as well.

Zs. B.

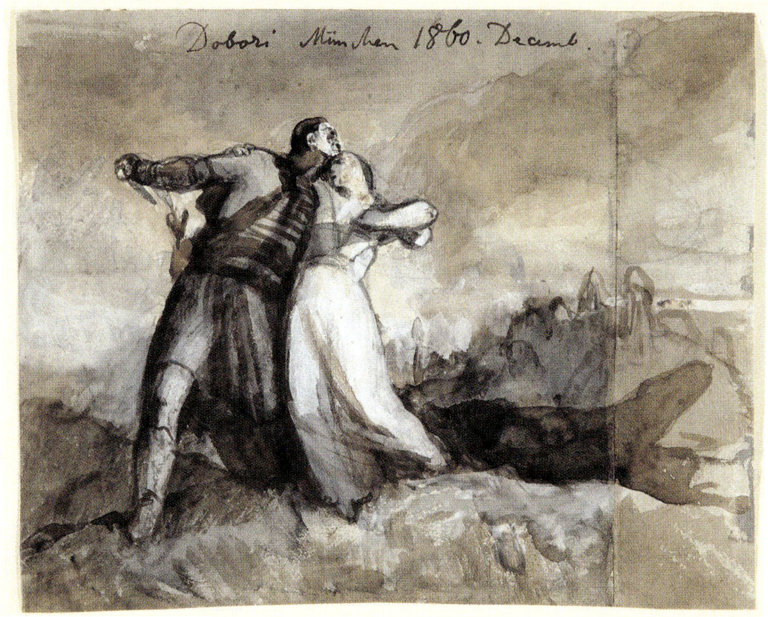

Bertalan Székely
(1835–1910)
Mihály Dobozi and His Wife
1860
Bistre and white body colour on paper
168 × 216 mm
Inv. no.: 1917-347

The monumental, premeditated, tranquil compositions of Bertalan Székely's history paintings were preceded by a lengthy period of planning. His artistic development in the early phase of his oeuvre—influenced by Munich history painting and his academic tutor Karl von Piloty—and his creative process are revealed by the diary he wrote at that time. The evolution and changes of a composition appear most spectacularly in the diary, including that of the painting entitled Mihály Dobozi and His Wife. According to a popular story, Mihály Dobozi was escaping on horseback from the Turks with his wife, but the enemy caught up with them, and the wife asked her husband to stab her saying she would rather die than be captured. Thus Dobozi killed his beloved wife and then died fighting the Turks. Székely prepared a unique series of sketches for the painting in each sheet of which he intensified the dramatic effect, the "shocking horror". He almost finalized some variations and then discarded them to get down to a new variant. The sketches all share the triangular block of the two protagonists in the foreground. In structuring the composition Székely probably adopted the "group theory" prevalent in his time: this stipulated that the secondary figures had to be arranged in relation to the central group in the picture. The series of only two figures throughout has some recurrent motifs such as the movement of the female figure tearing open her blouse: the woman offering, even demanding her death expresses in the most concentrated manner the tension of the dramatic moment.

O. H.

Károly Lotz
(1833–1904)
Horses in a Rainstorm
1862
Oil on canvas, 127 × 195 cm
Inv. no.: 2742

The scenery of the Great Plain with the long sweep-pole of the draw-well became the popular symbol of Hungarian landscape in the poems of Sándor Petőfi and János Arany, and in painting first in Károly Lotz's tempestuous puszta landscapes. The dual symbolism of the theme can be decrypted in both 19th- and 20th-century works: its unbounded vastness stood for both the sluggish barrenness of the "Hungarian wasteland" and for the Hungarians' unquenchable longing for freedom. Following his early successes after his studies in Vienna, young Károly Lotz returned home and got down to the depiction of the Hungarian rural scenery with a surprising freshness. Though most of his stormy landscapes still root in romanticism, but their natural dramatism, varied compositions and especially the colours borrowed from reality bring them closer to realism. He was particularly receptive to the atmospheric phenomena of the enormous firmament above the broad landscape. His swirling clouds of exquisite plasticity, the character and movement of horses, the peculiar sense of life of the people of the puszta could not be captured at the same level by any of his contemporaries.

A. Sz. M.

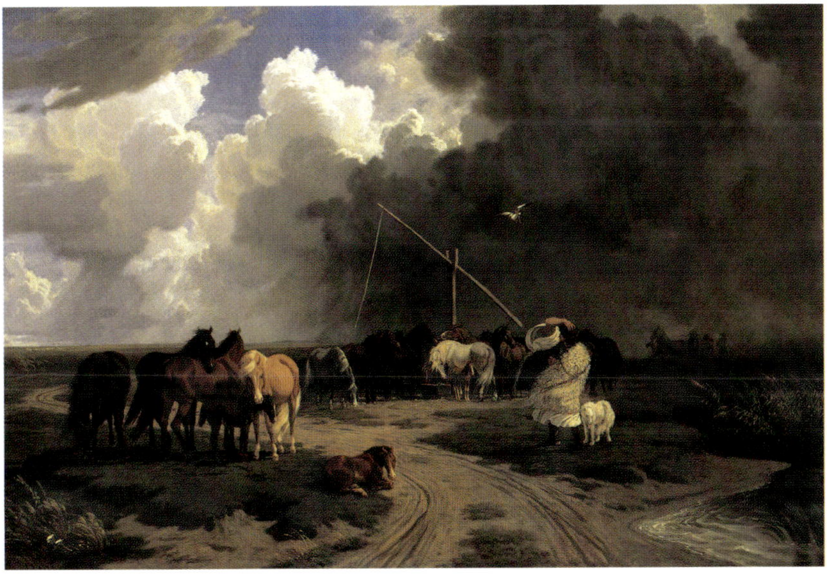

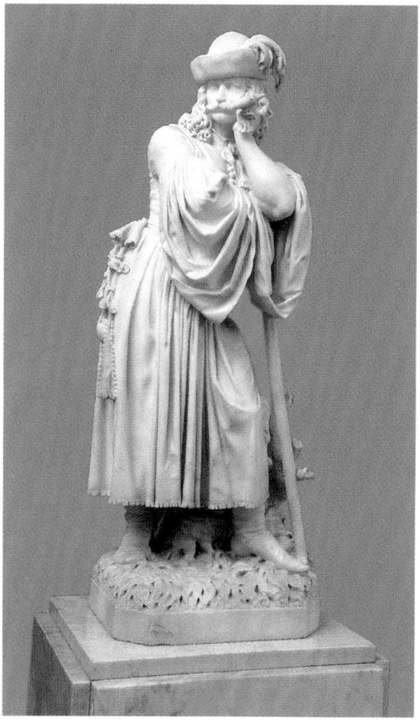

Miklós Izsó
(1831–1875)
Brooding Shepherd
1862
Marble, 35 × 28 × 95 cm
Inv. no.: 3338

Izsó made the first plaster variant of the statue in Munich and exhibited it at the Art Society of Pest in 1861 with the title Shepherd. As was customary at the Academy, he prepared model studies for the sculpture. Upon the request of manufacturer Mihály Gschwindt, he then carved in marble the piece in the Gallery known as the Brooding Shepherd in 1861. It was donated by Gschwindt to the National Museum of Fine Arts in 1864. Belonging to the group of rural genres, the sculpture condenses the sculptor's message in the sole figure of the shepherd. Izsó omitted from this larger work the accessory, explanatory-narrative motifs (such as the dog and flute) still included in the preliminary variant made in Munich. Some finely wrought details, however (the creases of the clothing, the tobacco bag on the right, the grassy texture of the base) set the figure into a subtly indicated narrative frame. The figure, his left elbow resting on his stick supporting his chin was modelled on a live sitter in original folk costume. To render an authentic figure, Izsó studied the life of shepherds in the puszta around Kecskemét. With a keen sense of plasticity and high technical expertise, he promoted the representative of this typical Hungarian occupation to a romantic hero.

J. Sz.

Mihály Zichy
(1827–1906)
Convivial Company
(Merry Fellows)
1865
Watercolour on paper, 175 × 250 mm
Inv. no.: 1955-5528

Best known for his illustrations made for the works of important authors János Arany and Imre Madách, Mihály Zichy spent most of his life after 1858–1859 in Russia where he taught and did various artistic services first in the grand duke's and later in the tsar's court. In 1859 Alexander II appointed him court painter; he served four tsars in his long career. After a West European tour he made in 1862, Zichy painted Convivial Company, which belongs with the group of It Has a Nice Colour, Yawning, Laughter or Falstaff with a Mug of 1873. From the 1860s, Zichy was intrigued by depicting guzzlers at merry-making, typical Falstaffian figures. From prints, photos, papers he must have indirectly kept watch on contemporary artistic trends and during his journeys he certainly met with 17th-century Netherlandish genre painting fashionable at his time. His sepia drawings and watercolours conceived in this spirit are also studies of physiognomy and mimic. The seven drunken figures of the Convivial company allow for a study of different variants and stages of laughter. The positioning of the figures around the table clearly adopt the compositional pattern of the Netherlandish examples. It is all but compulsory to have a male figure in front of the table, sitting facing the spectator, often smoking, playing some instrument or drinking, whose role is taken by a corpulent red-faced figure sprawling on a stool. A similar topos is the figure on the right who introduces the spectator to the company turning towards them, or the group of standing figures making a variety of gestures.

E. R.

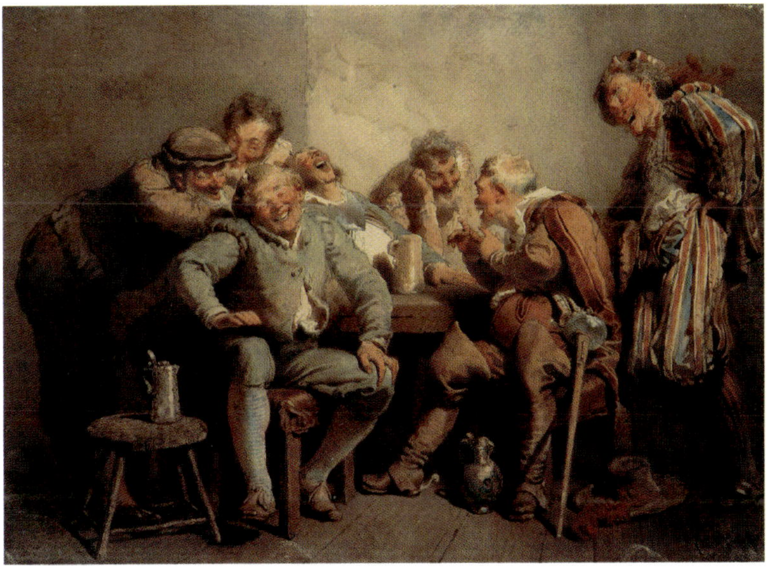

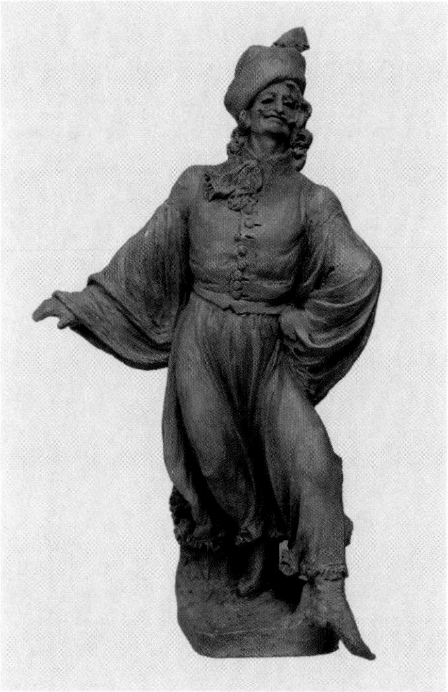

Miklós Izsó

(1831–1875)

Peasant Dancing II

1870

Terracotta, 7 × 7 × 28 cm

Inv. no.: 3347

A sculptor of 19th-century Hungarian romanticism, Izsó studied at Sárospatak and took part in the War of Liberation of 1848–1849 at the age of 17. After its crushing, he hid at various places and eventually settled in Rimaszombat where he carved building ornaments in the local stone carver's workshop. He also attended the local drawing class. Later he was the assistant of István Ferenczy and after Ferenczy's death (1856) he worked in János Marschalkó's studio. In 1857 he went to Vienna supported by Hungarian writers and poets making every effort to improve Hungarian fine arts. He worked at J. Meixner's and H. Gasser's workshops there. From 1859 he studied at the Munich academy from Max Widmann. He began making plaster sketches of Hungarian peasant characters after his childhood experiences. He returned home in 1862 and after a brief detour of Vienna and Italy he resumed his artistic programme begun in Munich. He modelled small terracotta figurines (20–30 cm) on themes taken from the life of the peasantry. Some of the types, e.g. the dancing peasant, he sculpted in more than ten variants. His terracotta studies of figures in movements of the popular dance of the 19th century, the verbunkos, are characterized by sweeping modelling, lifelikeness and an adequate surface finish for the materials. That implies the key and novelty of Izsó's sculpture, as they mark the break with the schematic, rigid modelling of academic classicism.

J. Sz.

László Paál
(1846–1879)
Noon
1870
Oil on panel, 36.5 × 53.5 cm
Inv. no.: 56.133

The painter of Transylvanian origin studied landscape painting at the Academy of Vienna and went on a long study trip to the Netherlands where this picture radiating the joy of the first-hand experience of nature was created. Quick and energetic improvisation, the capturing of large summary forms, the rendering of the exact tone values of the sunny landscape studded with deep shadows fascinated the artist in the first place, who was probably quite at ease in the scenery reminiscent of the flat Hungarian landscape. The small painting is the outcome of an unbiassed sovereign painterly approach, one of László Paál's most up-to-date works despite its seeming simplicity; a direct relative of Pissarro's and Sisley's landscapes painted a few years earlier, but unknown to Hungarian artists at that time.

A. Sz. M.

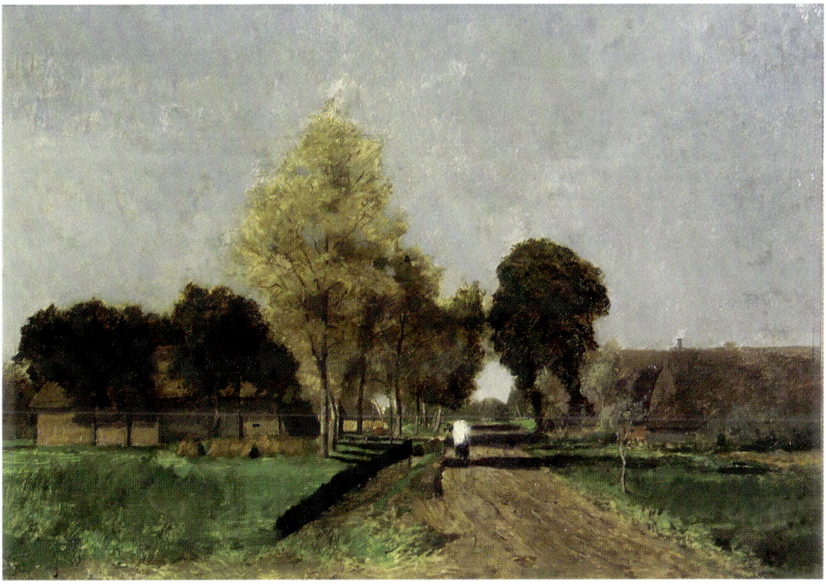

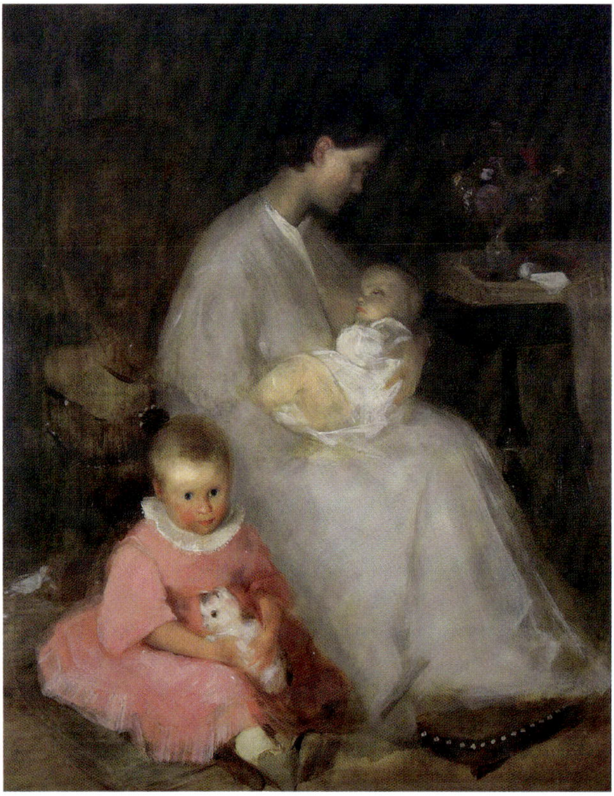

Géza Dósa

(1846–1871)

Mother and Children

1870

Oil on canvas, 146.5 × 118 cm

Inv. no.: 2001.2 T

Already in his works painted during his studies in Vienna and Munich the artist, who committed suicide at a mere 25 years of age, consciously avoided the then wide-spread theatrical, pathetic approach to history painting. His necessarily meager œuvre is crowned by his compositions of two figures radiating union which are even more laconic and unconventionally executed. His bold neglect of minute details was unparalleled in Hungarian painting up to then: he modelled the little family with broad, sweeping brushstrokes in blocklike masses. The gentle colour scheme enriched with faint whiffs of reflexions from the environment and the thin translucent layer of paint result in a relaxed overall impression diffused over the whole picture surface. Had Dósa managed to get to Paris—as he planned—he would certainly have had a great future as he was preoccupied by the same problems as the leading artists were the world over. The termination of his life with a tragic suddenness, however, nipped this development in the bud. If he had not given up the struggle for a living and acknowledgement so early, he might have become a comrade at arms of Szinyei in the struggle to disseminate modern painting in Hungary.

A. Sz. M.

Sándor Brodszky
(1819–1901)
View of Lake Balaton (Storm on the Balaton)
Early 1870s
Oil on canvas, 143 × 206 cm
Inv. no.: 2776

Brodszky, an artist showered with official acknowledgement for decades, became a popular painter of Hungarian castles and landscapes after returning from Vienna and Munich. This grand-scale rendering of the unparalleled panorama of the northern shore of the Balaton was commissioned by the state to enrich the stock of the National Museum. It was known that Brodszky had already scored successes with other views of the lake. He transferred his on-the-spot sketches to the canvas in the studio; after all, the large size, the stormy weather and the meticulous painting technique would not have allowed for painting in the open. He enhanced the monumental impression by thorough deliberation, the balancing of light and dark spots, stressed and unstressed details. The medieval ruins on top of the basalt cones rising out of the Tapolca basin—favourite protagonists of earlier and even contemporary heroizing history paintings—could also tell tales of the one-time glory of Szigliget and Csobánc, but the painter was more interested in rendering the rich natural formations and diverse atmospheric phenomena, treating the castle ruins as organic constituents of the landscape. Just like his example Carl Rottmann whose work he had studied earlier in Munich, Brodszky was a practitioner of late romantic landscape painting who already incorporated the effects of the real sight into his pictures.

A. Sz. M.

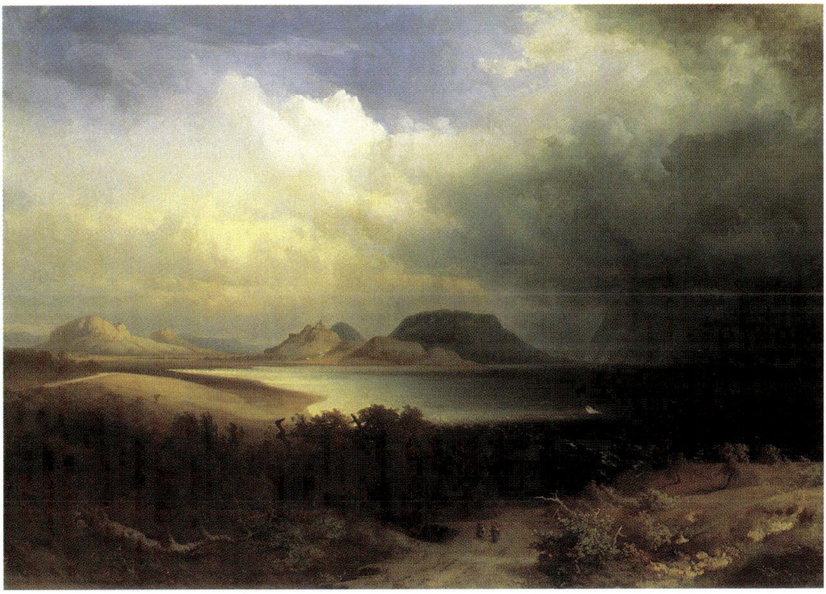

Pál Szinyei Merse
(1845–1920)
Picnic in May
1873
Oil on canvas, 127 × 162.5 cm
Inv. no.: 1547

Hungarian painting caught up with up-to-date European trends in the major works of Pál Szinyei Merse around 1870. Although he only got to Paris at an old age, he discovered plein air as a method of conveying the form-giving and colouring effect of sunlight more or less synchronously with, but independently of, the impressionists. He, too, created the harmony of sunsoaked colours dipped in diffuse light by considering complementary and contrast effects and tone values indicating the light saturation of colours. Unlike in the works of his predecessors and several of his contemporaries, the coherence of a Szinyei painting is not ensured by a single predominant tone but by the equal light values of many different colour patches. In his perfectly balanced compositions, every element refers to the union of man and nature. He painted Picnic in May—deemed by many to be one of the finest Hungarian paintings—upon a return to Munich, the venue of his academic studies, recalling his wanderings in Upper Hungary and the convivial picnics of the Munich artists. As he wrote in his autobiography, "I painted myself into the picture prone, munching away, with my back to the spectator. I must admit I was thinking of the critics who would dislike my picture." His guess was right: his contemporaries ridiculed him, his epochal significance only being slowly discovered half a generation later.

A. Sz. M.

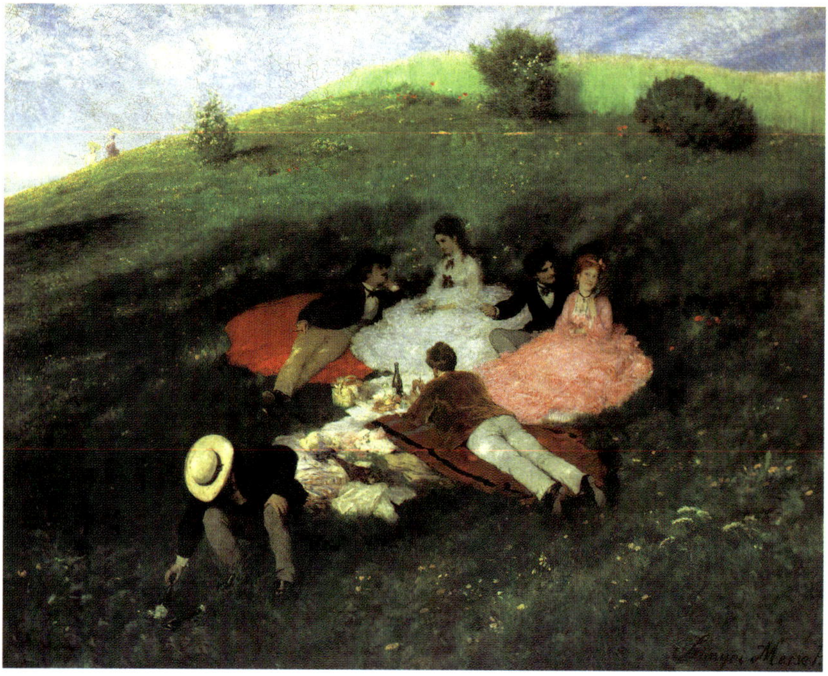

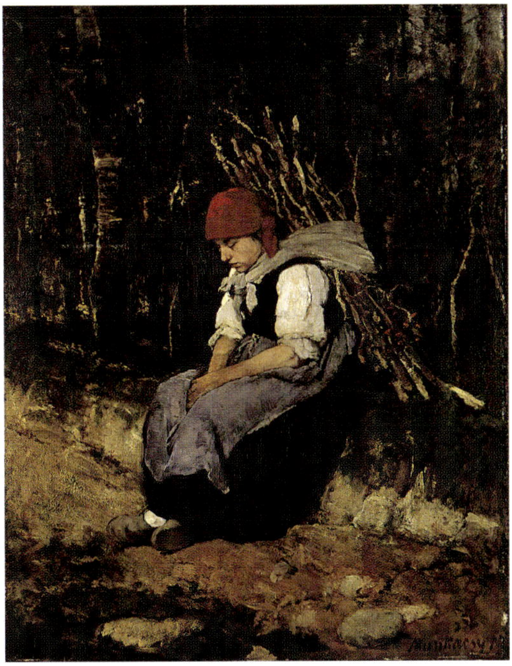

Mihály Munkácsy
(1844–1900)
Woman Carrying Brushwood
1873
Oil on panel, 99.7 × 80.3 cm
Inv. no.: 4647

Munkácsy moved to Paris for good in 1872, upon the call of his friend and fellow artist László Paál. However, they parted in France since Paál settled in the village of Barbizon in the Fontainebleau forest to live there all his short life, while Munkácsy stayed in Paris. Having set up for himself in Barbizon, Paál invited Munkácsy in a letter of 1873. Munkácsy accepted the invitation and stayed for a few months in the moody little sylvan village. Barbizon was made famous in the early 19th century by a group of French artists who substantially changed painting by advocating working in the open. In the pictures of Millet, Courbet, Daubigny and Dupré everyday scenes—people working, strolling, travelling—appear in a natural setting. The manner of painting also changed: the all-devouring gallery tone gave way to light-imbued colours and their tones to suggest atmospheric effects, the vibration of the air, the motion of light and shade. Woman Carrying Brushwood painted in Barbizon is already the outcome of this fresh approach. It shows a woman by a trail in the forest, resting from picking and carrying brushwood. The depiction of work-weary people without any beautifying is typical of realism, especially strongly represented without any lyricism by Courbet among the mentioned French artists. Munkácsy's painting is slightly melancholic, though the tired face, the stooped body and the rendering of the hand are tools of a representation devoid of idealization.

Zs. B.

Gyula Benczúr
(1844–1920)
Woman Reading in the Forest
1875
Oil on canvas, 87.5 × 116.5 cm
Inv. no.: 61.121

There are only one or two scenes in the open in Benczúr's oeuvre, although for his generation, beginning their career around 1870, upcoming impressionism was a hardly avoidable challenge. Around 1874–1875 Benczúr tried to capture the form-dissolving effect of light in several compositions, but he resumed his course by wholly discarding plein air painting. As his letters reveal, he exhibited the first variant of this composition in Vienna in 1873 and sold it in London in 1874. He probably repeated the picture showing his wife Karolina Max for family reasons in 1875. The multitude of sketches, pencil drawings made for the painting suggests the absorbed examination of the motif. The special appeal of the painting is the colour composition based on the fresh harmony of red and green, and the modern representation of women unconventional in the 19th century. The reading woman lying casually in the grass represents a modern intellectual type of woman that was hardly ever seen in earlier paintings. Among Benczúr's pencil studies one also finds a sketch of Karolina smoking a cigarette, which also shows the otherwise exemplary housewife as an early representative of modern women.

G. B.

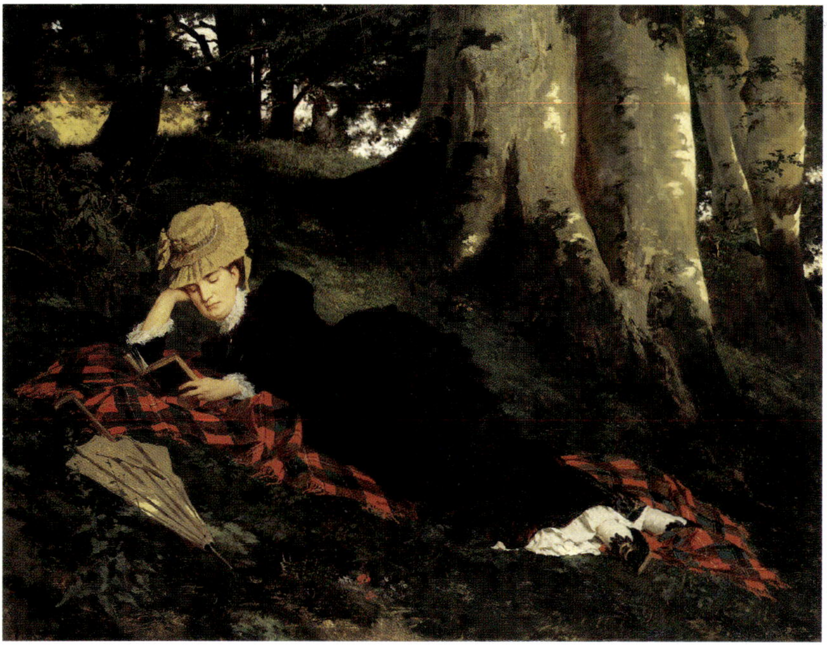

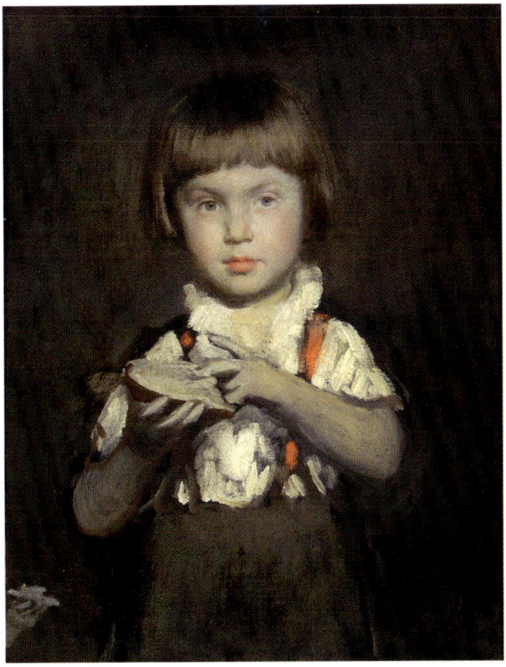

Bertalan Székely
(1835–1910)
Little Boy with Bread-'n-butter
Around 1875
Oil on canvas, 69 × 55 cm
Inv. no.: 55.716

Bertalan Székely was a prominent figure of Hungarian romantic painting, his oeuvre containing portraits, landscapes, genre scenes and, first of all, history paintings. His portrait and genre painting unfolding in the 1870s was largely influenced by his harmonious family life. He had four children: Árpád, Ákos, Ármin and Jenny. He depicted all his children in portraits. His third son Ármin was born in 1869 but died a few years later. This picture, traditionally said to depict Ármin is datable to 1874–1875 on the basis of the boy's age. Székely was a keen judge of human character. His portraits—commissioned or not—are never impersonal, the rendering always suggests a level of identification with the sitter which makes more profound and emphatic characterization possible. The little boy is not depicted in a carefully arranged pose but in a secretly observed situation. The artlessness of the movement, intimacy of rendering are rare even when compared to the rest of Székely's portraits. The bright white and red colours flashing up from the predominant grey—reinforced by the unfinished state of the picture—and the customary lack of idealization make this picture uniquely modern in his oeuvre and among the Hungarian portraits of that time. His use of colours and his manner of painting liken his portraiture to Manet's.

Zs. B.

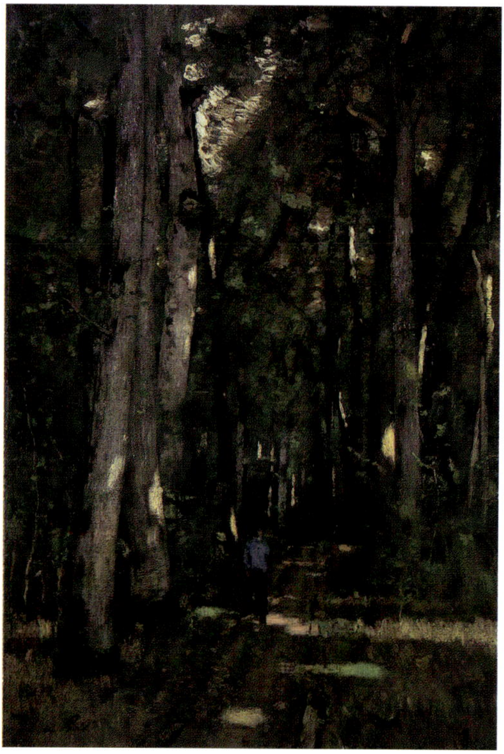

László Paál
(1846–1879)
Road in Fontainebleau Forest
1876
Oil on canvas, 91.7 × 63 cm
Inv. no.: 3822

In the spring of 1873 Lászlo Paál settled in Barbizon where he had been longing to go since he saw the landscapes of the artists working on the edge of the immense forest near Paris at an international exhibition in Munich in 1869. He arrived with a mature artistic stature, so he did not become the epigone of any famous artist working there. While in his pictures painted in the Netherlands he had depicted the selected details of nature from a broad view, in the forest of Fontainebleau—like in this chef d'œuvre—he rendered the thickness of the woods observed closely. In the dense forest the experience of enormous space—the infinity of nature—is felt. Paál, who died tragically young, was always relaxed by the mystic spell of the forest, which helped him sense the creative will permeating all nature. His longing for light often led him to depict the light phenomena, colour and tone value changes brought about by the sunrays penetrating the woods. He repeatedly returned to some pleasing detail to paint it at different times of day, in different light conditions. Though this method, the use of colourful shadows and several other stylistic elements brought him close to the impressionists, he never resigned from projecting his individual feelings into the landscape, thus saturating it with deep emotions.

A. Sz. M.

Géza Mészöly
(1844–1887)
Fishermen's Cottages at the Balaton
1877
Oil on canvas, 140 × 226 cm
Inv. no.: 2775

Copying Károly Markó the Elder's pictures in Budapest and the Zimmermann class at the Academy in Vienna both taught the lyrically tuned young man to depict nature in minute detail but also in its majesty. However, Mészöly already filled the pictorial schemes practiced on the basis of centuries-old traditions with life at the Academy. Back home, his only goal was to paint realistic, impressive pictures of the Hungarian landscape. He soon discovered the painterly potentialities of the Balaton and often returned to depict in series the quiet activities of fishermen and other people in the varied landscape. In his intimate paintings he showed simple people in an idyllic way, as natural beings, stressing their states of existence instead of the fashionable genre-like approach. Even far removed from his country, in his studio in Munich and Paris, he was preoccupied by the scenery around the Balaton and the Tisza river. His excellent memory of form and colour and a great deal of on-the-spot sketches and study drawings helped him achieve the realistic effect. One of his favourite compositional devices was to double a huge tree in the mirror of the water surface in the middle of the composition. This device which lent a diversity to the composition and allowed for subtle plays of tones and forms, is also applied in this large painting which he meant for the National Museum.

A. Sz. M.

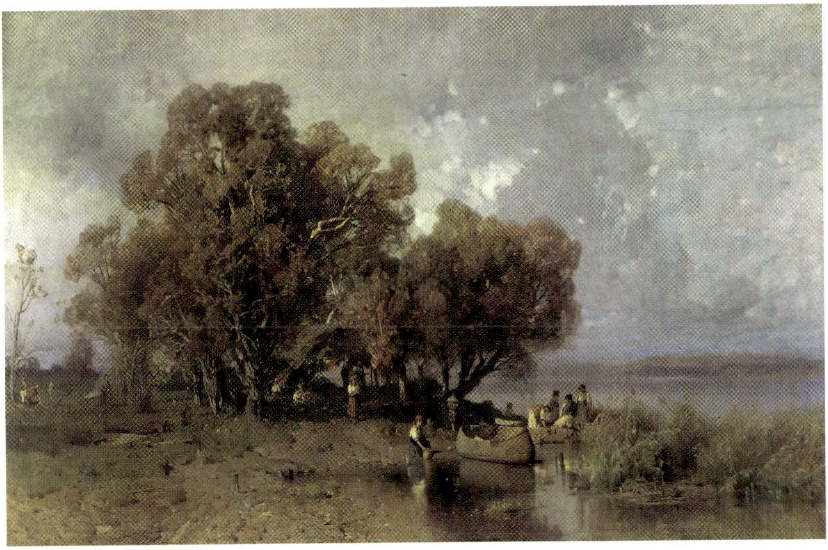

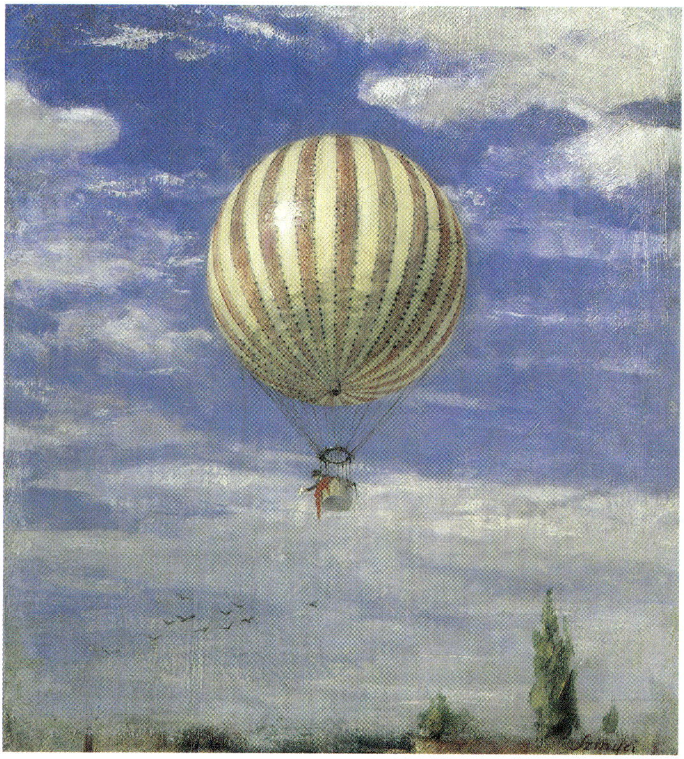

Pál Szinyei Merse
(1845–1920)
Balloon
1878
Oil on canvas, 42 × 39.3 cm
Inv. no.: 4648

Deliberately opposed to the public tastes worshiping traditions blindly, Szinyei left Munich after completing Picnic in May and did not return before his old age when he was given an award. Instead of going to France like several of his compatriots to draw inspiration for his innovative art, he withdrew to his native land to get married. The growing family, the everyday cares and the uninspiring village environment at Jernye prevented him from profound artistic absorption. In 1878, however, the boldness of his youthful paintings gushed forth again: his optimistic mood is proven by one of his most original themes, the Balloon. He was seriously intrigued by technical innovations—during his academic years he tried to construct an airplane—so his brother-in-law's balloon trip immediately electrified him. He would have gladly joined him, for a man flying high need not be interested in the trifling affairs of his fellowmen swarming down on the ground. That is how the floating airship overcoming the force of gravity became the symbol of the flight of human thought and artistic freedom.

A. Sz. M.

József Engel
(1816–1901)
Eve (Eve Awakening to Life)
Around 1880
Marble, 58 × 57 × 211 cm
Inv. no.: 3666

József Engel made the first version of his statue Eve or Eve Awakening to Life in Rome in 1864. Commissioned by János Pejacsevics, he carved the composition into marble in two-thirds life-size. The count had it erected in his Buda palace but it was devoured by fire there in 1872. Eve was one of the first works by Engel that arrived in Hungary from Rome. In 1866 Engel won the competition to design a monument commemorating István Széchenyi—an important politician and patron of arts and sciences in the first half of the 19th century—and moved to Pest. After the original plaster cast he carved the Eve statue in marble again, now slightly larger than life-size. He put it on display at the 1885 National Exhibition. Eve is not only the Biblical figure identified by her attributes but also the allegory of the domination of female beauty over the world. The finely modelled body, the carriage of her head and even her facial features adapt details of the Venus of Milo in the Louvre—the statue is Engel's paraphrase of the classical work. The arms of the Greek original are missing, so Engel modelled Eve's arm gestures from studying Venus' arm stumps. He omitted the drapery from the lower part of Venus' body. Eve's bare right foot steps forward on a spherical section symbolizing the globe and used as the plinth. The serpent wiggling forth from under the woman's feet warns that although female beauty dominates the world, it is at the same time the origin and cause of sins.

J. Sz.

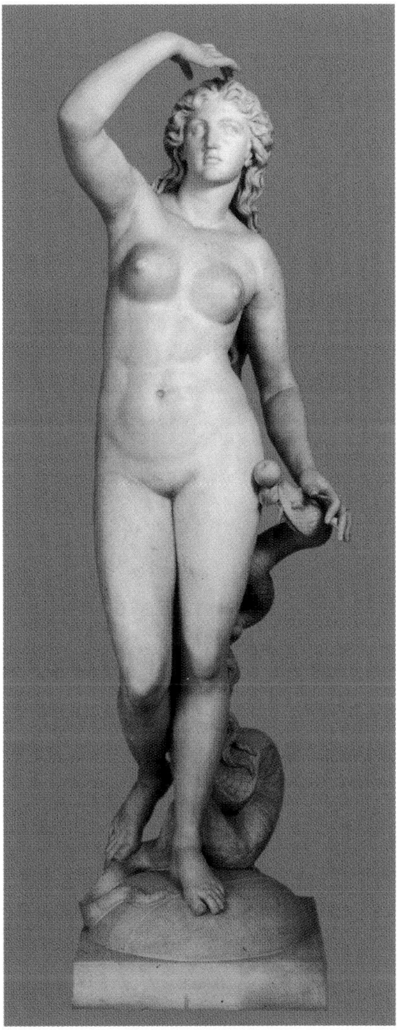

Alajos Stróbl
(1856–1926)
Luischen
1884
Marble, 48 × 33 × 25 cm
Inv. no.: 57.21-N

Stróbl was fond of making portraits, as the set of hundreds of registered works in his oeuvre proves. Salient among them are the intimate portraits of his family members: freshly and vigorously modelled portraits based on sincere emotions and thorough psychological observations. "In this profuse series of portraits many are excellent and some are real gems," Károly Lyka, one-time pupil, then fellow professor and noted art writer said. Such a real "gem" is the portrait of Lujza (Alojzia) Kratochwill, the sculptor's future wife, carved in Carrara marble, exposing all the fine qualities, beauty and warmth of the material. Modelled with affection and great mastery, the charming head of fine features is an authentic child portrait, the characteristics of this age being especially conspicuous in some parts of the face as the slightly open mouth, and the shoulders. A coloured plaster variant of the statue is also known, because Stróbl sometimes used discrete and careful colouring, conjuring up a typical aspect of antique Roman portrait sculpture.

G. Sz.

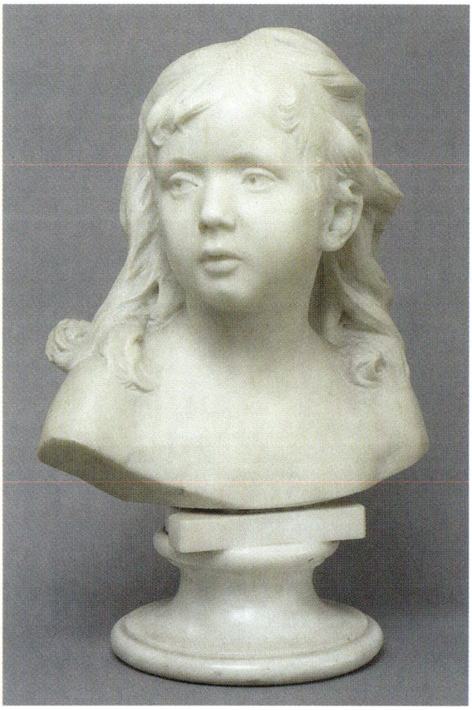

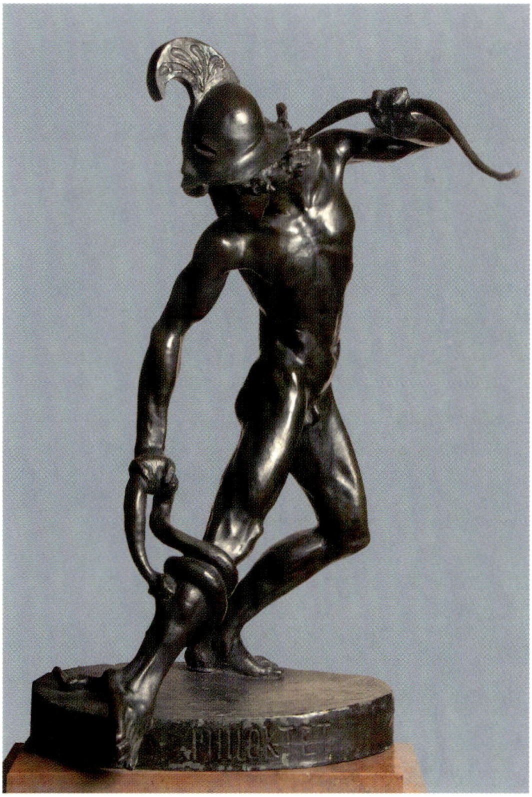

György Zala
(1858–1937)
Philoctetes
1884
Bronze, 35 × 25 × 64 cm
Inv. no.: 87.2-N

Hungarians interested in art studied at the academies of Vienna and Munich in the first half of the 19th century, thus György Zala (then called Mayer) also learnt in Vienna—from Edmund Hellmer—and later in Munich from Joseph Knabl and Syrius Eberle. From the Academy of Munich he sent home—still in plaster—his Philoctetes, the Greek mythological hero, to the autumn exhibition of the Art Society in 1884. His work combines historicizing romanticism and its cult of heroes with the allegorical approach typical of the neo-baroque. Philoctetes of Thessaly was a hero of the Trojan war: his wound bitten by the poisonous serpent of Lemnus only healed after killing prince Paris in Troy. His figure was perpetuated by Homer's epic poems, and Sophocles wrote a play about him. The figure fighting with the snake—a symbol of both life and death, victory and defeat—was probably inspired by the Laocoon group. The antique theme allowed for anatomical studies, the presentation of construction (contrapposto); apart from the accurate rendering of the work of the muscles, some slight disproportion is sensed. The statue —probably a diploma work for the academy—is not known on a larger scale.

G. Sz.

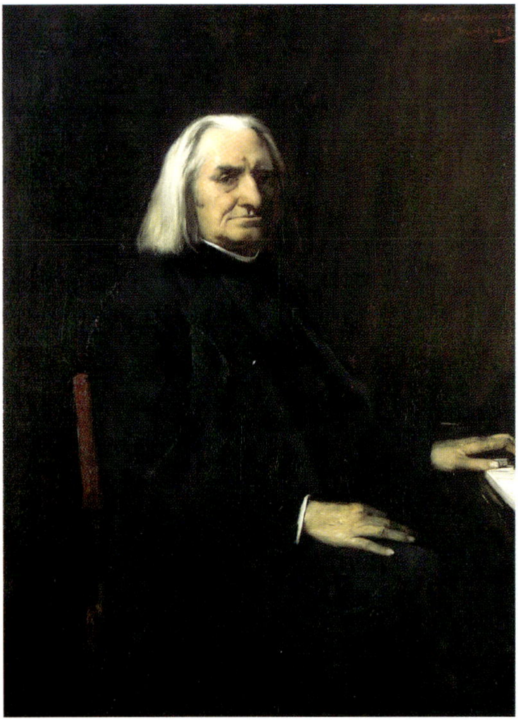

Mihály Munkácsy
(1844–1900)
Portrait of Franz Liszt
1886
Oil on canvas, 130.5 × 99.5 cm
Inv. no.: 2820

The genre pieces and landscapes of Munkácsy represented the Hungarian variant of French realism, while his portraits, his three paintings of Christ and the ceiling fresco of the Kunsthistorisches Museum in Vienna are high-quality works of historicist academism. Munkácsy lived a luxurious life with his French wife in Paris from 1872. Especially from the 1880s their Thursday soirées were visited by distinguished guests from all over Europe: aristocrats, statesmen, artists, including naturally Hungarians. They were visited by the archbishop of Kalocsa Lajos Haynald and Ferenc Liszt serveral times. Liszt visited the Munkácsys in March 1886. On the 23rd, Mrs Munkácsy organized a grand banquet with a concert, then on the 25th another concert at the St Eustache church where Liszt's Esztergom Mass was performed. Munkácsy began his portrait of Liszt during the March visit and finished it relatively quickly, in two weeks. It is the last portrait of the composer: Liszt died in Weimar in the summer. This depiction of the old master is the best portrait in the oeuvre of Munkácsy, a sensitive judge of the human soul. The dark background and dark clothes accentuate the whiteness of the composer's hair and face, throwing not only the facial features into deep relief but also putting the stress on characterization.

Zs. B.

László Mednyánszky

(1852–1919)

Oak Woods along the Tisza

Late 1880s

Pencil, ink and white body colour on paper, 282 × 400 mm

Inv. no.: 1902-1077

A great portion of Mednyánszky's almost incomprehensibly large œuvre comprises drawings. In addition to the multitude of studies and sketch-books, an important group of works consists of the drawings for the engraved illustrations of Az Osztrák–Magyar Monarchia írásban és képben [The Austro-Hungarian Monarchy in Words and Pictures], a monumental series of 23 volumes published over 25 years. First appearing as booklets and later bound in book-form, it was the major source of popular knowledge in the age initiated and patronized by the heir to the throne, Rudolf. It was launched on December 1, 1885, in parallel German and Hungarian editions. Seven of the published volumes were devoted to Hungary with illustrations by the most outstanding artists and draughtsmen of the period. These were mainly landscapes, veduti, depictions of folk costumes. The drawings meant for the illustrative engravings have a conspicuous feature, the technique: Mednyánszky almost always used ink, watercolour, white body colour and their combinations. They also testify to balanced composing skills and mature draftsmanship. He produced illustrations for the volumes using the technique he elaborated for this purpose for fifteen years. Oak Woods along the Tisza is one of the best known pieces. It is more than a topographic representation, his all but stylized trees convey Mednyánszky's devout attitude to nature. Owing to the technique, the black and white contrasts create a highly sensuous, closed space.

O. H.

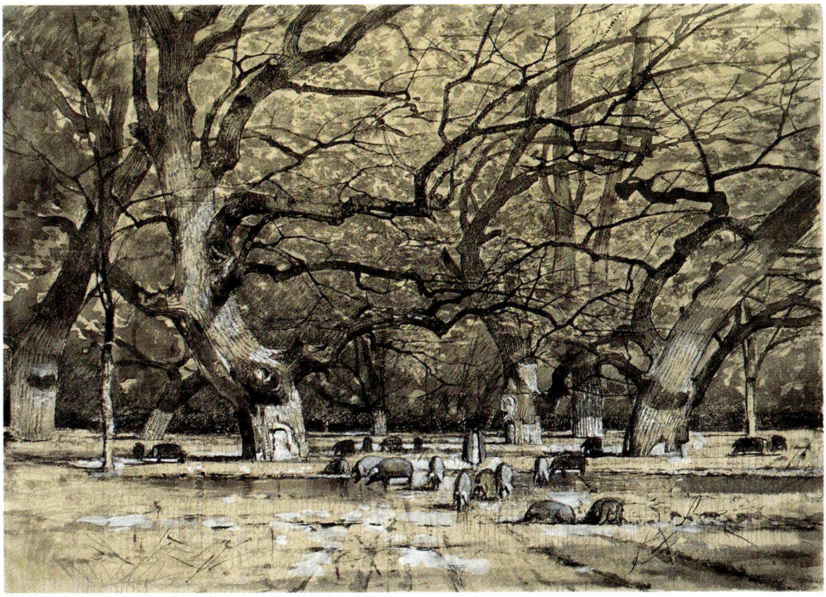

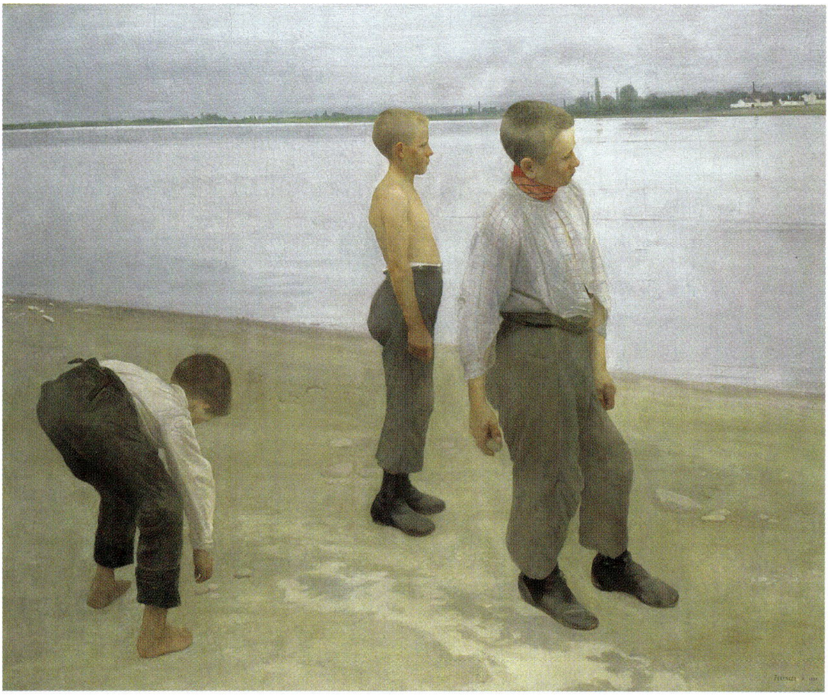

Károly Ferenczy
(1862–1917)
Boys Throwing Pebbles
1890
Oil on canvas, 119 × 149 cm
Inv. no.: FK 3778

Károly Ferenczy was the leading figure of the unfolding and consummation of plein air painting in Hungary, the most outstanding artist of the group and style known as the Nagybánya school, so called because the group founded an artists' colony in Nagybánya (today Baia Mare, Romania) in 1896. After years of studies abroad, he settled with his family in Szentendre, close to Budapest. As he attended Simon Hollósy's art school in Munich, he was drawn under the influence of Jules Bastien-Lepage for a time and made his first works at home in his style. The four years in Szentendre comprise a separate chapter in Ferenczy's œuvre. He picked his subjects from everyday life showing the figures in ordinary activities. In the spirit of the painting traditions of Munich he depicted genre scenes on the canvases, but he deliberately avoided stories with a point to them. He watched his figures from afar, concentrating on states rather than actions. A clearly composed world painted with puritanic simplicity appears, the figures being enveloped in a strange sadness and lyricism. The triangle of Boys Throwing Pebbles adjusts to classic compositional principles. In the wake of Bastien-Lepage Ferenczy muted the colours with a nacreous lustre; the various hues of grey endow the painting with a lyrical dimness. Everything seems to be covered by a veil of mist, the forms being painted in it with ethereal subtlety.

M. G.

István Csók
(1865–1961)
Orphans
1891
Oil on canvas, 121 × 136 cm
Inv. no.: 2863

In his memoirs István Csók narrates the story of Orphans in detail. The mother and daughter visiting the artist in his Munich studio appeared like an apparition from the netherworld in the mysterious bluish twilight of dusk. Csók first depicted this experience in a symbolic painting, envisioning the girl as the spirit of the dead child next to the mother reading the Bible. However, he soon repainted the "visionary" picture, turning the figures into orphaned siblings. The socially sensitive subject was just as typical of naturalism around the 1890s as was the photographic accuracy of painting. Several Hungarian and foreign contemporaries of Csók adopted this painting style at that time. By the bold effects of illumination and the highlighting of a single colour—blue—Csók created a more exciting composition than his fellow artists of similar schooling, the representives of the so-called "painting without shadows". The peculiar lighting which the brushwork captured perfectly scored great success at exhibitions in Munich and Vienna. As Csók recalled, there were lamp-lit pictures galore at the exhibitions of the Glaspalast in Munich and "blue was the dominant colour" in Viennese showings after this painting. In the winter exhibition of the Hungarian National Art Association in 1891 it was awarded the grand prize, the most prestigeous artistic prize in Hungary.

G. B.

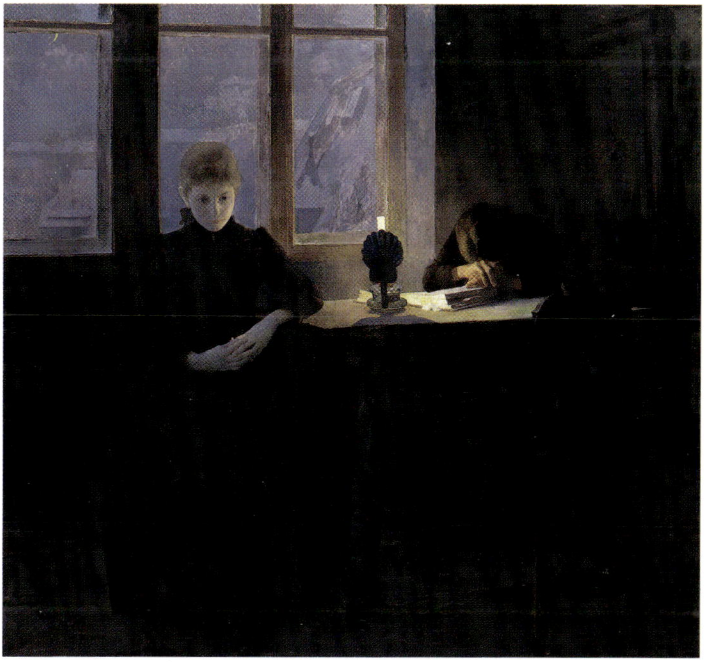

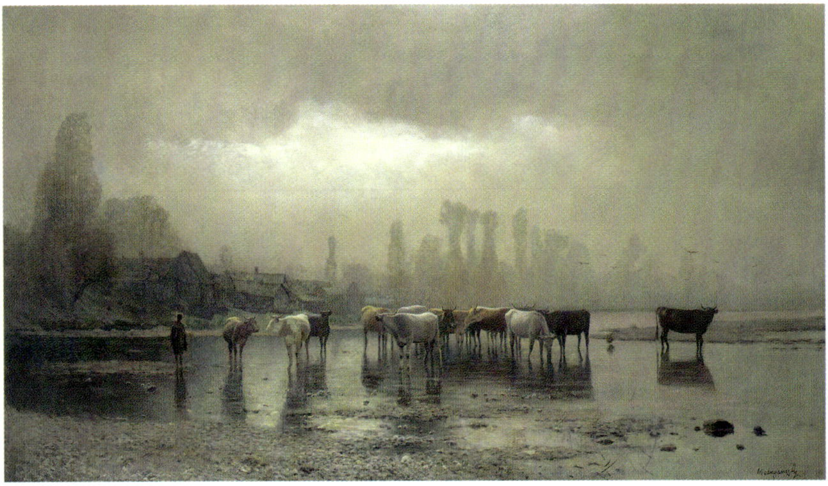

László Mednyánszky
(1852–1919)
In the Vicinity of Munkács (Watering-place)
1891
Oil on canvas, 114 x 201 cm
Inv. no.: 55.849

In the early 1890s László Mednyánszky was making landscape sketches and studies around the Verecke pass for the enormous cyclorama of Árpád Feszty, The Entry of the Hungarians. That was certainly when he got to Munkács where he painted this accurately localized picture. It is a specific feature of Mednyánszky's paintings that unlike most of his contemporaries, he avoided personal details, close views, the intimate, "interior-like" grouping of the motifs of the scenery. Even in his depiction of the inside of a forest, which allows for greater intimacy, he always left a crack in the composition towards the infinite. Instead of manifesting the late romantic longing for infinity, the openness and vastness of his landscapes convey the need to create optimal harmony between heaven and earth. For Mednyánszky, who built his whole painting activity on firm principles of colour and form symbolism, this also meant the effort to harmonize the mundane and the spiritual components. Although perfectly fitted to the thematic range of late 19th-century naturalism, Watering-place painted near Munkács is a fine specimen of atmospheric painting of Austrian roots with its subtle light effects, while its mysteriousness built on grey can also be interpreted in the terms of symbolism.

G. B.

Gusztáv Magyar-Mannheimer
(1859–1937)
Factory on the Outskirts of Budapest
1893
Oil on canvas, 86 × 131 cm
Inv. no.: 1507

His restless nature drove the painter, who won many prizes in his age but whose fame has slightly dimmed by now, to try out several styles. As a born colourist, he usually started out of from colour and arrived at surprisingly light-handed, airy solutions. At the same time, he was also characterized by a dampened colour scheme saturated with emotions, verging on romanticism. This landscape rises high above his average oeuvre: such expressive depiction of poor outskirts like this was to come only far later in Hungarian painting, in the work of István Dési Huber and his fellows. The broad panorama with Váci road and the Ördög (Devil) Mill includes the puffing engine of the circular railway on the left, and shanties in front of the faraway mills and factory plants with a man and child standing on the road. A remote echo of the social interest of European painting spreading at that time can be felt in the painting, but the artist did not dig deeper into the implications but offered the pleasure of pure visuality. The riot of fantastic sunset colours and the trans-figuration of the prosaic environment were the artistic problems to be solved here.

A. Sz. M.

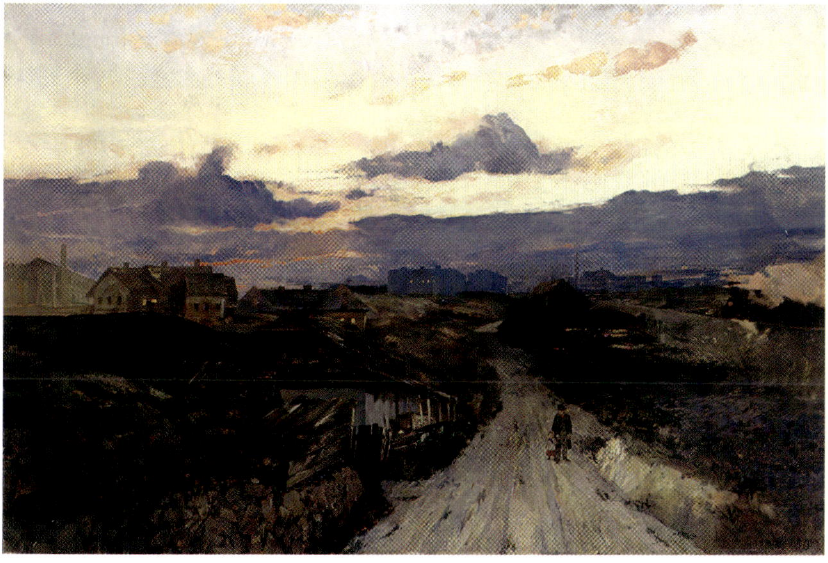

János Thorma
(1870–1937)
Portrait of Irén Bilcz
1892
Oil on canvas, 110 × 96.5 cm
Inv. no.: 78.149 T

The painter learnt in Simon Hollósy's private art school in Munich in 1888–1890, then he was trained at the Julian Academy in Paris in 1891. From 1884 he and his family lived in Nagybánya (Baia Mare, Romania) where he was one of the artists who prepared and then founded the artists' colony aimed to bring to efflorescence the Hungarian plein air endeavours. In Munich he came to know Jules Bastien-Lepage's naturalist paintings, his works of the early 1890s testifying to the assimilation of this style. A unique masterpiece of Thorma's early period is the portrait of Irén Bilcz, which regrettably passed unnoticed at that time. His contemporaries failed to take note of it, thus this initiative was not continued in his œuvre. There is an interesting duality in the picture: while in the modelling of the sitter and her clothing the naturalist approach is predominant, the golden background and subtle art nouveau arm support already anticipate the decorative style of the turn of the century. Looking for analogies, one is prompted to name Klimt's works of stylistic duality made in the early 1900s. The depicted young woman, Irén Bilcz was the daughter of the Greek Catholic priest of Nagybánya. Later she married a noted artist of the colony, Béla Iványi Grünwald, who perpetuated the graceful figure of his wife in several paintings.

E. P.

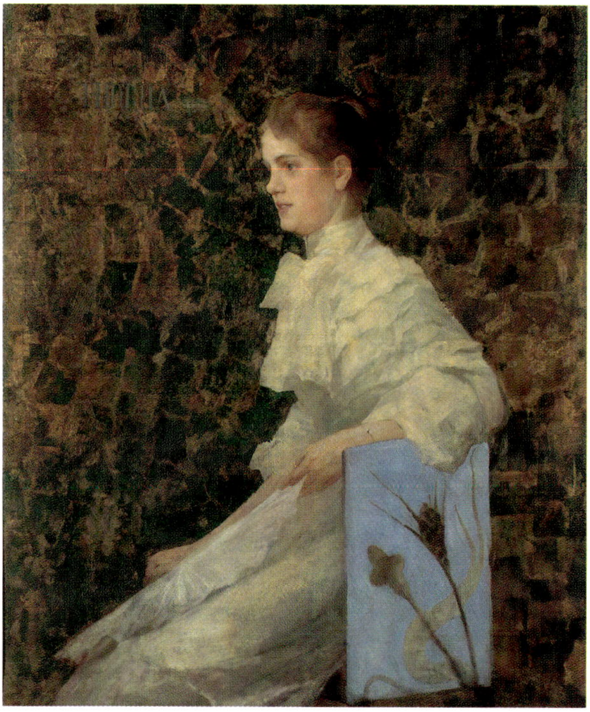

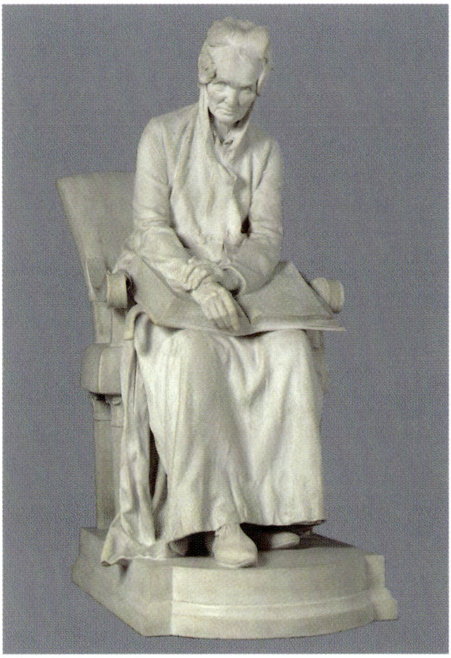

Alajos Stróbl
(1856–1926)
Our Mother
1894
Marble, 69 × 103 × 161 cm
Inv. no.: 1610

This is one of the best-known, most often reproduced works of 19th-century Hungarian sculpture. The old woman modelled with great affection and reverence was the artist's mother Karolina Wirosztek. She married twice, her granddaughter from her first marriage, Lujza Kratochwill became Alajos Stróbl's wife later. Her second husband was József Stróbl, a bailiff at the Habsburg archduke Albrecht's estate in Liptó county. They brought up four children. The cares and worries left their mark on the mother's face. The dense web of wrinkles, hollow eyes, the slack, baggy skin are keenly observed details which the artist transfigured into a higher quality with the help of his modelling skills, exploiting to the full the structural potentialities of white Carrara marble, and thus he created a portrait not only of his mother but also of old age. The model rests her hands on a book with a clasp, probably the family Bible, looking pensively into the memories of the past. The ribbons of her outdated bonnet are loosened for the period of relaxation, her very simple clothes the lifelikeness of which praises Stróbl's mastery and the "fine naturalism" of the unfashionable, old, worn laced boots show kinship with the theoretical ideas of the founder of the Nagybánya artists' colony Simon Hollósy. First shown to the public at the millennial exhibition in 1896, the sculpture won the Grand Prix at the Paris World Exposition in 1900.

G. Sz.

Károly Lotz
(1833–1904)
Kornélia Lotz in Black
1896
Oil on canvas, 163.8 × 82 cm
Inv. no.: 3531

The most-sought-after fresco painter in the 1870s–1880s, Károly Lotz turned to portraiture more intensely in the 1890s. His sitter was most often his foster daughter Kornélia. His portraits of Kornélia coalesce into practical series, but it is not so much the character of the beautiful young lady that is represented but the sensual and spiritual beauty of the female sex. The greatest appeal of Kornélia even to the present-day spectator is not so much her personality but her professional capability of adapting. She is a bathing nymph and goddess, bacchante and grand lady, innocent virgin and a serious woman all at the same time. It is hard to make out from Lotz' portraits what Kornélia was actually like—we just take her as the changeable woman, dame and diva, enticing beauty and the sheer subject of lust, the type of ideal woman at the turn of the century. It is fascinating that the modern female personality permeates even the old-fashioned, historicist milieu in the Kornélia portraits, in anticipation of the great female types of the 20th century. The narrow standing format of this portrait of Kornélia in a black dress, the graceful harmony of the mirror frame in the background with the subtly swaying forms of the sitter already point to the forms of art nouveau, the colour scheme predominated by black also being in line with the tendencies around the turn of the century.

G. B.

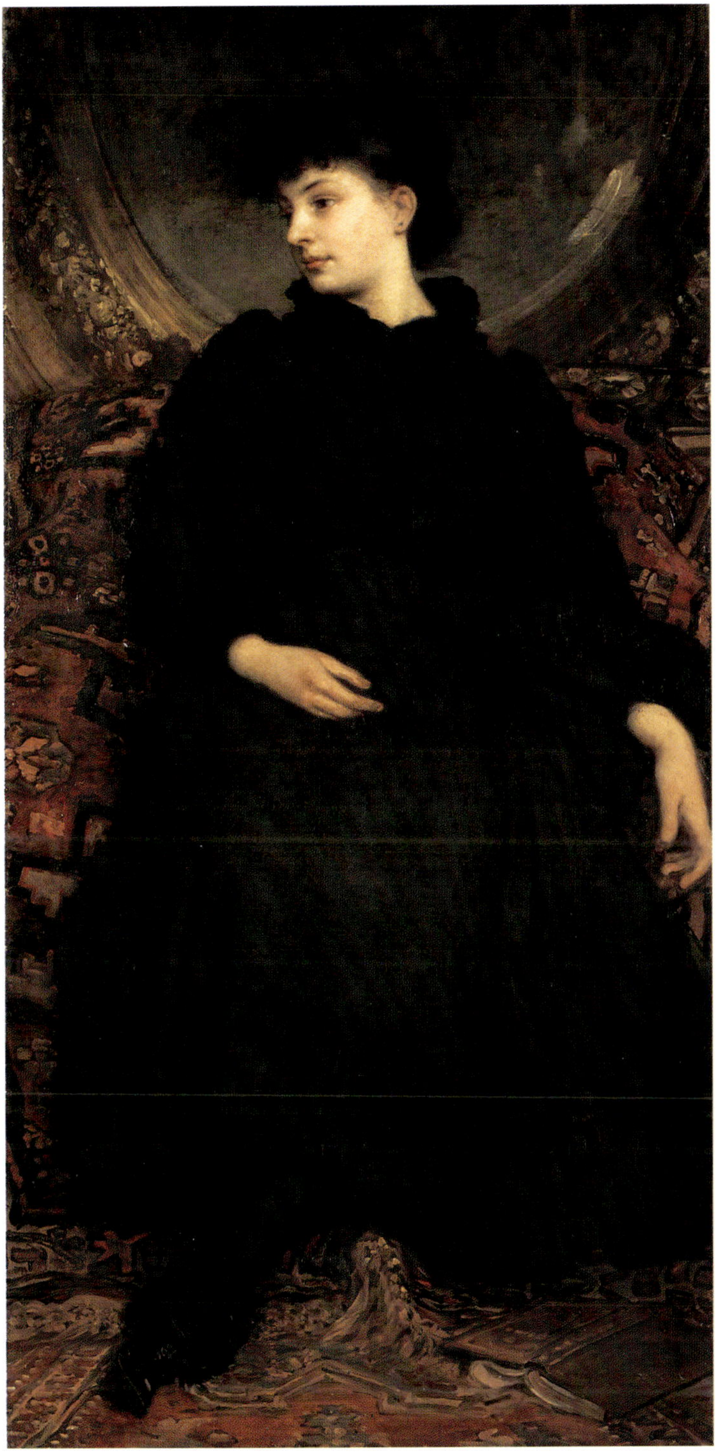

Gyula Benczúr
(1844–1920)
The Recapture of Buda Castle in 1686
1896
Oil on canvas, 707.9 × 351 cm
Inv. no.: FK 2867

Benczúr's historical composition is the last great summary of 19th-century Hungarian history painting. It synthesizes the main characteristics of the genre and terminates its further possibilities. The intention to experience the national past and visualize it connects the work with the great romantic compositions of the 19th century. Individualizing the figures after contemporaneous portraits and basing the composition on thorough investigations for the sake of historical authenticity reveal the unshakable ties with reality, a basic lineament of historicism. In the weapons, clothes, flags and other accessories objects shown at the 1886 historical exhibition commemorating the siege can be recognized. Benczúr's painting is no less than the condensation of the age's knowledge of the 1686 siege. The peculiar solemnity of the work, the absence of real "action", of the narrative and emotional tension, the passivity of the victorious heroes all anticipate deheroization, a sign of the crisis of history painting which the new generation, intent on renewing the genre, had to face up to at the turn of the century. The enormous painting was commissioned by the municipality of Budapest to commemorate the bicentennial of the recapture of Buda from the Ottomans (1686). The picture was completed for the millenary celebrations in 1896. It boosted the popularity of the painting at home that in 1900 it received the Grand Prix at the Paris World Exposition.

G. B.

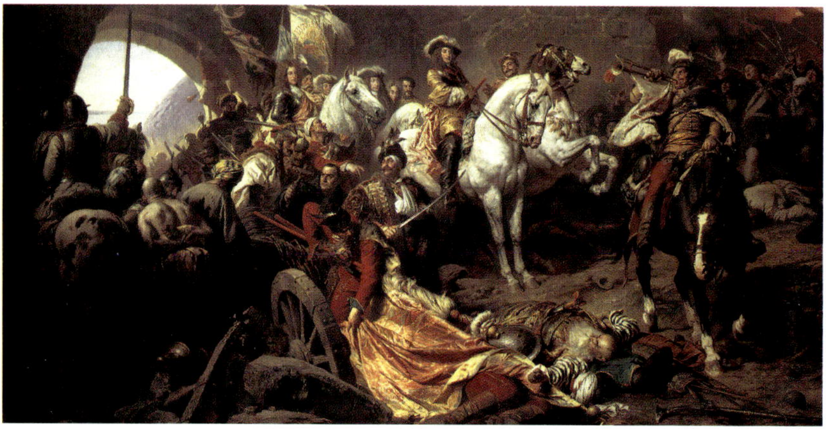

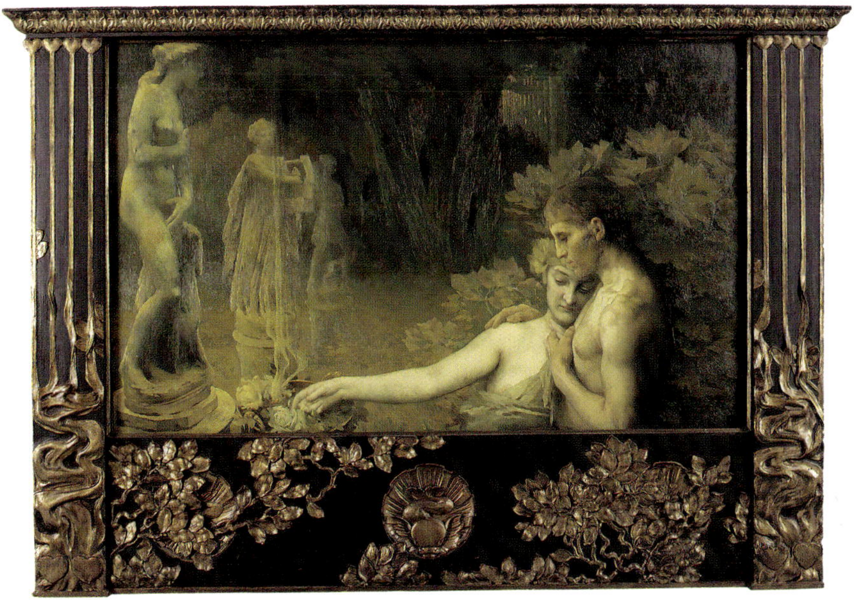

János Vaszary

(1867–1939)

Golden Age

1898

Oil on canvas, 92.5 × 156 cm

Inv. no.: 1614

The first mature period of the painter between 1895 and 1905 was characterized by representative panel paintings and naturalistic rural genre pieces belonging to the current of international art nouveau. The main creation of Hungarian symbolism, Golden Age, was first exhibited in Műcsarnok [Palace of Art], Budapest in 1898, then it was shown to the European public at the Paris World Exposition in 1900. The peculiar atmosphere and subtle sensuosness of the painting derives from the counterpoint between modelling forms as dictated by the academic traditions and an art nouveau decorative character. The picture is in kinship with the naturalism-tinted symbolism of German Jugendstil. The embracing human couple in the foreground of the park lined with antique statues—of Apollo, Diana—offers a sacrifice to the goddess of love, Venus. The opaque green colour scheme elicits a dreamlike, mystic atmosphere, while the contrast between the dark green background and the almost fluorescent naked bodies is profoundly erotic. The richly carved frame was also designed by Vaszary as an integral part of the composition. The art nouveau motifs of the canvas, the wavy line of the sacrificial smoke meander onto the sumptuously decorated frame.

E. P.

Miklós Ligeti
(1871–1944)
Portrait of József Rippl-Rónai
1900
Bronze, 50 × 30 × 44 cm
Inv. no.: 56.426-N

Ligeti began his studies with Lajos Mátray at the School of Applied Arts and then he was apprenticed to Alajos Stróbl. After Vienna and Munich he went to Paris in 1894 to study at the Julian Academy. Rodin's work and approach put some—undeniable—imprint on Ligeti; some sources claim that he also met the French master in person. The painter Rippl-Rónai also lived in Paris at that time. He had already had his first exhibition and precisely in 1894 his painting My Grandmother received very appreciative reviews in the French press. They may have become acquainted then or perhaps at Rippl-Rónai's first Hungarian public showing (Budapest, Royal Hotel, 1900) when Ligeti purchased one of his paintings. In the vigorously animated portrait of the painter literally bearing the modelling sculptor's fingerprints, the painterly effects of the play of light and shade are predominant. Ligeti's work is impressionistic. This kind of modelling characterized a brief early phase of his career (the portrait of the painter Béla Iványi Grünwald, 1901, is similar). His affinity to a painterly attitude found an outlet in the 1910s and 1920s in the products of the Angyalföld Workshop of Artistic Ceramics which he founded.

G. Sz.

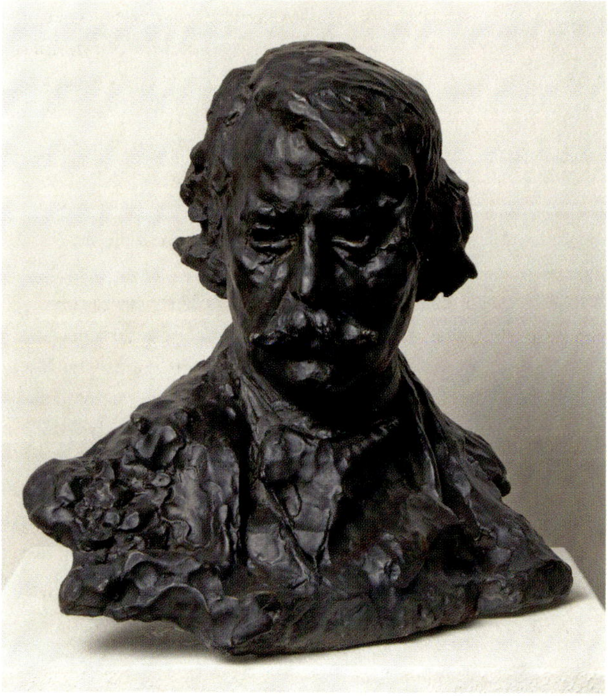

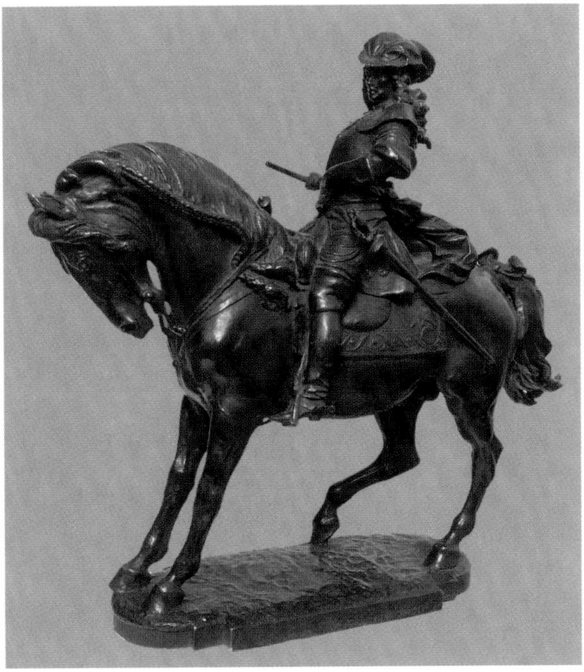

József Róna
(1861–1939)
Equestrian statue of Prince Eugene of Savoy
Around 1900
Bronze, 16 × 38 × 53 cm
Inv.no.: 56.547-N

József Róna's statue of prince Eugene of Savoy is an 1:10 diminished variant of the monument of the prince now in front of the main entrance to the Hungarian National Gallery. It was customary in the age to make reductions of monumental sculptures (identical variants on a far smaller scale), but it was also general practice to make small models of planned monuments. The bronze variant of the Prince Eugene statue might both be a reduction or a preliminary model. At the spring exhibition of 1899 both variants (the small and the large one) were presented simultaneously, so the small one was probably the model for the monument. József Róna made the statue, an expensive undertaking, upon commission from the town of Zenta, but the town was unable to pay for it. Róna was saved from bankruptcy by prime minister Kálmán Széll's proposition for it to be purchased by state and erected outside the palace of Buda. The rearing horse arching its neck, its tail fluttering, carries the commander leaning slightly back, dressed in armour, a large hat and enormous boots, holding a staff in his stretched out right hand. The model for the horse was a Lipitzaner owned by count Tivadar Andrássy, while the horseman was modelled after a young trainee at the Spanish Riding School in Vienna. The sculpture was well received in the artistic circles at its first showing.

J. Sz.

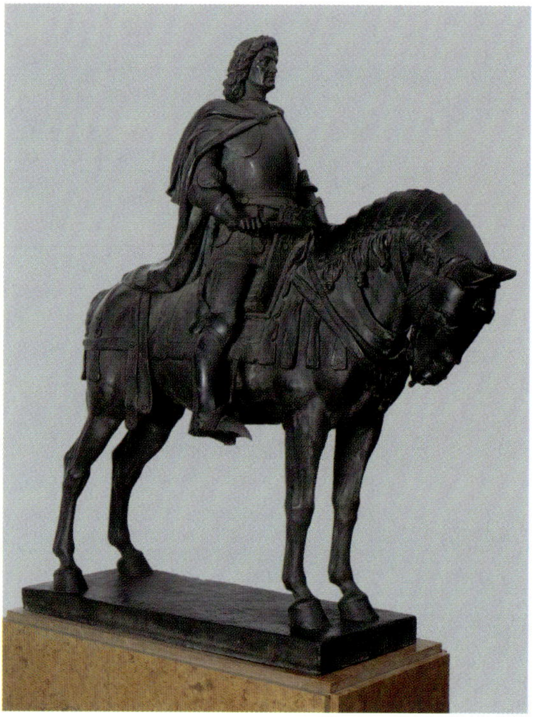

János Fadrusz
(1858–1903)
Equestrian statue of King Matthias
1902
Bronze, 44 × 110 × 158 cm
Inv. no.: 65.45-N

János Fadrusz was a decisive figure in the monumental sculpture of late Hungarian historicism at the turn of the 19th and 20th centuries. His twice life-sized statue of Matthias was erected in the native town of the king, Kolozsvár (today Cluj-Napoca, Romania), outside the south front of the St Michael church in 1902. In this composition, Fadrusz broke spectacularly with neo-baroque restrictions, adopting the monumental form creation of classicism. At the time of the inauguration of the Matthias monument the sculptor received a state commission to produce the reduced variant of the public statue for the so-called Hunyadi room created in the extension of the Royal Palace. Since in a public statue erected on a tall pedestal some distortions are necessary to achieve the required view, these disproportions become disturbing on a reduced scale. That is why there are conspicuous misproportions in the diminished variant of Fadrusz' equestrian statue. The face of the young king sitting in armour in a tall-backed saddle is stern, his wavy hair coming down to his shoulders is crowned by a laurel wreath. The equestrian statue is grand, dignified, radiating power and resolve just like the large public monument which it was based on. The composition is harmonious and solemn also on the smaller scale, but its monumental effect is lost.

J. Sz.

Lajos Gulácsy
(1882–1932)
Na'Conxypan
1902
Pastel, cardboard, 368 × 334 cm
Inv. no.: FK 5233

The realm of Gulácsy's imagination, Na'Conxypan, somewhere between Japan and the Moon is a town whose inhabitants he described in stories and depicted in drawings and paintings. They are both ordinary people and fantastic heroes of tales, kindly figures usually rendered with a naive charm, sometimes clad in exotic clothes. The streets of the town evoke his Italian memories, the sources of his playfulness, humour, grotesque figures are the character types of commedia dell'arte and the world of E. T. A. Hoffmann's stories, but they also have kiship with Jacques Callot's engravings and the art of the Netherlandish painters. Drawings and stories of Na'Conxypan keep recurring throughout Gulácsy's whole oeuvre. This pastel piece is an early example: the figures passing in the street in peculiar hats are outlined with fine contours and the crayon creates a very finely homogeneous atmosphere.

E. R.

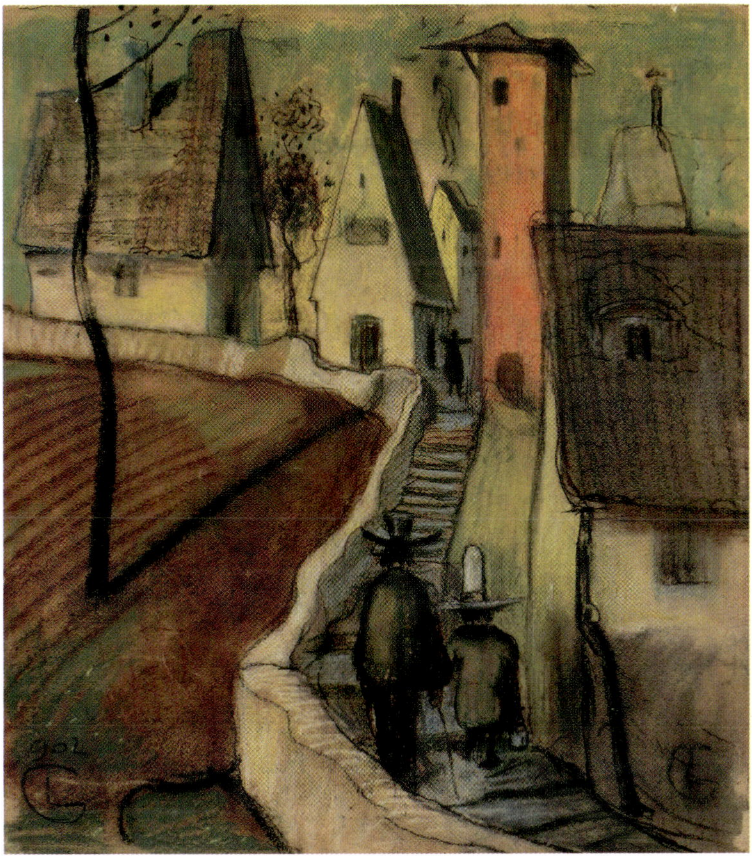

Miklós Ligeti
(1871–1944)
Anonymus
1903
Bronze, 73 × 52 × 56 cm
Inv. no.: 2072

One of the so-called "king's statues" represents the anonymous author of Gesta Hungarorum, the chronicle narrating the story of the Hungarians' conquest of their future country. Francis Joseph I decided about the king's statues (hence the name) shortly after German emperor William's visit to Budapest in 1897. Rumour has it that the guest made a pitying, disdainful remark about the bare, unadorned squares of Budapest. The royal rescript addressed to the prime minister lists the persons to be represented and their merits, noting that the costs were to be charged on the court budget. Modelling the anonymous chronicler was not easy as there was no depiction or description to base the features on. Ligeti therefore—disagreeing with the statues committee who proposed modelling a "typical Hungarian" face—retained the anonymity of the chronicler, the romantic envelope of "facelessness". The play of light and shade on the surface of the bronze statue erected at a well-chosen site in the City Park in 1903 turns the slightly stooped pensive figure of the scholarly monk timeless, unapproachable, somewhat out of this world. The inscription registered the research findings about the person of Anonymus: "Gloriosissimi Belae regis notarius". Small eosine-glazed variants of the statue were marketed by the Zsolnay Factory of Pécs, and porcelaine versions made at Herend are also known.

G. Sz.

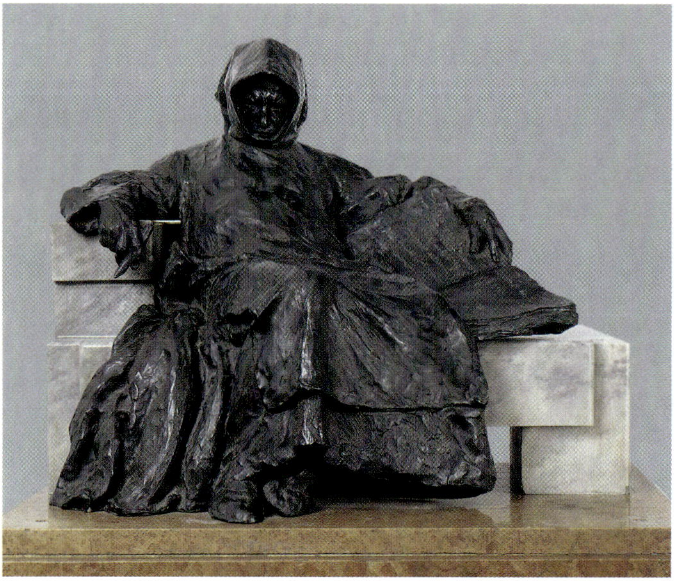

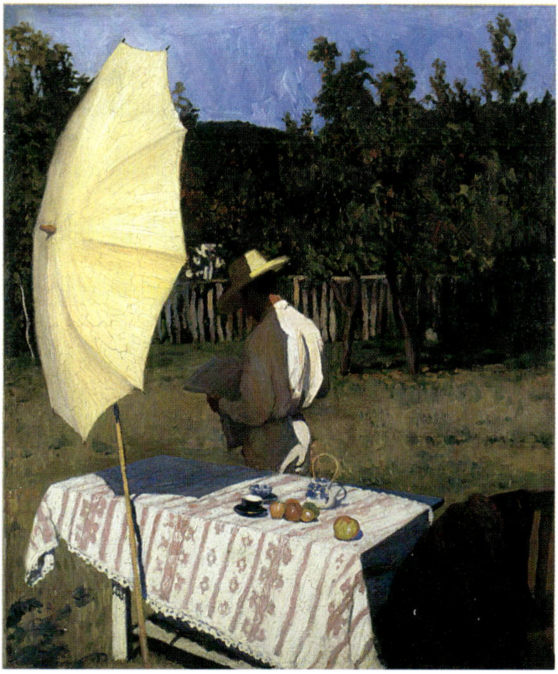

Károly Ferenczy
(1890–1920)
October
1903
Oil on canvas, 126 × 107 cm
Inv. no.: 59.44 T

Károly Ferenczy was in the search of perfection devoid of artfulness and conventions. The intellectual tensions, the sensuous and rational force of his paintings derive from the simultaneity of formal and emotional harmonies, from the courage not to sacrifice anything of the complex human character of his figures for the sake of arbitrary artistic form. The figures of Károly Ferenczy's paintings are in perfect harmony with nature while they preserve the integrity of their human characters and do not mar nature at all. Although we sense that the reading man is the owner of this piece of nature, he merges with the luxurious autumn scenery with self-evident naturalness. He is half in the shade, turning into himself, ignoring the surrounding world. He has become part of nature, but not via a formal degradation—contrarily, through an intellectual activity. The apples on the table suggest the beauty-creating power of nature and the regulating will of creative man. Each motif is important in the composition, and each is subordinated to the rest. A sort of paternal providence characterized Ferenczy as the head of the family guiding and watching the fate of his children, and it was present in his whole œuvre. Everything is important in the picture, every motif preserves its individuality and subordinates itself to a superior order. This "familiar" attitude to the world, to nature produces the emotional surplus to Ferenczy's composition which is peerless in Hungarian painting.

G. B.

Simon Hollósy
(1857–1918)
Peasant Farmyard with Cart
1910–1912
Oil on canvas, 80 × 100 cm
Inv. no.: 57.71 T

The once prophetic teacher of the private art school in Munich and highly influential leader of the Nagybánya artists' colony (started in 1896) founded new artists' colonies at various places after 1902, last at Técső (today Tyachev, Romania) in Máramaros county, with little success. The crisis his painting and teaching method underwent in Nagybánya did not leave him for years. He began painting landscapes at Técső on the Tisza: the cone of the Nereszen perhaps reminded him of the Kereszthegy (Cross Mountain) at Nagybánya. Nevertheless, Hollósy never fully appreciated landscapes, the remainder of his life being spent in realizing the never completed great work, the Rákóczi March. Despite its late date, Peasant Farmyard with Cart is one of the peaks of the master's plein-air painting, testifying to a persistent attachment—reminiscent of the old Monet's—to the natural sight already using the tools of impressionism. The vibrating air dissolves the objects into soft, almost immaterial shapes in the dazzling sunlight, and we almost feel the heat of the carriage mountings on our skin; the eye wanders over the blinding surface of the whitewashed wall and we can almost hear the sizzling dryness of the cornfield behind the houses. The painting was exhibited at the jubilee showing of Nagybánya in 1912 where—in István Réti's recollection—it appeared faded and melancholic among Ferenczy's and Iványi Grünwald's serene, sunny pictures.

Gy. Sz.

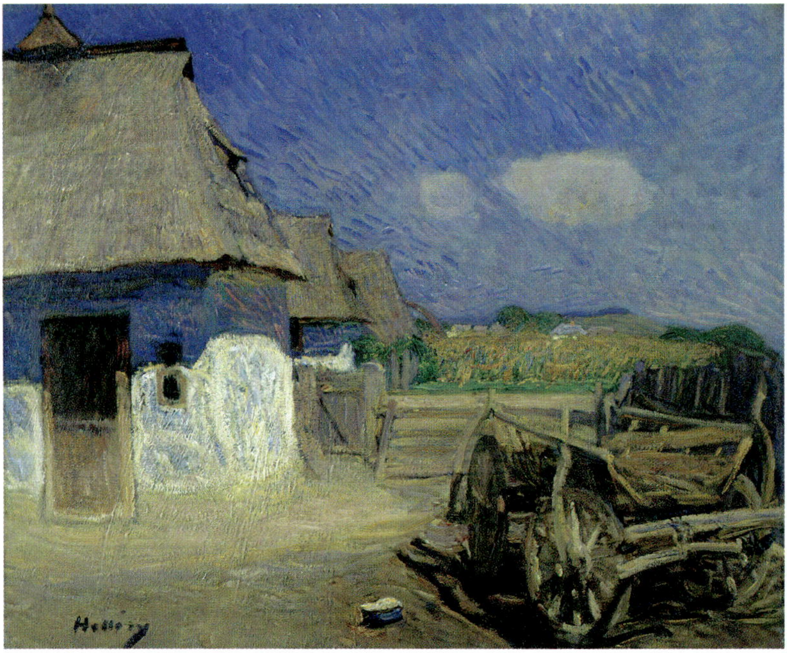

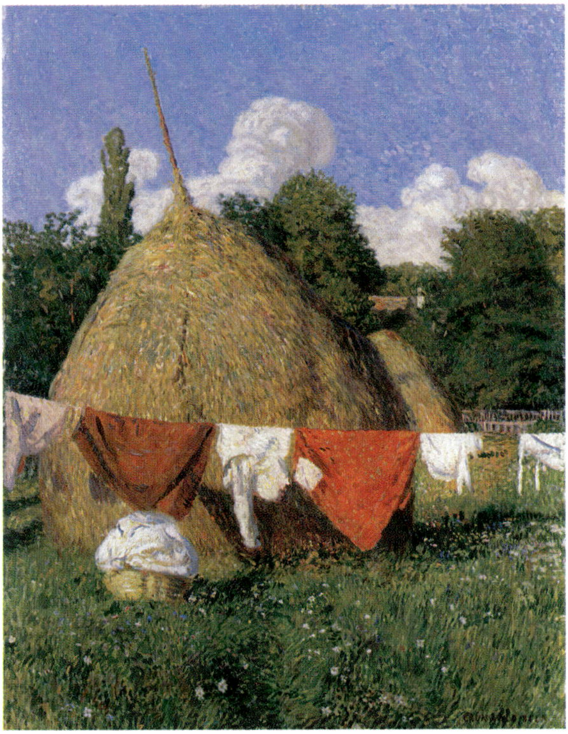

Béla Iványi Grünwald
(1867–1940)
Drying the Laundry
1903
Oil on canvas, 166 × 133 cm
Inv. no.: 2480

After Simon Hollósy left in 1902, Ferenczy, Réti, Thorma and Iványi Grünwald undertook to run the art school at Nagybánya (Baia Mare, Romania). Tutoring the students, correcting their works took up much of Iványi's energies, yet 1903 was one of his most successful years. The familiar environment of Nagybánya, his harmonious private life—his son was born in the previous year—and the impressions of a trip to Africa and Turkey all urged him to register his external and internal experiences in fresh, optimistic landscapes. The pictures painted in this period include decisive pieces of the œuvre such as the masterpiece of plein-air moods, Spring Outing (HNG), The Three Magi (private property) setting the biblical story in Nagybánya, on Virághegy (Flower Mountain), and a depiction of haystacks—emblematic since the impressionists—, Drying the Laundry. The forms all but dissolve in the glaring sunlight; the blue of the sky, the ochre of the typical haystack, the garden full of wild flowers and the bright colours of the drying garments merge into a vibrating surface, almost like a mottled woven fabric. The artist already experimented with a variant of the painting in the previous year, but only presented the final mature version at the Autumn Exhibition in Műcsarnok (Palace of Art) in 1903 where the state purchased it.

Gy. Sz.

Tivadar Csontváry Kosztka
(1853–1919)
Pleasure Drive in Athens by the Light of a New Moon
1904
Oil on canvas, 92 × 72 cm
Inv. no.: 95.1 T

In Csontváry's oeuvre the night landscapes—Trau, Castellamare, Taormina, East Railway Station in Budapest, the Cairo pictures, Athens, Jajce and other nocturnal scenes painted at unknown places—are not merely supplements to the series of "daylight" compositions but provide the thematic frames to the elaboration of autonomous pictorial problems. One of the central problems of Csontváry's oeuvre was the objective possibility and subjective ability of painting light, first of all sunlight. In his nocturnal pictures he also examines the nature of light from a very modern point of view. Csontváry was preoccupied by night not because of the darkness, nor because of its mysticism or romantically animated symbolism. His pictures are about electric light, or the conflict of electric and natural light effects. In all his nocturnal pictures man-made artificial light and people moving at ease in the dark have distinguished roles. The fishermen, café guests, workers at the power plant, people idling around the railway station in other night-scenes fill the realm devoid of sunlight with life just as naturally as do the idyllically naive figures of the promenade in Athens. In his day pictures light consecrates the landscape and divine energy radiates to the earth from the fantastically colourful skies, but Csontváry leaves the night to man as a human territory.

G. B.

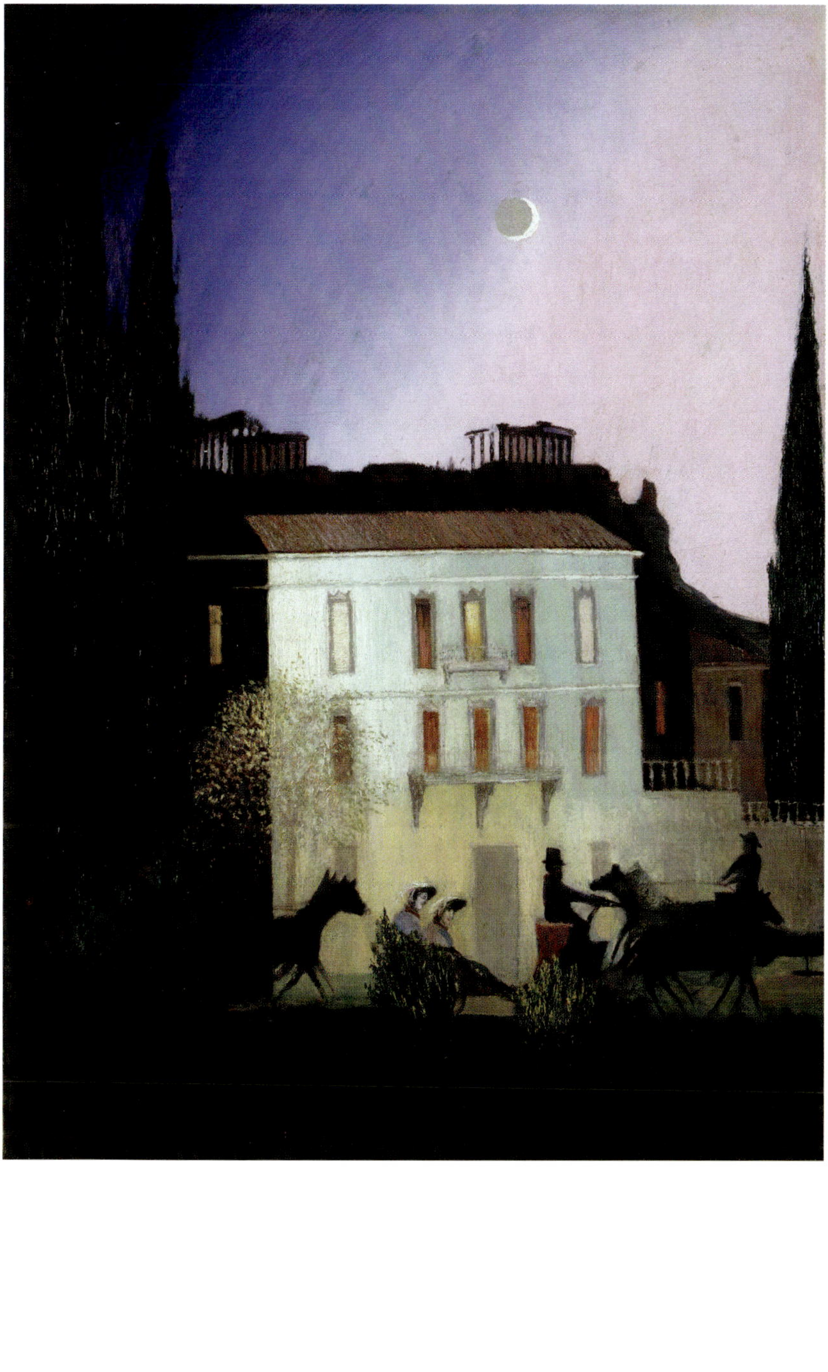

Tivadar Csontváry Kosztka
(1853–1919)
Ruins of the Ancient Greek Theatre at Taormina
1904–1905
Oil on canvas, 302 × 570 cm
Inv. no.: 93.32 T

Csontváry's painting of nearly 20 square metres is one of the best-known Hungarian works. Its appeal owes not only to its enormous size but also to the over-mystification of the painter's person. The peculiar life story of the painter, his visionary calling to become a painter, the well-nigh miraculous survival of his oeuvre all fed the emergence of legends around the artist. Yet he was very much the offspring of the turn of the century. His oeuvre united in an idiosynchratic manner the universal individualism of romanticism and modernism's search for collective ideals. Csontváry's painting aimed at a thematic and optical totality. Roaming all Europe and the eastern Mediterranean in search for the great motifs, he depicted an almost encyclopaedic list of tourist sights. The unusual and conspicuous colourfulness of his pictures encompassing the entire spectrum derives from his special colour theory, his "solar road painting". The ruins of the theatre at Taormina inspired several Hungarian painters from the mid-19th century. Csontváry depicted the ruins from the optimal vantage point that was discovered by the 19th-century romantic painters. Yet the colossal size, the resultant panoramic illusion and the decorative colour scheme displaying the impact of post-impressionism made it wholly novel and unique.

G. B.

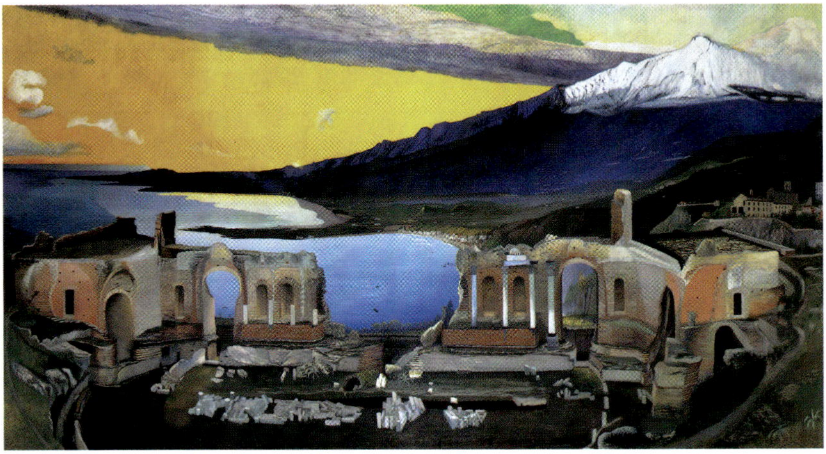

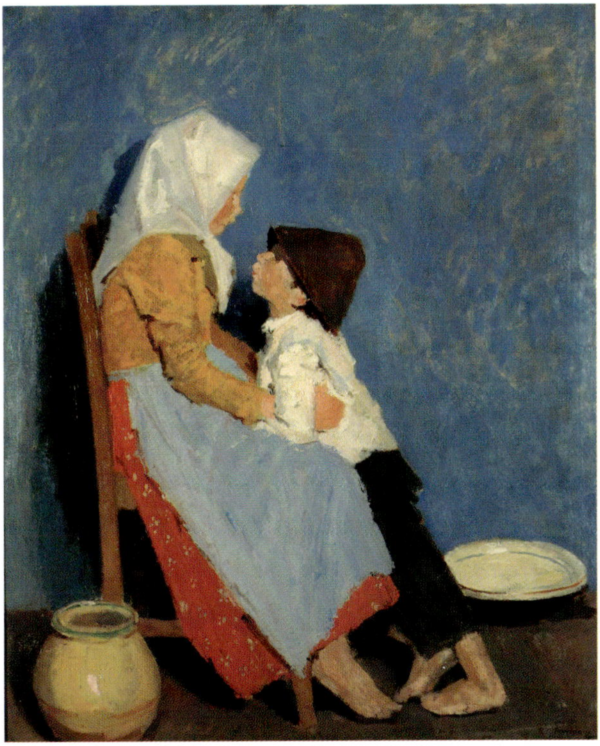

Adolf Fényes
(1867–1945)
Siblings
1906
Oil on canvas, 125.5 x 106 cm
Inv. no.: 3276

The artists' colony of Szolnok, an art centre fostering the realistic traditions of genre painting, was established in 1902. One of the decisive figures of the colony was Adolf Fényes, associated with the town for nearly four decades. In his period between 1897 and 1908 he painted his series Life of the Poor with deep commitment and empathy. The genre scenes of the cycle divide into three distinct stylistic groups. In the realistic works of the initial years the dramatic character of the monumental peasant figures is enhanced by the use of dark brown and black colours. From 1903 his palette brightened and the motifs were soaked in sunlight. By 1906 Fényes arrived at a post-impressionist approach to the picture. Siblings belongs among the masterpieces of the latter period. In the crystallized composition decorative forms bring forth the figures of the siblings against a homogeneous blue background. In the works of this period, Fényes usually depicted one typical figure or typical moment. The concise indication of the interior allows a glimpse of the everyday life of the poor peasantry, of their simple but noble material culture. The noted art writer of the period Károly Lyka wrote about Fényes' paintings in 1905: "He achieves increasigly more with increasingly less."

E. P.

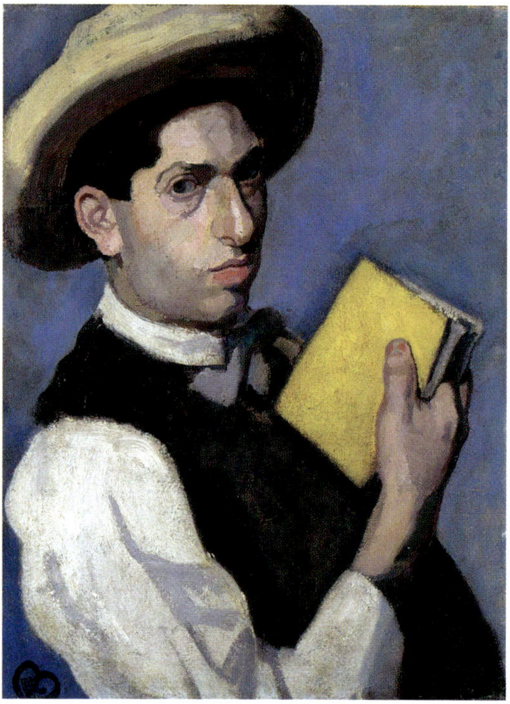

Róbert Berény
(1887–1953)
Self-portrait in a Straw Hat
1906
Oil on canvas, 59.5 × 44.5 cm
Inv. no.: 56.208 T

The youngest member of the group Nyolcak (The Eight), Róbert Berény began his studies at the Julian Academy in Paris in 1905, but he was more interested in the fermenting art life and the contemporary works he saw at exhibitions and in private collections. In 1906 he already presented some paintings at the Salon d'Automne and in October he summarized his efforts in his Self-portrait with a Straw-hat. The narrow frame of the bust seemingly follows the traditional self-portraits of artists facing the spectator self-consciously, but Berény seems to have been more intrigued by the correlation between the primary colours of the background and the book cover than the precise rendering of the environment of the young man who, having just reached manhood, is already acknowledged as a painter. The painterly contrast of the dark vest and the glowing white shirt is perhaps a vestige of the tradition of Mihály Munkácsy, but the tilted and carefully balanced vertical axis alludes to the knowledge of Cézanne's compositional order while the ever braver use of colours suggests acquaintance with the results of the Fauves. Berény's early self-portrait paves the way for his diverse series of painted and drawn self-portraits often characterized by irony, playfulness or the use of various modernist stylistic elements.

Gy. Sz.

Béla Czóbel
(1883–1976)
Sitting Man
1906
Oil on canvas, 169.5 × 79.5 cm
Inv. no.: 55.752

Béla Czóbel, who studied in Nagybánya under Béla Iványi Grünwald in the previous years, exhibited in the Salon d'Automne in Paris in 1905 in the company of the French Fauves led by Henri Matisse. The real breakthrough came in the next year when he introduced his compositions built of colourful, glaring, large patches at the artists' colony, providing an example for the young "Neos". He sent these pictures to the Salon d'Automne too, including Sitting Man, a portrait of his brother-in-law. One of the major works of 1906 is the garden scene of Painters in the Open (Centre Pompidou, Paris), although he was mostly preoccupied with the problem of half- or full-length portraits in closed spaces at that time. The accessible works and those only known from reproductions document how his art based on the traditions of Nagybánya and the example of Rippl-Rónai grew ever more brave and colourful upon the impact of Van Gogh, Gauguin and Matisse, and how it became increasing more original as Czóbel departed from his chosen "masters". In the character picture of the Sitting Man the geometric pattern of the carpet, the still-life details in the background and the change of viewpoints exemplify how the "savage" colour use of the period and the direction of further development—the decorative approach—are synthesized at a higher level.

Gy. Sz.

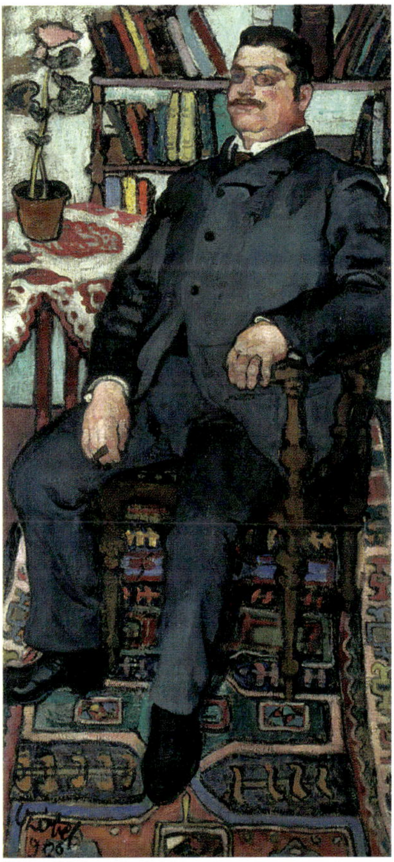

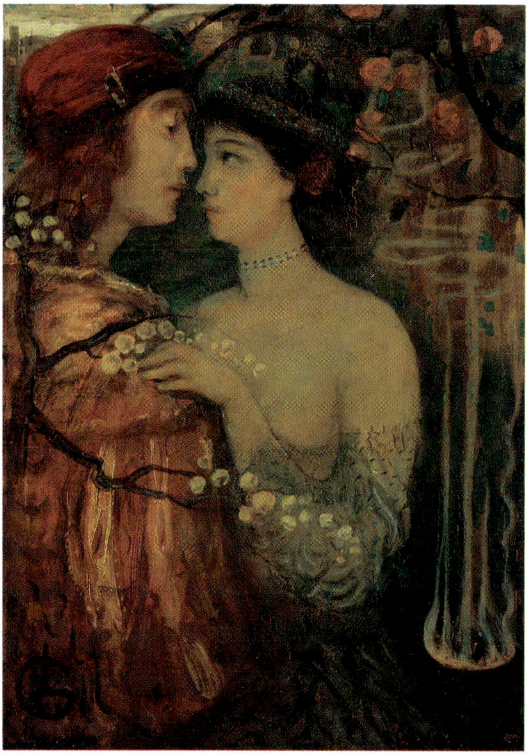

Lajos Gulácsy
(1882–1932)
The Garden of the Magician (Enchantment)
1906–1907
Oil on canvas, 85.5 × 63 cm
Inv. no.: FK 10.197

It decisively determined Gulácsy's approach that he spent nearly thirteen years in Italy with short interruptions between 1902 and 1915. The works painted at the beginning of the century display the fertilizing effect of the English Pre-Raphaelites in the first place. In the female figure of this picture Dante Gabriel Rossetti's model of a fine-cut profile is reborn—her features appear in other works by Gulácsy as well. The couple engrossed in one another is surrounded by a natural setting, a garden of a mystic atmosphere. The flowers unfolding from the rampant vegetation and the swirling ribbon of smoke at the right suggest roses and the fragrance of incense. In the wake of French symbolist poetry Gulácsy often appealed to various senses of the spectator, eliciting different sensations. The reddish overall tone mirrors the pantheistic unity of man and nature. The picture also formulates the existential experience of secessionism, the longing for an idyllic life. His friend the poet Gyula Juhász wrote about Gulácsy: "...he was very far from the world that kept teeming and whirling around him." The painting was first shown to the public with the title Enchantment in the Gulácsy exhibition at the Uránia art gallery in March 1907.

E. P.

József Koszta
(1861–1949)
The Three Magi
1906–1907
Oil on canvas, 121 × 125.5 cm
Inv. no.: 3692

Rising from poverty, Koszta attended all major schools and could even gain experience at the leading art centres of Europe, and yet he became one of the most independent Hungarian painters. When in Rome on a grant in 1905, he immersed into individual questions of creation. The religious composition to be created as a requirement in return for the grant was developed from a variant of his only picture on a historical theme, the meeting of King Matthias and his wife Beatrix. He envisioned the first version of The Three Magi as a fresco, which is perhaps why this work is more compact than his paintings up to then. Koszta's pregnant chiaroscuro contrasts were supplemented here with the contrasts of complementary colours; the dramatic clashes of dark and light patches were to characterize nearly every subsequent painting. This picture also marks a turning point by the discovery of the enhanced light intensity of glowing local colours. The compact forms of the intimately solemn peasant Madonna and the oriental kings resembling shepherds assert themselves wonderfully in the slack rhythm of heavy masses of bright colours against the backlight.

A. Sz. M.

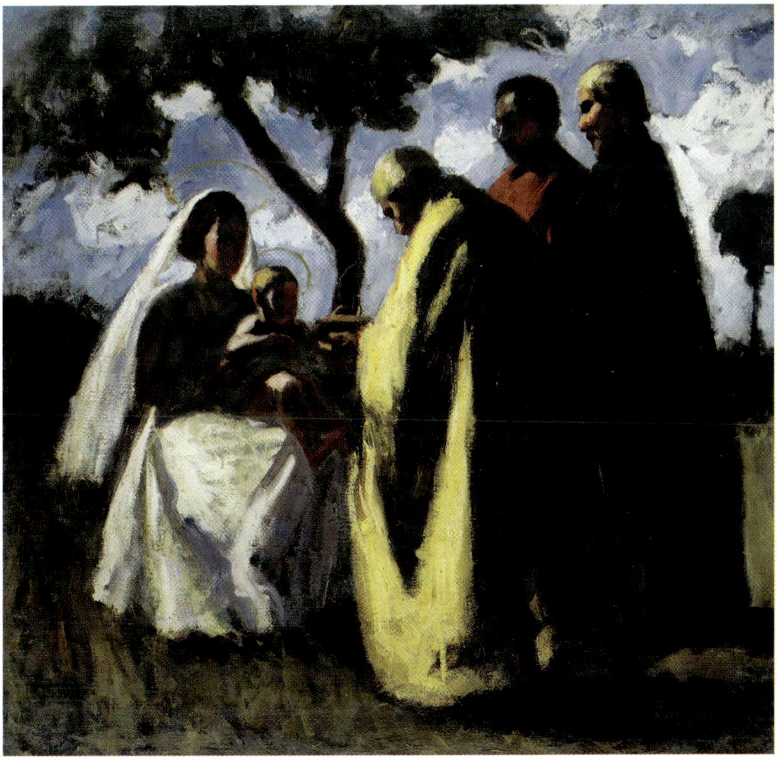

Dezső Czigány
(1883–1938)
Burial of a Child
Around 1907–1908
Oil on cardboard, 60.7 × 76.2 cm
Inv. no.: 89.52 T

Formerly a pupil of Hollósy, Czigány studied at the Julian Academy in Paris in 1905 and exhibited portraits in the Salon des Indépendants already the next year. He shared a flat with his friends Róbert Berény, Lajos Gulácsy and György Bölöni in Paris. Back home, he visited Nagybánya again in 1906 and chose Károly Ferenczy as his master. Taking stock of the influences manifest in his art, one may list Velázquez and Rembrandt of earlier ages and Cézanne and the Fauves from among his contemporaries. He remained loyal to his chosen examples throughout his life as confirmed by his role-playing self-portraits emanating various moods and his precisely elaborated still lifes. Burial of a Child is almost unparalleled in his oeuvre despite the fact that some motifs (field with stacks, roadside cross) cropped up in his earlier paintings as well. The direct influence of Gauguin can be discerned in the painter, who had a larger selection on display at the exhibition of French painters in Nemzeti Szalon (National Salon) in 1907. Although the overall tone is dark, the colour contrasts almost glow in this balladistic work which narrates the frequent event of a child's death in rural life. The coffin hiding the innocent child, the mourning parents are united by the white colour of the tin Christ, producing a verbally unspeakable moment of redemption.

Gy. Sz.

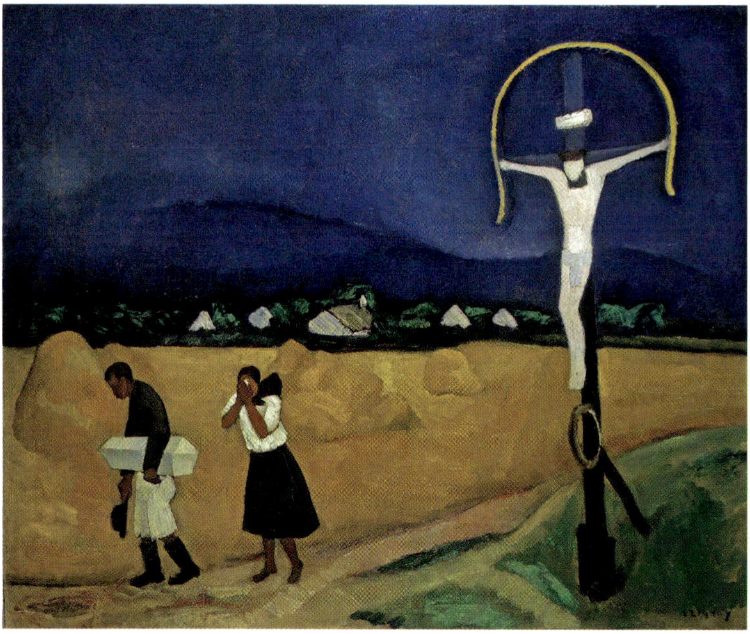

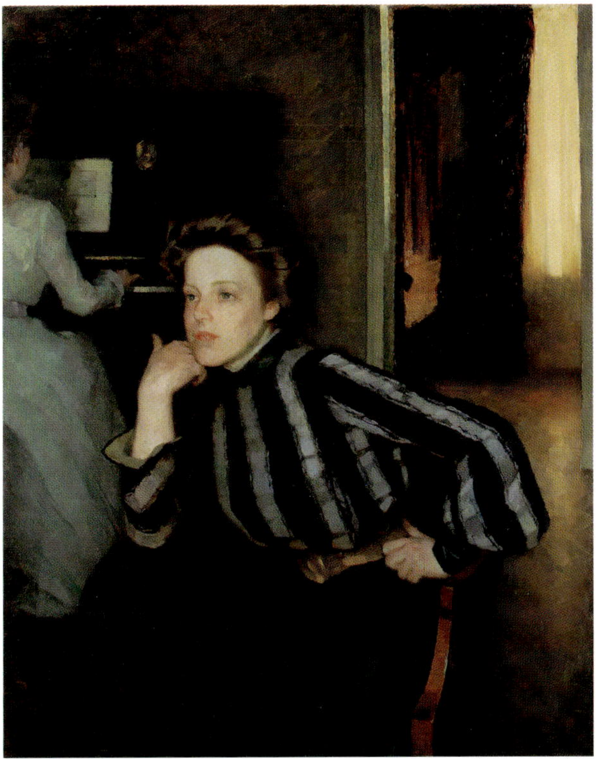

Frigyes Strobentz
(1856–1929)
Adagio
1909
Oil on canvas, 127 × 103 cm
Inv. no.: FK 2247

After studies in Dresden and Düsseldorf, Frigyes Strobentz studied in Munich where he lived nearly all his life, with some interruptions. He was a founder and regular exhibitor of the Sezession of Munich and the artists' colony at Dachau. In the artistic revival at the turn of the century music played a central role, representing the "pure", direct and universal art form that the visual arts of the period also wished to achieve. Musical similes, notions, titles multiplied not only in poetry and painting but also in journalism. Frigyes Strobentz's painting is not only about music but elicits strong musical notions. The difference in scale of the human figures, the rhythm of the interior space, the top view all lend a curious dynamism to the picture. The meditative glance and hesitating movement of the woman sitting in the foreground, the hazy figure of the other woman depicted from behind emanate sadness. The uncertainty of the strange movements is enhanced by the closed, sultry atmosphere of the interior with a door opening into another closed space. The Hungarian interiors painted around the turn of the century usually suggest the warmth of the protective home, but in Strobentz's oeuvre the interior expresses suffocating solitude.

G. B.

Sándor Galimberti
(1883–1915)
Townscape (Nagybánya)
Around 1909
Oil on canvas, 72.5 × 194 cm
Inv. no.: 87.22 T

The pupil who departed most from the plein air naturalism of the founding masters of the Nagybánya artists' colony was Sándor Galimberti. He and his wife Valéria Dénes jointly elaborated a pictorial language comprising more and more abstract landscape elements, "constructive" composition incorporating the achievements of cubism, and a conscious colour reduction. His talent was taken note of by József Rippl-Rónai, but after Nagybánya and Técső, his most thorough studies were pursued in Paris where he exhibited at the Salon d'Automne and the Salon des Indépendants from 1907. With his fellow painters Tihanyi and Ziffer, Galimberti adapted to Nagybánya the townscapes from a high vantage point characteristic of the French impressionists and further developed by the Fauves. They painted their innovative veduti, often combining various points of view, from the István Tower rising above the historical centre of the town. Galimberti's Townscape shows a corner of the quadratic main square with the Calvinist church with a red tower cap in the background and greenish slopes on the other side of the river Zazar. The colours are adjusted to the basic colours of the Fauves' palette, but a shift away from the specific scenery towards a more abstract landscape structure can already be discerned.

Gy. Sz.

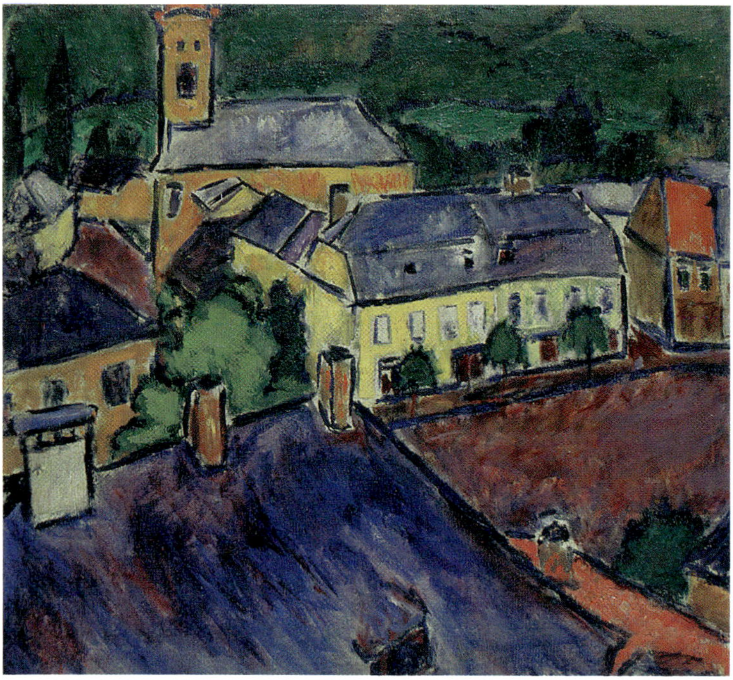

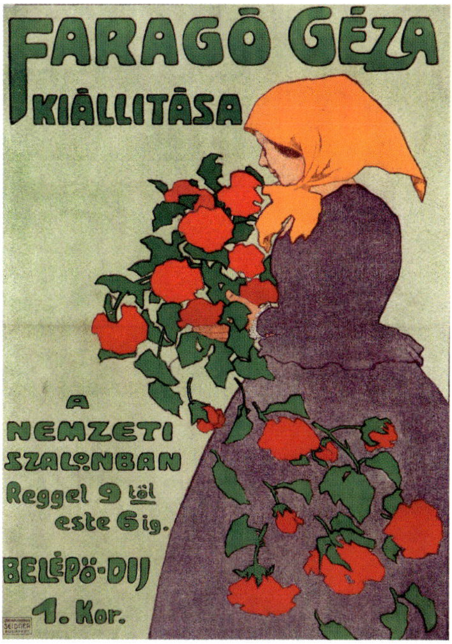

Géza Faragó
(1877–1928)
Géza Faragó's Exhibition at the National Salon
1910
Lithograph on paper, 95 × 63 cm
Inv. no.: XY. 58. 116

Géza Faragó was already a famous and popular designer of humorous commercial adverts and theatre bills in Budapest in 1910. His farcical ideas, gags, caricaturistic figures were widely known. But his fame equally depended on entertainment and an ability to couple satire with the decorative linearity and subtle colour realm of art nouveau. He masterfully exploited the potentialities of colour litography, delighting the spectator with sophisticated tone combinations and the lively play of surfaces of different patterns. He presented another little known facet of his versatility at the exhibition at Nemzeti Szalon (National Salon), showing his paintings next to his posters. Several paintings were made in the countryside, mainly in the art colony at Szolnok, based on observations of nature and idyllic village and small-town life. This set of experiences was emphasized by the poster of this exhibition, showing a girl with a scarf, holding flowers, depicted with touching lyricism. Being a born designer, Faragó stylized the model into pale lilac and red colour planes and fleeting lines. The contrast of lilac, red and green colours, the rendering of the figures in patches and the finely traced letters ensure that the poster can be comprehended, "read" by the eye from a distance—the elementary requirement of posters. Yet the young woman and the flower are more than just a pleasing sight: they symbolize harmony, art.

K. B.

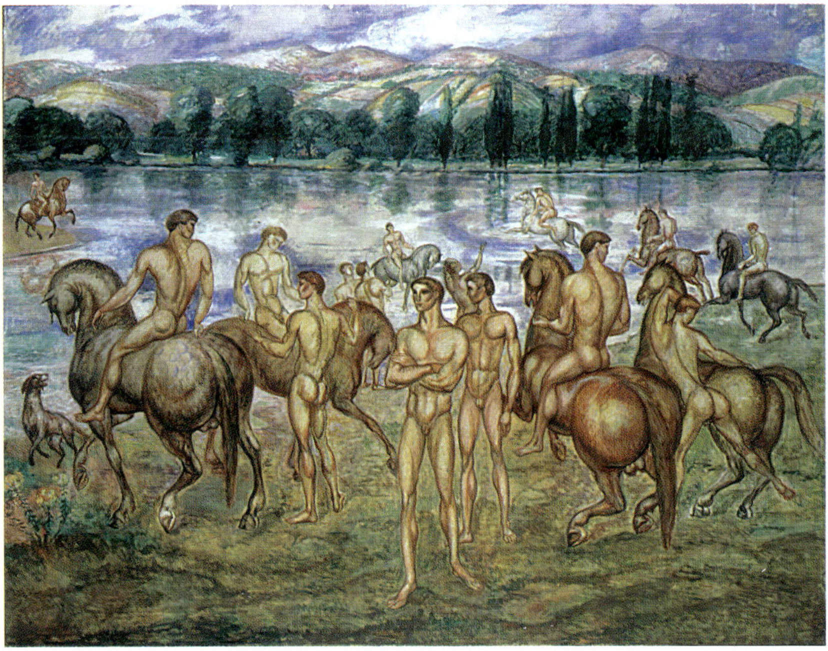

Károly Kernstok
(1873–1940)
Riders by the Waterside
1910
Oil on canvas, 214 × 292.5 cm
Inv. no.: 59.34 T

Before becoming the leader of the artists' group Nyolcak (The Eight) emerging around 1908, Kernstok had gone through all phases and tried out all stylistic variants of Hungarian art history accumulating since the late 19th century, from Munkácsy's dark-toned genre scenes through the atmospheric painting of Nagybánya's plein air naturalism to the brave and dynamic colour spectrum of French Fauvism mediated by Czóbel (Nude Boy Leaning against a Tree, around 1908–1909). Presented at the 1911 exhibition of The Eight, Riders on the Waterside, soon taken for the emblem of the exhibition, indicated a new change of approach and need for synthesis, not only in his individual œuvre. Kernstok's friends, the progressive theoreticians and art writers of the age (György Lukács, György Bölöni) advocated a new worldview, a radical break with the earlier naturalist-impressionist aesthetic. The new painters "drawing from Nature using the intellect"—The Eight—aimed again at stability, a formal order in accord with Cézanne's ideals. In their pictures the stylized human figures not adjusted to realistic anatomy are gradually spiritualized, thus becoming heralds of a new Arcadia, a new society. Kernstok's large painting is an indicator of this transformation: he painted the recognizable Danubian landscape in serene, impressionistic colours, the foreground has a reserved tonal range, while the graphic riders and nude boys already point at a monumental art that he was to realize in the stained glass window he designed for the Schiffer Villa in Budapest the next year.

Gy. Sz.

Ödön Márffy

(1878–1959)

The Old Customs House at Vác

1910

Oil on canvas, 70 × 91 cm

Inv. no.: FK 1065

Having spent several years in Paris on the scholarship he received from the municipality of Budapest, Márffy returned to Budapest in the autumn of 1906. After the most systematically spent years of study—he attended the École des Beaux-Arts in Paris and inquired into the art of Van Gogh, Matisse, Gauguin and Braque—he developed his individual style back in Hungary. In Paris he also met the poet Endre Ady, as well as painters Róbert Berény and Lajos Gulácsy, with whom he remained in contact. From 1908 he often visited Károly Kernstok in his manorial house at Nyergesújfalu frequented by progressive thinkers and future members of Nyolcak. His contemporaries already noticed his ability to balance between powerful Fauvist colours and constructive composition. The compositional order of the old custom-house of Vác is depicted from a deliberately indicated upstairs window. The heaviness of the building blocks is suggested by the ochre-brown colour effect outlined by greens. Márffy was not intent on assuming several vantage points for this top view as his contemporaries Tihanyi and Galimberti did. The proportions of the painting indicated by the slightly marked strolling figure and the almost accurate perspectivic structure of the space ensure the stability of the picture, while the cut-off buildings, the half of the window frame suggest momentariness, the actual meeting between painter and sight.

Gy. Sz.

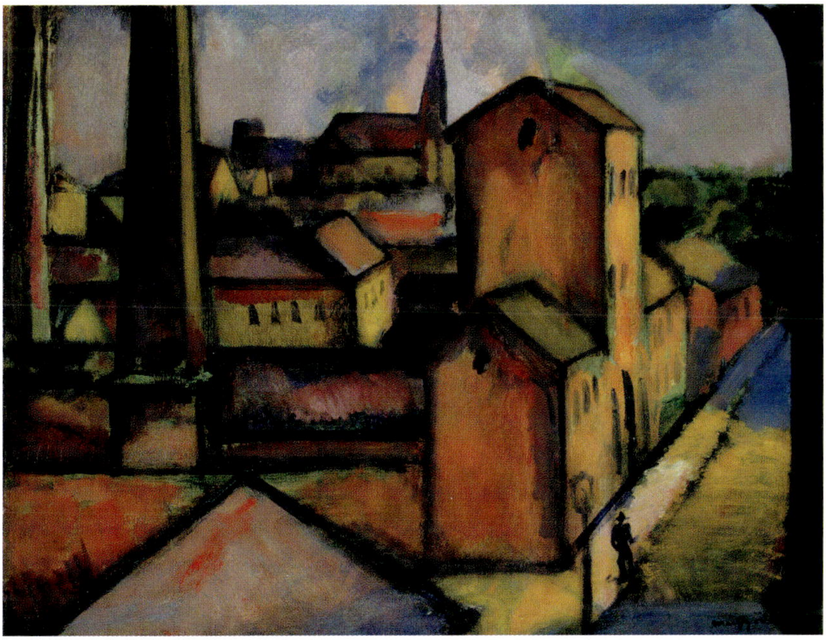

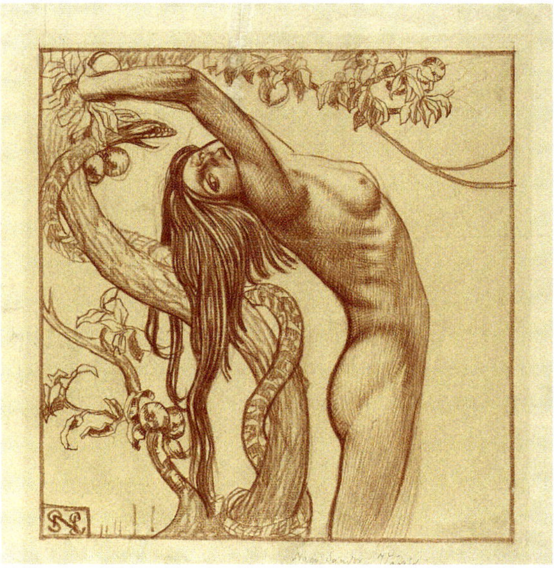

Sándor Nagy
(1868–1950)
Longing
Around 1910
Red chalk on paper, 335 × 346 mm
Inv. no.: 1926-1238

Next to the founder Aladár Körösfői-Kriesch, Sándor Nagy was the leading personality of the Gödöllő artists' colony. The subtle red chalk drawing repeats a popular theme of symbolism, the Fall of Eve. Revealing Nagy's virtuosity as a draftsman, the picture also affords an insight into the process of creation. The female figure leaning back was probably drawn first; the semicircle of her body is repeated by the undulating tree trunk around which the serpent is coiling in another wavy line. The branches on the left and on top, mainly used to fill space, rhyme with the trunk and the female body, while the hair rhymes with the arch of the serpent. In this drawing Eve is not the sinful woman of the Bible or the femme fatale luring men into sin so frequently represented by his symbolist contemporaries. Several artists of the Gödöllő colony including Sándor Nagy adopted the reformed way of living spreading around the turn of the century. Also working in the colony, Mariska Undi held lectures on female gymnastics and Isadora Duncan's novel dance art in 1908. Duncan's pupil Valéria Dienes, the creator of orchestics, was invited by the Gödöllő artists after her return from Paris in 1912 to give a demonstration of this new art of dancing. The movement of Eve is a dance movement; in the idiom of dancing, this movement is not artificial but expressive. Sándor Nagy, who also reformulated the theme of the Annunciation in his picture Ave Myriam showing himself and his wife, probably wanted to give an individual new meaning to the Biblical story in Longing, too. It must be the longing of unspoilt humanity represented by the first woman for the fruit of the tree of knowledge, for life made full by the Spirit.

G. T.

Sándor Ziffer
(1880–1962)
Landscape with a Fence
Early 1910s
Oil on canvas, 91.5 × 109 cm
Inv. no.: 60.26 T

Ziffer met Béla Czóbel as a pupil of Hollósy in 1906. Czóbel had called him to Nagybánya, from where the road led straight to Paris. His sudden encounter with the latest French trends fundamentally determined his subsequent work: the Fauvist works at the Salon d'Automne, the commemorative exhibition of Gauguin and allegedly Matisse's encouragement persuaded him to change his naturalist style established in Hollósy's school. Back in Nagybánya, he created the cream of his oeuvre in 1907–1908, including landscapes and townscapes which are closer to Lajos Tihanyi's works painted at that time than to Czóbel's. Landscape with a Fence captures an exact topographic site: a small street lined with miners' houses winding towards the foot of Kereszthegy (Cross Hill). However unintentionally, the picture is like the summary of his career so far, since in the next years the artist's interest turned increasingly to Germany, on account of his German wife. The cold blue contours, the contrasting glowing reds, the sharply drawn shadows in the oblique sunlight evidence his attempt at reviving naturalist landscape painting and the comprehension of the stylizing, decorative approach of the Fauves and Gauguin, at the same time.

Gy. Sz.

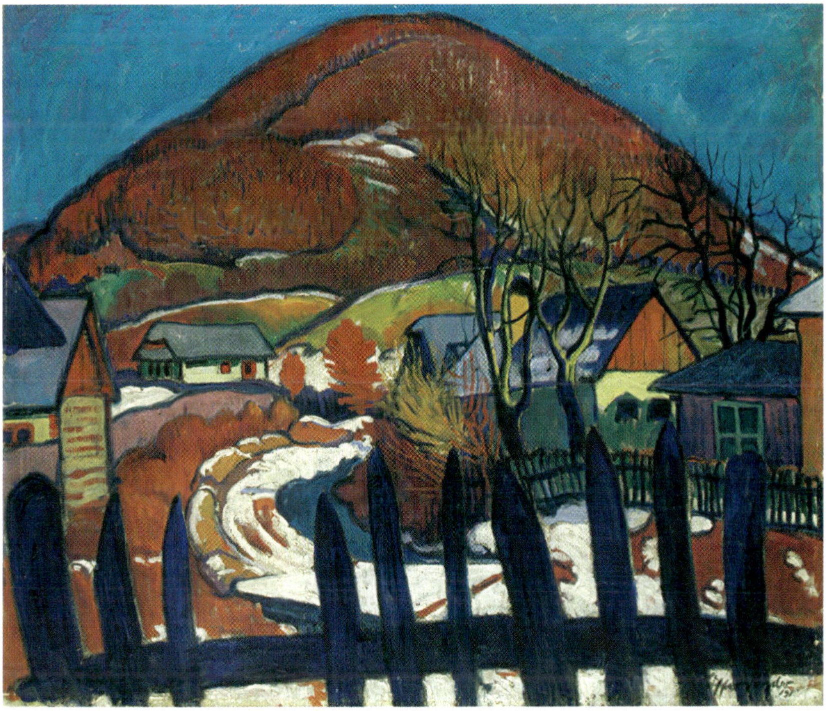

Aladár Körösfői-Kriesch
(1863–1920)
The Story of Klára Zách I
1911
Oil on panel, 102 × 194 cm
Inv. no.: 6077

Aladár Kriesch settled in Gödöllő with his family in 1901 and founded the art colony of Hungarian art nouveau imbued with a Tolstoyan spirit. His example was the romantic historicism of the Pre-Raphaelites and his aim was to create a typically Hungarian style. He saw the possibility of unfolding a national art in Hungarian historic legends and he created an art nouveau formal idiom combined with folklore elements to depict stories of the ancient past. The impact of Pre-Raphaelite art and the cult of the middle ages are most obvious in his two large panel pictures elaborating the story of Klára Zách, for which he made innumerable graphic studies. The theme leads the spectator into 14th-century Hungarian history. Klára's father, Felicián Zách attacked the royal family in revenge for the defilement of his daughter. In retaliation, his whole family and clan were murdered. In Körösfői's paintings beauty and youth symbolized by the young woman fall victim. On the left the figures of Casimir and his sister, the Queen, embody intrigue and seduction, while the graceful company of ladies-in-waiting are depicted well separated from them. The figures are outlined by decorative art nouveau wavelines. The archetype for the painting in art history was Botticelli's Primavera.

E. P.

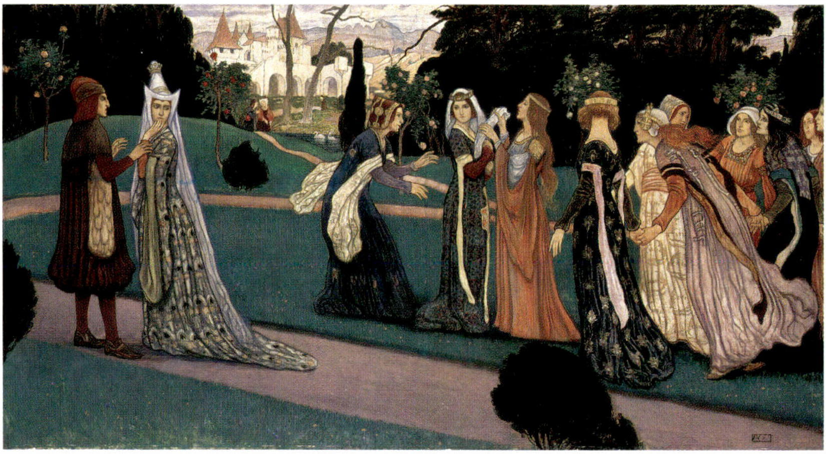

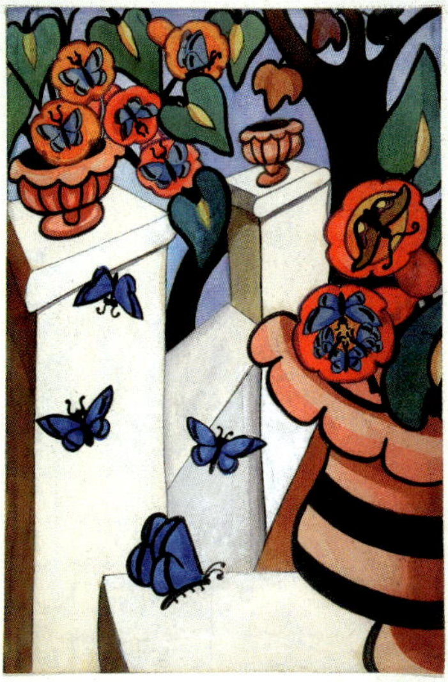

Anna Lesznai

(1885–1966)

Journey of the Little Butterfly in Leszna and Neighbouring Fairyland

1913

Ink, aniline and tempera on paper, 370 × 255 mm

Inv. no.: F.76.184

Anna Lesznai was an active member of the major intellectual movements at the beginning of the 20th century, e.g. the Sunday Circle, her friends included poets Endre Ady and Béla Balázs, for whose books she designed covers. Her poems were published in the periodical Nyugat (West), but she was also invited to exhibit in the company of the progressive artists of the group Nyolcak in 1911. Apart from folkloristic-art nouveau embroideries, she made several illustrations for her own poems in the 1910s (Days of the Baby in Swaddling Clothes, Tale of the Pieces of Furniture and the Little Boy, Tale of the Strawberry-sized Heart). The first to be published was Journey of the Little Butterfly in Leszna and Neighbouring Fairyland (Vienna, 1913), the original illustrations of which are partly in the Lajos Hatvany Museum (Hatvan) preserving her estate and partly in the Hungarian National Gallery. The eight large-sized—mostly full-page—emphatic compositions are more than sheer illustrations: they add up to a cycle of paintings each having an artistic value of its own. The picture discussed here—The Little Blue Butterfly Finds Relatives in a Flower Vase—is the third sheet of the series. Boldly simplified yet abounding in minute details, the sensitively painted pictures of the series take us to magic venues, to an intriguing and exciting realm in which the objects, plants and animals have souls and inextricable existence. Anna Lesznai's illustrations express her eternal nostalgia for a harmonious world so much unlike the real, a world idealized to a fairyland that captures the children's imagination but enchants the adults as well.

F. Zs.

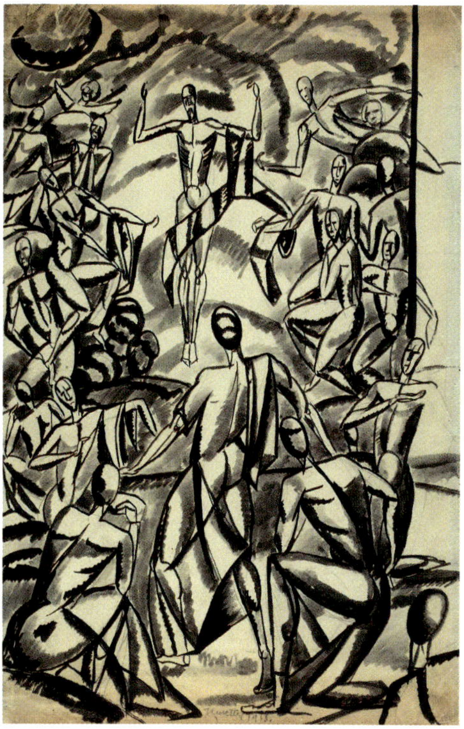

János Kmetty
(1889–1975)
Ascension
1913
Washed ink, brush and pen on paper,
502 × 333 mm
Inv. no.: F.62.185

The large ink drawing is an equivalent of the diverse painted variants of the theme. It is not just a preliminary study but an autonomous work, a definate stance in the history of Hungarian Activism—an avant-garde movement centred around the periodical MA (Today)—where the role of drawing becomes accentuated on account of the potentiality of immediate and powerful expression. Kmetty radically reformulates the traditional theme of the Ascension: the conventional representation of Jesus gives way to new man (new messiah) changing life and art. A thematic precedent is his drawing Self-portrait with Apple (HNG) in which he shows himself as new Adam. The substitution is obvious in the Ascension, too, as he doesn't change the compositional layout, using the upward thriving symmetrical layout brought to full bloom in the baroque. The elongated forms and the twisting of the draperies relax the rigorous compositional order of the puppet-like figures. Kmetty's synthesizing endeavour of the 1910s was expressed typically in his attempts to merge the painting of the old masters (first of all Leonardo and El Greco) and the formal language of cubism. Ascension is connected to one of the most important programmes of the Activists, the one aimed at the creation of 20th-century monumental art.

A. K.

László Mednyánszky
(1852–1919)
In Serbia
1914
Oil on canvas, 67.6 × 100 cm
Inv. no.: 5245

The last period of László Mednyánszky's œuvre comprises war sketches, drawings, paintings. War had attracted the artist from his youth. He noted in his diary in 1884 that the contrast between peaceful life and the excitement of war "constitutes the essence of my life". Aged 62 at the outbreak of World War I, Mednyánszky volunteered for the army, reporting to a newspaper about the fronts in Galicia, South Tyrol and Serbia. Always on the search for the union between the material and the spiritual, Mednyánszky did not make any concessions for the sake of sentimental or patriotic narratives. He summed up his deepest and innermost experiences of the relationship between nature and man in the following words in the summer of 1917: "Every material thing is complex, everything that constitutes our sensuous world breaks down to particles and dissolves in the primaeval material it grew out of." In the midst of wartime massacre Mednyánszky was scrutinizing the face of nature, in his war pictures decay, death is also part of the great cycle of nature. He noted in his diary with seemingly indifferent objectivity: "beside the dreariness of the war, one must see its poetry as well; certainly, one must not be completely overcome by the details." Even if he seemingly only concentrated on the artistic problem, his picture In Serbia is one of the most shocking mementos of war in Hungarian painting.

G. B.

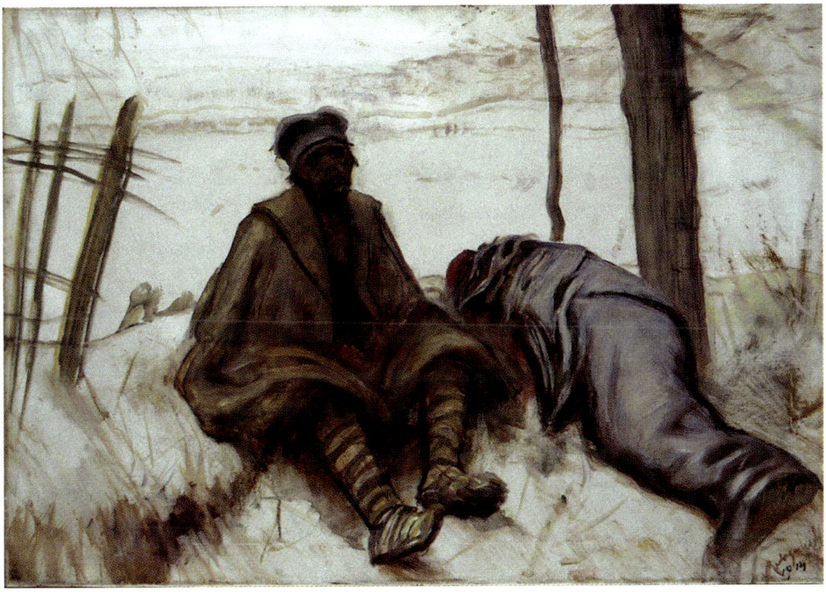

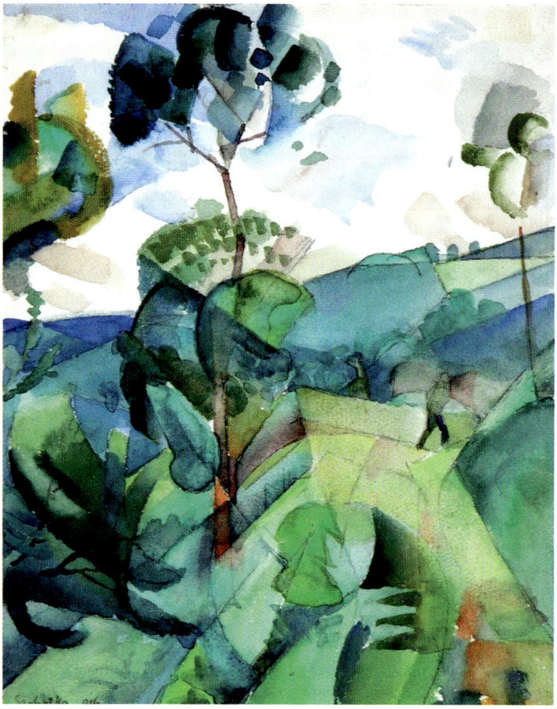

Imre Szobotka
(1890–1961)
Landscape with a Tree (Landscape at Saint-Brieuc)
1916
Watercolour and pencil on paper
200 × 160 mm
Inv. no.: 1954-4861

Having finished the School of Applied Arts, in 1910 Szobotka arrived in Paris upon the invitation of sculptor József Csáky where he could see most diverse variants of cubism in exhibitions. In the painting school La Palette led by Metzinger and Le Fauconnier he could learn the basic principles of the trend and in 1913 and 1914 he could exhibit works in the Salon des Indépendants. The outbreak of World War I found him in a small village in Normandy, Saint-Brieuc, from where he was interned as a citizen of an hostile country. The intellectual and artistic continuity during the next four and a half years of internment was ensured by ever fewer watercolours for shortage of paper, first of all illustrations to Paul Claudel's Annunciation. Szobotka painted landscapes combining the rational constructing principles of cubism with the colourfulness of Fauvism. This is where his creative method balancing between the hardly recognizable but originally realistic landscape elements (trees, houses) and the self-governed pictorial structure is most conspicuous. After his post-war return to Budapest, the naturalistic strain of his painting strengthened and the process of abstraction was reversed: in his later works the distinct cubist language turned increasingly into stylistic memories to convey concrete reality.

Gy. Sz.

József Nemes Lampérth
(1891–1924)
Standing Female Nude
1916
Oil on canvas, 131 × 79.5 cm
Inv. no.: 59.147 T

Short-lived József Nemes Lampérth already debuted with a mature style in 1911, at the age of 20. His subjects were restricted to the most laconic genres, still-lifes, portraits, nudes and landscapes. He transposed the concise and expressive style of his nude drawings into his paintings which preserved the sweeping hatched modelling characteristic of his drawings, but at the same time exchanged the scratchy texture of drawings for relief-like impasto treatment of oil surfaces. The two basic components of a studio situation: the background and the figure are in strong contrast. In front of a dark green undulating drapery a female nude of radiant body colour takes shape in the light falling slantwise from above. The forms of the woman standing in contrapposto are simplified, the superimposed planar surfaces of various tone and colour degrees emphasize the plastic values of the masses. The face indicated by a few schematic patches is in shadow, the robust body coalesces into an apparently finite architecture of forms. The S-lined pose of the figure implies stability and balance, while the dramatic light-and-shade contrasts and the rhythm of the thick paint spread with arched brushstrokes suggest suppressed tension.

A. Z.

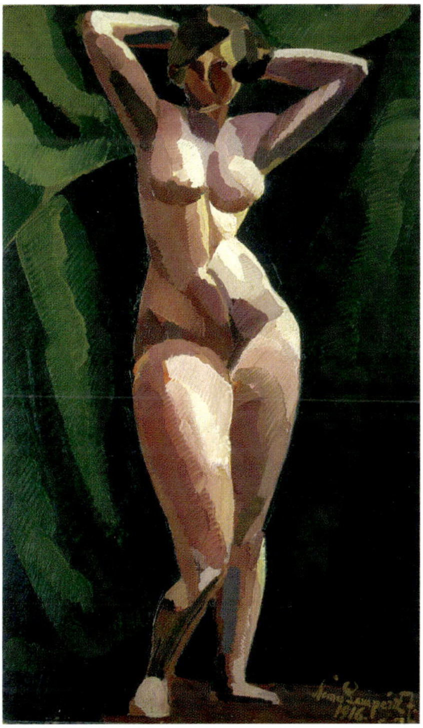

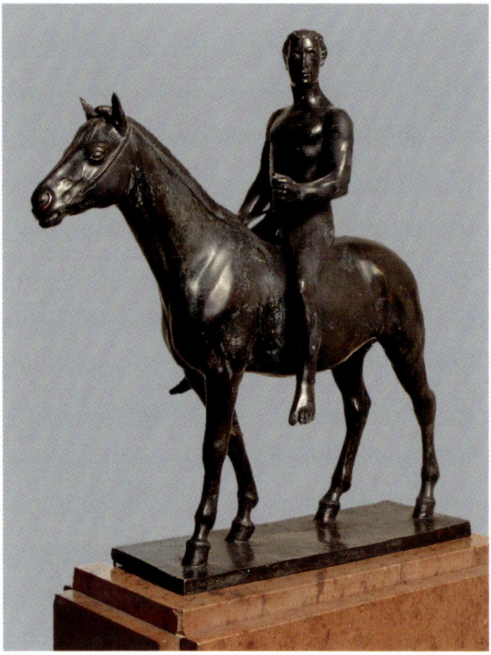

Márk Vedres
(1870–1961)
Youth on Horseback
1917
Bronze, 15 × 45.5 × 60.5 cm
Inv. no.: 52.158

Márk Vedres studied in the special pottery school in his native Ungvár (today Uzhgorod, Ukraine) and worked in the ceramic factory there. In 1895 he attended Simon Hollósy's art school in Munich, in 1897–1900 he was a student at the Julian Academy in Paris, where he got acquainted with Rodin who corrected some of his works and largely influenced him at that time. From 1899 to 1907 he frequently exhibited at home and in 1911 he was also invited for the exhibition of the group of artists Nyolcak (The Eight). In 1902–1914 and 1925–1934 he lived in Florence where he made the acquaintance of German sculptors living there, all followers of Adolf Hildebrand. Apart from them, ancient classical art and renaissance small bronzes influenced him decisively. He worked out some characteristic motifs (dancing, bathing, piping, riding nudes) variations of which are present throughout his oeuvre. The riding figure modelled in Budapest between the two stays in Florence depicts a classically idyllic state while the structurality of the bodies indicated by crystallized forms points towards some post-cubist abstraction. Underlying this might be Vedres' association with the radical bourgeois intellectuals at home. He made several funerary monuments and sculpted ornaments for buildings during his stay at home. That may also have contributed to the somewhat larger scale of Youth on Horseback compared to his earlier small nudes made in Florence.

J. Sz.

János Mattis Teutsch

(1884–1960)

Landscape

Around 1917

Oil on paste-board, 48.5 × 50 cm

Inv. no.: FK 772

The expressive linocuts of János Mattis Teutsch who was born in Brassó (today Brašov, Romania) were first published in Lajos Kassák's Activist journal MA (Today). The first Budapest exhibition of his collected works was held in the exhibition space of the periodical in 1917. A year later MA published an album, and two of his prints were reproduced in Der Sturm in Berlin. His pictures are the most painterly of all the works of the Activists. In his decorative landscapes of bright colours painted in this period, thin-trunked trees are swaying in the wind amidst the undulating land strips. The tradition of art nouveau planarity, the winding, linear structures are enriched with the powerful gestures of painterly expression in Mattis Teutsch's pictures. The lively flow of interpenetrating amorphous colour strips is counterpoised by the vertical rhythm of interlacing tree groups. The softly merging organic forms of the landscape visualize human emotions, the innermost happenings of the soul. The powerful colours proclaim the dynamism of life. In addition to symbolist and art nouveau precedents, his pictorial world was influenced by the Munich expressionists (Der Blaue Reiter). Later his visual thinking became more abstract, but the inspiration based on experiences of nature ran throughout his artistic career.

M. G.

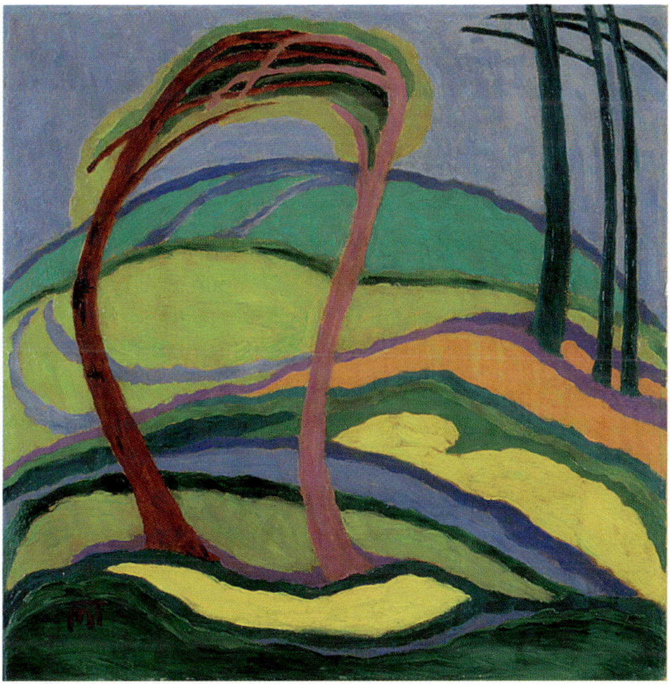

Lajos Tihanyi
(1885–1938)
Portrait of Lajos Kassák
1918
Oil on canvas, 86.6 × 70 cm
Inv. no.: 70.134 T

Tihanyi scored his greatest success with his series of expressive portraits of the leading men of letters, musicians, artists, theoreticians of the age. He held a mirror to the sitters in which he did not only show their characteristic features but also the personalities hidden behind colours and forms. He was interested in the anatomy of the head, the structure of the face, the liveliness of the eyes, but first of all the psychological features of the character. The leader of the Hungarian avant-garde movement Lajos Kassák is shown first of all as the devoted spokesman of social progress. Depicted in the typical Russian shirt, with straight long hair, bright broad forehead and a strictly serious glance the poet implies the asceticism of missionaries. Tihanyi was in personal contact with the poet as he also belonged to the Activists. Several of his works were reproduced in MA (Today), the periodical edited by Kassák and he had a one-man show in the exhibiting space of the journal in 1918. Tihanyi was chiefly inspired by the expressive portraits of Oskar Kokoschka. His Austrian fellow-painter was primarily interested in the momentary psychological state of the model. In Tihanyi's portraits the hidden dimensions of the personality are more emphatic, the determining features of the sitter's character are accentuated.

M. G.

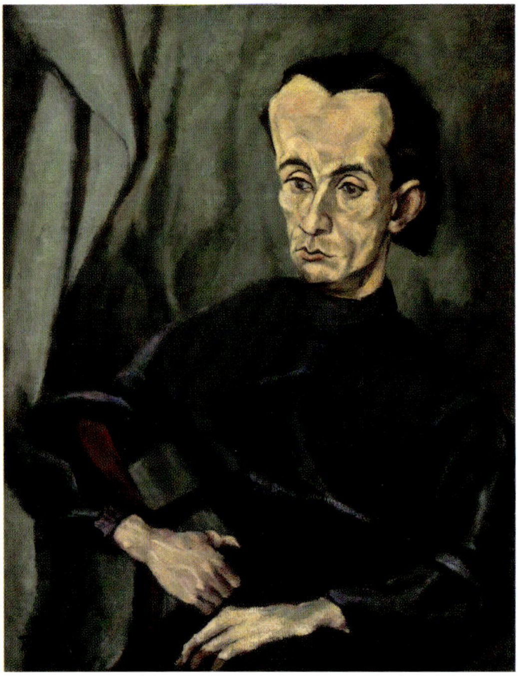

László Moholy-Nagy
(1895–1946)
Sitting Man
1919
Pencil on paper, 332 × 253 mm
Inv. no.: 1919-589

Relatively few mature pieces like this one survive from the early Hungarian period of the great master of international avant-garde. Having recovered from his wound received on the front in World War I, Moholy-Nagy turned more and more intensively to literature and fine arts. In 1918 he studied in Róbert Berény's private school and learnt from him dynamic, expressive draughtsmanship without academic shackles. After the rather amateurish drawings on the postcards sent home from the front, in the first year of peace his futuristic works had already incorporated the effects of the avant-garde trends. In 1919 he joined the activist artists rallied around Lajos Kassák and his periodical, and emigrated like most leftist intellectuals at the end of the year. After a brief sojourn in Vienna he went to Berlin, presenting his dadaist and later constructivist works in the periodical and gallery Der Sturm between 1922–1925. Seeing them, Walter Gropius invited him to teach at the Bauhaus. This drawing was purchased with a few other pieces right after its completion by the revolutionary Art Directory for the Museum of Fine Arts in 1919, but it remained unknown until the Hungarian avant-garde exhibitions organized in the last decades of the 20th century.

É. B.

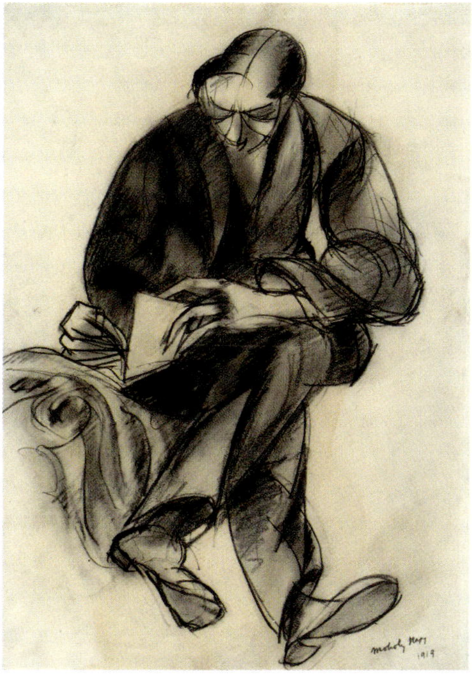

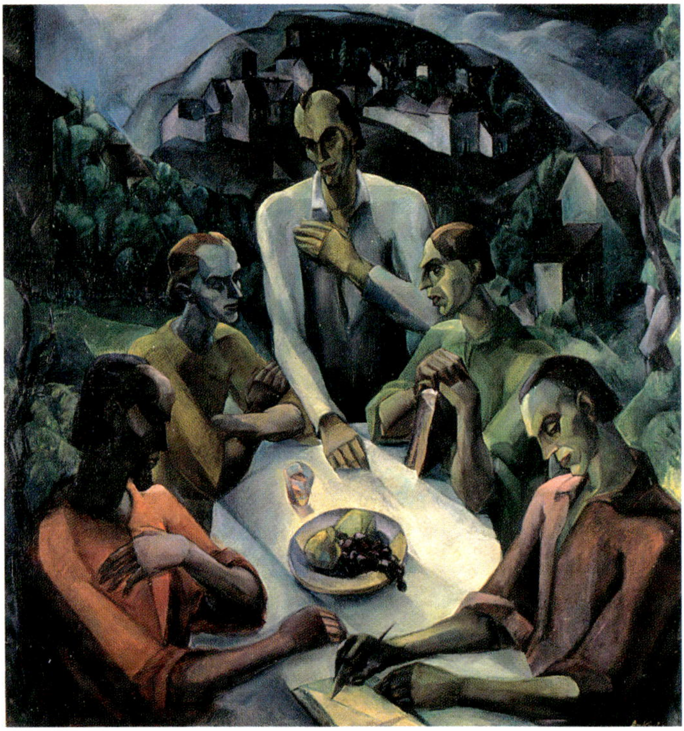

Gyula Derkovits
(1894–1934)
The Last Supper
1922
Oil on canvas, 150 × 145 cm
Inv. no.: 54.326

Mustered out from World War I for ill health, Gyula Derkovits, who worked as a joiner, trained himself at private art schools. He took the subject for his early masterpiece, Last Supper, from the Bible and like so many of his contemporaries, he turned to the world of the old masters from the misery of the war and the following years. Apart from the theme, however, he did not adopt the traditional patterns. The style of the picture reflects the impact of contemporary efforts, the human figures broken up into cubistic forms are set against an expressive landscape. At the apogee of the strictly symmetrical pyramidal composition Derkovits himself can be recognized with head bent to one side and hand held at the chest. The Hungarian and foreign representatives of the classicizing trend of the 1920s often painted elevated self-portraits showing themselves in different roles. This painting is also such a hidden self-portrait. The painter standing as Christ at the head of the table is accompanied by four seated figures in modern clothes, the marked features of each resembling Derkovits'. The artist's wife later recalled the genesis of the painting as follows: "The theme of the supper had long preoccupied him because it conjured up old family memories. On Saturday evenings in the old times, he and his brothers sat around the table, and there were heated and fertile discussions during supper."

A. Z.

Béla Uitz
(1887–1972)
Icon Analysis on a Purple Ground
1922
Oil on canvas, 158 × 141 cm
Inv. no.: 72.36 T

Béla Uitz was an outstanding artist of the Hungarian Activist movement. In this picture he exemplifies the combination of tradition and modernity in a peculiar manner. He lived in Vienna in 1920–1924 and painted his large Icon Analysis there after returning from Moscow in 1921. His personal experiences led him to turn to the old art relics of the Eastern Orthodox Church when he got acquainted closely with the Russian avant-garde. He eagerly visited the churches and exhibitions in Moscow. He was fascinated by the constructivist works of Malevich, Rodchenko and their colleagues whom he met personally. Uitz combined in a unique manner these two kinds of influence. As he admitted, he did not want to analyze a concrete icon but tried to create a new modern composition through expressive empathy, through painterly transfiguration. He experimented by varying different geometric elements and colour and texture relations. In addition to the objective analysis of art, he also modelled the order of the universe, in the wake of Malevich. Uitz' main achievement was the synthesization of the different endeavours. He carefully kept his icon analyses born of the individual union of intuition and reason in all stations of his emigration, hiding them in Moscow during the persecution of abstract art and donating three of them to the National Gallery at the end of his life.

É. B.

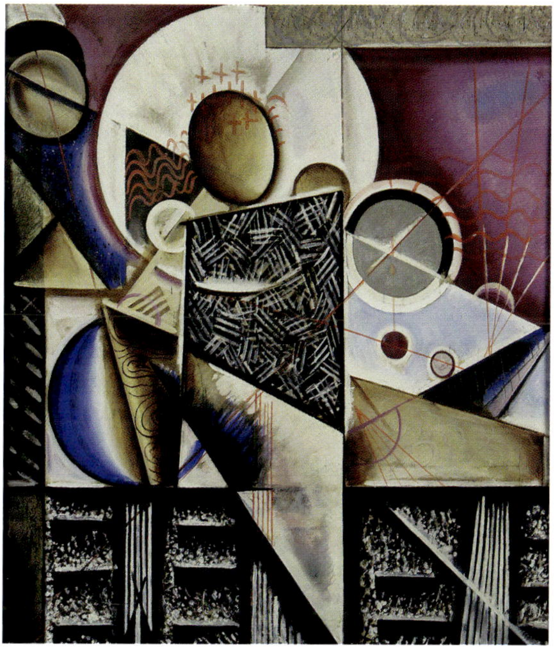

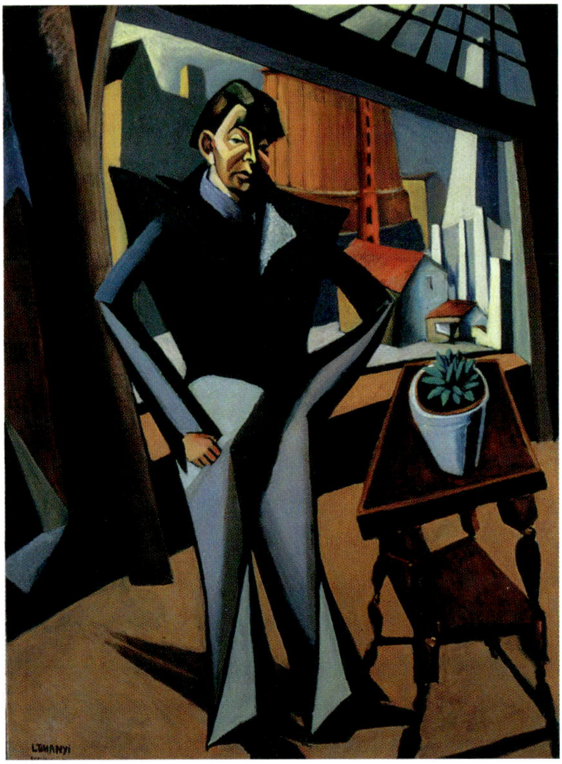

Lajos Tihanyi
(1885–1938)
Man Standing at the Window (Self-portrait in Berlin)
1922
Oil on canvas, 140.5 × 105.5 cm
Inv. no.: 70.180 T

Lajos Tihanyi was a salient figure in the Hungarian avant-garde movement unfolding in the 1910s. He presented rigorously constructed still-lifes, landscapes and expressive portraits at the exhibitions of The Eight, the group of constructive artists breaking with impressionism. His painting incorporated elements of expressionism, fauvism, cubism and futurism. As a leading figure of the Hungarian Activists, he joined Lajos Kassák's circle. In 1918 he had a one-man show in the exhibiting room of the periodical MA (Today). After the fall of the Commune in 1919, most leftist intellectuals had to go into exile. Tihanyi went first to Vienna and in the early 1920s to Berlin. His full-length self-portrait shows him in his Berlin studio, by the huge glass window overlooking the factory buildings in the outskirts. Objects represented from various viewpoints, the splintery break of planes and distorted forms were characteristic devices of avant-garde painting at that time. The analytic approach of the cubists is combined here with the dynamism of the futurists and the intense colourfulness of the expressionists.

M. G.

Farkas Molnár
(1897–1945)
Spatial Composition
1922
Linocut on paper, 250 × 247 mm
Inv. no.: G 2004.8

The artist and architect born in Pécs studied at the Academy of Fine Arts in Budapest in 1915–1916 and later at the Technical University. His art unfolded among the expressionists of the Pécs Artists' Circle in 1920–1921. The group toured Italy together: his cubo-expressive drawings made there were the basis for his subsequent richly coloured landscapes and his lithographs made in the graphic workshop of the Bauhaus in 1921–1922. In addition to etching, he mainly tried his hand at linocuts. These prints, several of which were published by Kassák's MA (Today) in Vienna, emanate the spirit of constructivism. As an adherent of Dutch Theo van Doesburg, he searched for the order of absolute forms and their relations in Weimar. With his colleagues including other Bauhaus members from Pécs they established the international KURI group (Constructive, Utilitarian, Rational, International) in opposition to the expressionist attitude. Their principles—leaving utopias behind for practice—are represented by this print. The strictly rectangular units cut out along the liner suggest constructivist order, the contrasts of white and black details represent dynamism, the space organization in isometric perspective stresses the architectural idea. Working in Gropius' office, Molnár increasingly turned to architecture, producing works of art ever more rarely. Relatively unknown and recently purchased by the Gallery, this sheet is a good example of small-series hand-made prints. It is peerless in Hungarian art in representing the that-time ideas of utopistic world construction.

É. B.

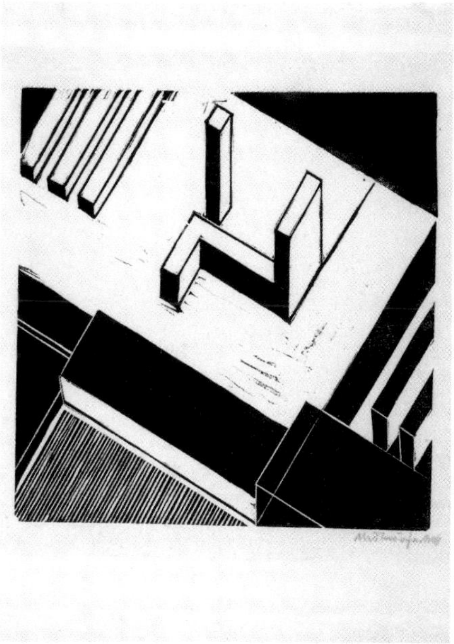

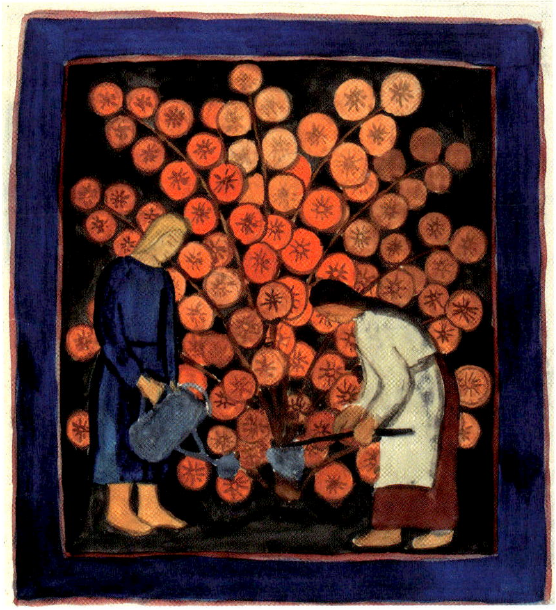

Noémi Ferenczy
(1890–1957)
Gardeners
1923
Watercolour on paper, 398 × 371 mm
Inv. no.: 1925-1141

Noémi Ferenczy was an exemplary master of 20th century Hungarian textile art. The unity of design and execution was realized in her works as she executed her own designs. Her tapestries were planned as autonomous pictures and already at the time of creation, they were put on display in exhibitions of fine arts instead of applied arts. It was not only the final textile that was exhibited but also the large painted cartoons documenting the process of creation, together with small composition and colour sketches. The fresh watercolour sketches of firy colours made with a brush on tracing or parchment paper of a silken lustre are perhaps the artist's most captivating works. There are several colour sketches made for large tapestries in the Gallery's collection. One of the most significant early works is Gardeners made in 1923, probably during her stay in Vienna, for a large tapestry entitled Gardening Women (1924) in a German private collection today. Simply dressed women are tending, watering and hoeing in union a large decorative bush whose bright red radiant blossoms fill nearly the whole surface. The monographer of Noémi Ferenczy, Júlia Jankovits presumes that the composition is related to a latent work also exhibited in Moscow at the 5th International Party Congress in 1924 with the title Worker and Peasant Woman Tending the Tree of Revolution.

F. Zs.

Ferenc Medgyessy
(1881–1958)
Female Nude (Leaning Woman)
1923
Bronze, 13.5 × 12 × 48.5 cm
Inv. no.: 56.55-N

A graduate of the University of Medicine, Medgyessy began his art studies at the Julian Academy in Paris right after finishing his medical studies in 1905.
In 1909–1910 he lived and worked in Florence. With their rich museum collections, art works and lively art life these two cities decisively influenced his whole life.
He arrived home with a resolute artistic program in 1910 and began work committed to it. He knew what to do to develop a singular style. His aesthetic norm was the simplicity and majesty of ancient oriental art to which he tried to adjust his own works. His stone sculptures are characterized by monumentality, lack of decoration, blocklike appearance and one predominant view. He returned even to the techniques of Etruscan, Roman and Greek art. In addition to the mythological figures and subjects of the archaic ages as well as work, man at work, his favourite subject was the female body. He elaborated this theme in many statues and reliefs, usually making several variants of the same position and figure, and sometimes he executed a composition on various scales. Leaning Woman exemplifies well that Medgyessy's small-scale sculptures also imply monumentalness, that is why they were well suited to be produced for public spaces.

J. Sz.

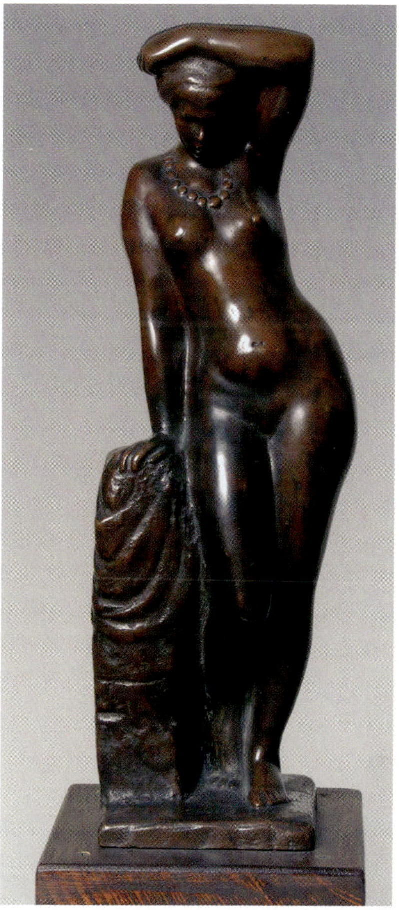

Dezső Bokros Birman
(1889–1965)
Ady
1924
Bronze, 21 × 22 × 37 cm
Inv. no.: 56.133-N

Dezső Bokros Birman studied ornamental sculpture at the School of Design in 1908–1910. In 1911–1912 he lived in Paris where he was mainly influenced by the Greek collection of the Louvre and the East Asian statues in Musée Guimet. In 1914 he learnt stone carving in Ruskicabánya. From 1915 he was conscripted and acted as war painter from 1916. In 1919–1921 he lived in Berlin and got acquainted with the post-war trends of expressionism. Between 1926 and 1932 he alternated between Budapest and Slovakia, and also visited Vienna and Paris. In Pozsony he was in contact with the leftist Sarló (Sickle) movement and in Budapest with the Group of Socialist Artists in 1932–1936. Bokros Birman's works can be ranged in thematic groups, the main types often recurring during his career. One recurrent theme was the human face, he was an excellent portraitist. He visualized the character traits of the faces and plastic, static values of the structure of the head, as well as the depths of the human character even if he had to disrupt the plastic unity. The basis for the sculpted head of the poet Endre Ady was probably the multiply copied and disseminated death mask of the poet well-known in the 1920s. The majestic calm, classic proportions, crystallized forms of the closed block of the face with closed eyes turn the work into a metaphor of poetry. The peculiar patina covering the bronze surface enhances the harmonious impression.

J. Sz.

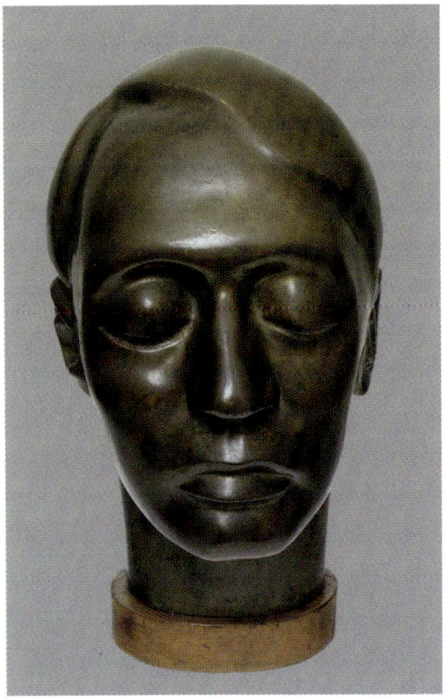

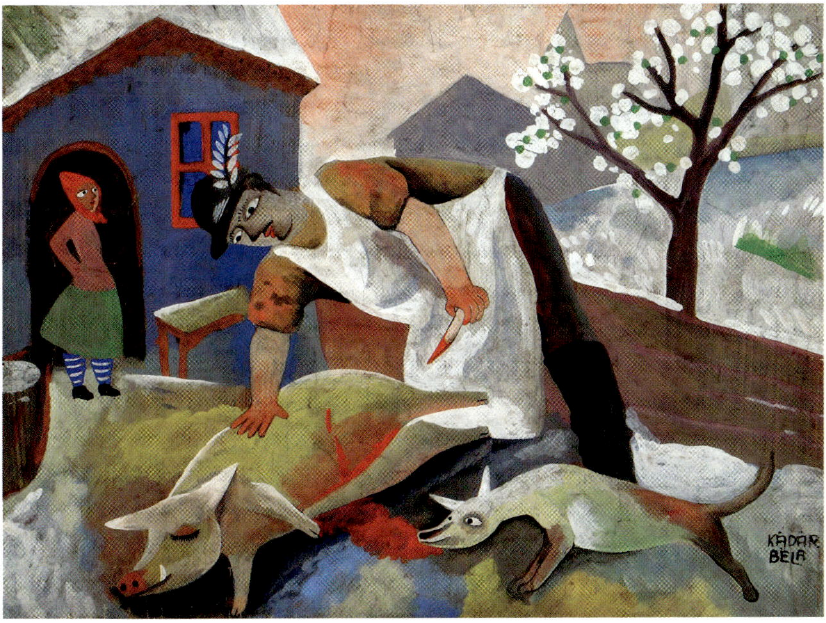

Béla Kádár

(1877–1956)

Pig-killing

Around 1924

Tempera on paper, 351 × 487 mm

Inv. no.: F.83.92

Béla Kádár's career began in the early 1920s with expressionist prints. Unlike his fellow avant-gardists, he did not live in emigration, although he worked mainly for Herwarth Walden's Der Sturm gallery in Berlin. Pig-killing is one of the finest pieces of the artist's "Sturm-like" compositions, a relative to the folklore-inspired surrealistic works of Franz Marc, Heinrich Campendonk and Marc Chagall. Kádár set his scenes elaborated as effective stories in rural main streets with church towers or village courtyards amidst peasant women in kerchiefs, horning cows and happily frisking dogs. He transformed the schematic motifs of Hungarian folklore into an easily encoded pictorial system. In building a composition, shaping stylized figures, dynamizing decorative planar surfaces he drew on the formal innovations of contemporary painting. With the light-handedness of masterful draftsmanship he arranged the coloured surfaces, creating a harmony of the decorative patches by the virtuosic use of tempera. He was both nostalgic and up-to-date, his pictorial imagination conveying the events of everyday life so diversely that he could conquer the metropolitan public accustomed to modern sights.

M. G.

Lajos Kassák
(1887–1967)
Bildarchitektur V
Around 1924
Oil on cardboard, 28 × 20.5 cm
Inv. no.: 70.130 T

Lajos Kassák is internationally acknowledged as an avant-garde classic, his art organizing efforts, theoretical and artistic activity being mentioned on a par with Mondrian's, Malevich's, El Lissitsky's. The diverse endeavours of the artists in the Activist movement led by him radically modernized Hungarian artistic thinking so that an exceptional synchrony emerged between Hungarian art and the progressive European trends. After the fall of the Republic of Coucils in 1919 Kassák was forced into emigration and resumed the edition of MA (Today)—one of the highest quality art magazines by European standards—in Vienna as it was banned in Hungary. In the 1920s he made constructivist works he called "Bildarchitektur". He rejected the traditional pictorial arsenal of painting. In the intellectual process of creation the avant-garde artist also brought about a new relationship with the surrounding world. Instead of the sensuous representation of nature, he strove to create "picture-objects" on equal value with reality. Kassák's compositions are visual models of the construction of a new world order, within the frames of planarity. The dynamic ensemble of geometric shapes put together like building blocks, the balanced coloured elements, overlapping surfaces and linear structures imply the pure spirituality of a sensible construction.

M. G.

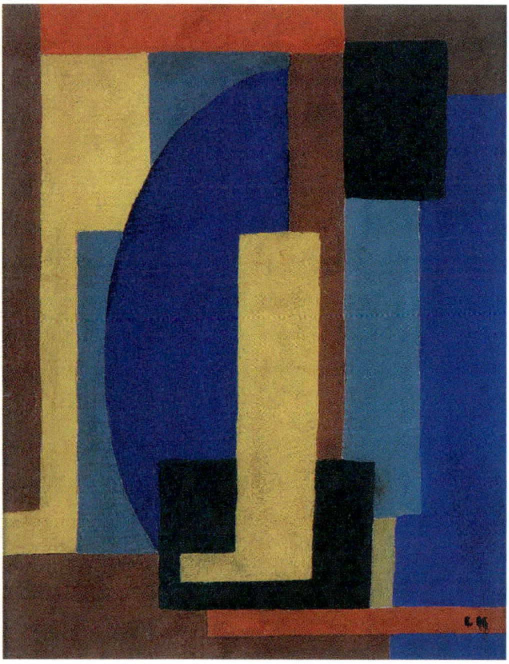

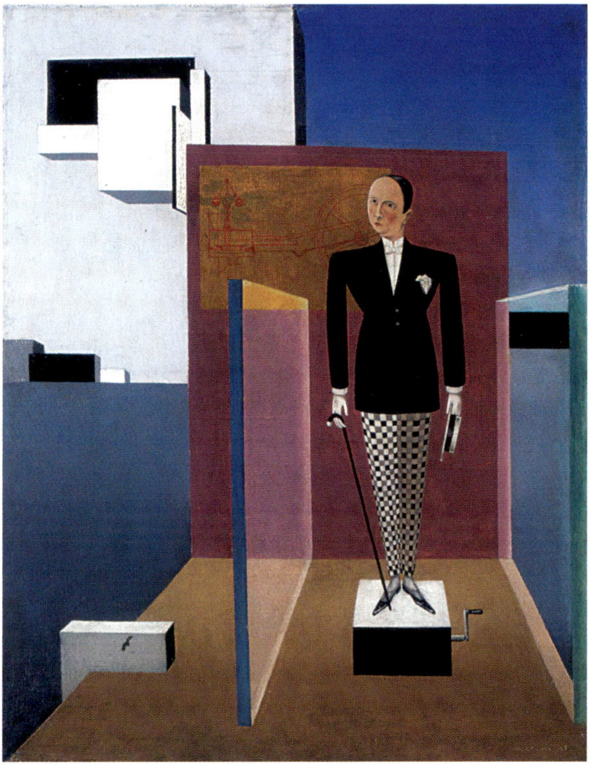

Sándor Bortnyik
(1893–1976)
The New Adam
1924
Oil on canvas, 48.3 × 39 cm
Inv. no.: 64.85 T

Sándor Bortnyik joined the circle of activist artists around the journal MA (Today) in 1918, contributing his dynamic works fusing cubism and expressionism in an individual manner. Forced into emigration in 1919, he—like many of his fellow artists—was attracted by the international constructivist movement. In 1922–1924 he lived in Weimar and kept in contact with the artists of the Bauhaus. He painted abstract two- and three-dimensional compositions and inserted objects and figures into them. The New Adam is one of these works. In this ironic painting he reveals a critical attitude to the constructivists' "brave new world". His wind-up mechanical figure resembling a mannequin is set in the abstract composition like a puppet on the Bauhaus stage. Is this perfectly functioning fop the new man created by modern art? Is this crystalline but lifeless setting the new city? asks Bortnyik. It is, however, perceptible that the artist relished in elaborating precisely the details of planes and spatial forms, and the balance and colour harmony of the abstract composition delights the viewer as some of the best achievements of constructivist painting. Bortnyik is ironic about the utopistic ideals but cannot remain indifferent to them as he was also a contributor to the emergence of the "new world".

K. B.

Aurél Bernáth
(1895–1982)
Riviera
1926–1927
Oil on canvas, 130 × 150 cm
Inv. no.: 6370

Riviera marks a turning point in Bernáth's career: it closes off the harrassed landscape visions of the German expressionist period. It underscores the significance of the picture that he regarded it as "the first work of his life". It is associated with the painter's trip to Italy, but as he recalled, the picture had already been formulated on his mind on the way there and he was searching for and found motifs to this inner picture. In this way, the picture is not the representation of a real sight. It divides into two distinct spheres: the tectonic orders of pale brown rocks and the saturated immaterial blue patch of the sea and sky are contrasted. All other motifs are subordinated to this antithesis: the barren scenery is enlivened by the spot of a single green plant, the white grill of the thin railing is consumed by the large colour surfaces. The cliffs falling steeply into the sea are divided into two by a horizontal path with a sweeping arch, pointing at the horizon where sea and sky meet. A few human figures are also included in the cosmic world but their presence lacks accent: the closest figures are just leaving the picture, the old couple on the bench merge with the shadow of the cliff, the faint patches of two figures on a distant balcony dissolve in front of the blue background, and it is hard to decide whether the farthest figure is a human being or a stone column. Their colour, schematic sketchy forms, rigid movements and faceless existence liken them to inanimate nature, to minerals.

A. Z.

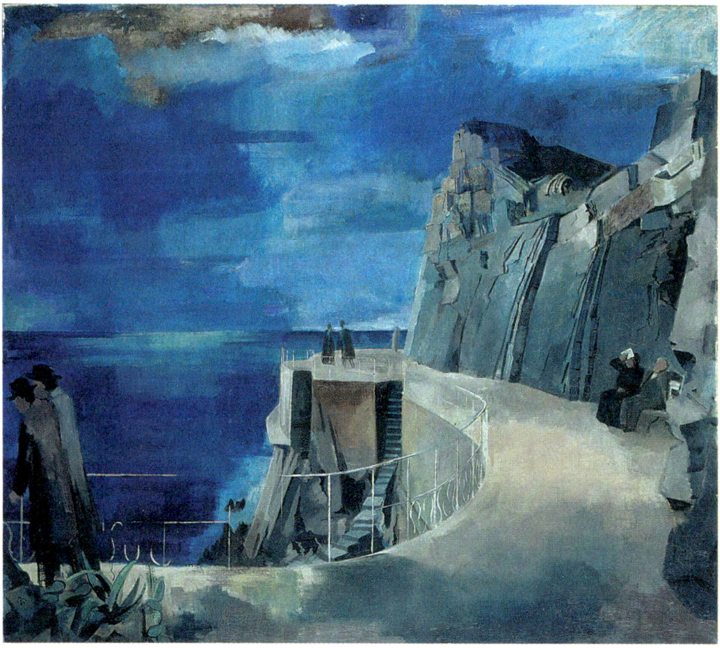

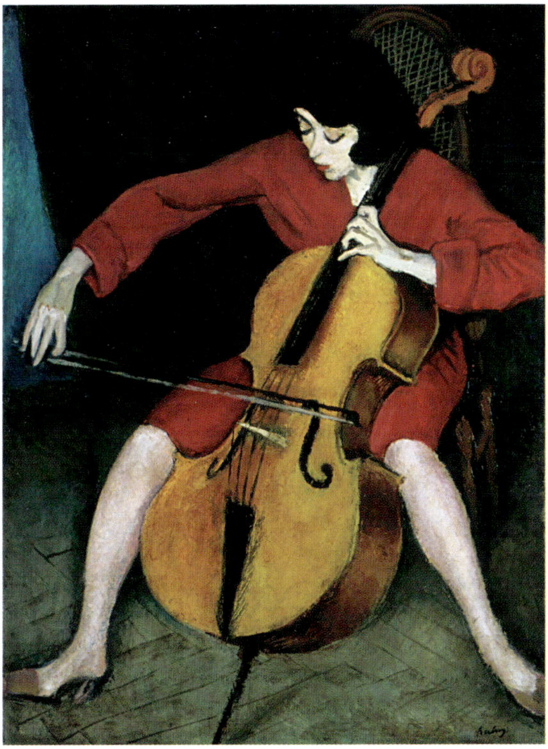

Róbert Berény
(1887–1953)

Woman Playing the Cello

1928

Oil on canvas, 133.5 × 100.5 cm

Inv. no.: 63.70 T

Returning from an emigration of several years Berény's career turned back to the representational idiom of post-impressionism after his avant-garde phase. The picture of the cello-player, the painter's wife, is built of intense colour patches which are structured by dynamic lines of forces in combination with a system of exposures and cuts-offs. The red patch of the dress is cut into two by the emphatic diagonal of the cello, an elbow and foot of the woman "stick out" of the picture. The basic form of the instrument, its alternating concave and convex arch is repeated in the modelling of the female figure. The plasticity of the cello is in contrast with the planarity of the rest of the motifs which are given stress by the large continuous surfaces of the background and are balanced by the organic forms of the sketchy pattern of the parquet and the scamped indication of the matting of the chair-back. The spatial values are overshadowed by the logic of the harmonization of the planar surfaces, which has superiority to the rules of anatomy and perspective, so the length of the thighs can be disproportionate, the cello can oddly foreshorten. The textural effects have a salient role in the picture: the artist scratched back the paint at places and at others he incised into the still soft surfaces with the brush handle.

A. Z.

István Szőnyi
(1894–1960)
Burial at Zebegény
1928
Oil on canvas, 100 × 125 cm
Inv. no.: 63.137 T

Szőnyi, who lived in Budapest until the age of 30, moved to a small village in 1924 and lived there with some interruptions till his death. By the end of that decade, he gradually returned to the traditions of the Nagybánya school; his melted pictorialness concentrated on the subtly matched colour tones and the solving of compositional problems, and the sensitive effects of the texture were coupled with intimate lyrical moods. The central motif of his pictures painted in Zebegény is the Danube bend depicted from a variety of vantage points and amidst most diverse light conditions. Another major group of works shows the everyday life of simple villagers. These two picture types—landscape and genre-piece—are combined in Burial in Zebegény. Built on the contrast of whites and blacks, the picture only tolerates a few other colours, most emphatic of which is the patch of the dirty yellow sky weighing down on the mountain range of a lilac tone. The composition is built of spatial layers wedged into one another, their horizontal strips being counterpoised by the thin black sticks of the tree-trunks. The participants of the funeral progress carefully in the snow, leaning forward, the dark patches of their clumsy figures meander towards the depth of the picture space following the arch of the equally black fence; their figures remind the spectator of Pieter Brueghel the Elder's Winter kept in the Kunsthistorisches Museum in Vienna.

A. Z.

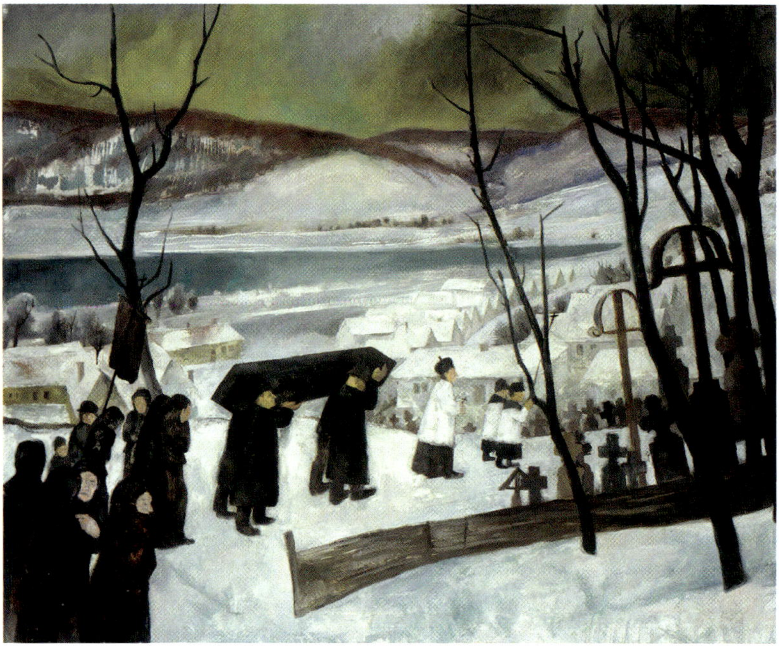

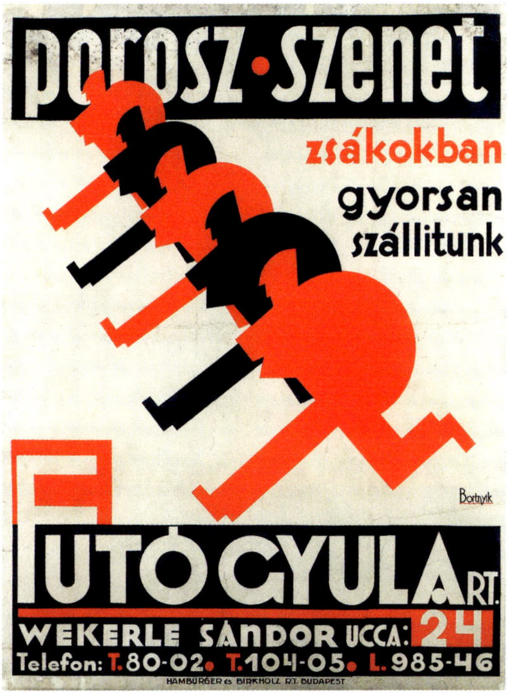

Sándor Bortnyik
(1893–1976)
We Transport Prussian Coal Quickly in Sacks. Gyula Futó Co.
1928
Lithograph on paper, 126 × 95 cm
Inv. no.: XY. 60.67

Having returned from his emigration in Austria and Germany, Bortnyik exhibited abstract works as well as paintings, prints, scenery designs combining abstract and figural elements in Budapest in 1925. His exhibition was not as successful as expected because it ran contrary both to the official cultural policy and the public taste. Also exploiting his German experiences, Bortnyik now turned to graphic design, the profession he had practiced in his youth. What was rejected in the exhibition rooms was accepted in the street: his posters were a great success. One of his first clients was the coal merchant Gyula Futó, for whom he designed several handouts, adverts and posters from 1926. Bortnyik did not hesitate to incorporate the meaning of the client's name ("futó" means 'runner') as a running figure carrying a sack of coal: it is both humorous and illustrates an important element of slogan: "quickness". He converted the typical, emblematic figure of the Budapest streets, the coal-man, into the a figure of utmost abstraction, a red and blue patch like a sharply outlined paper cut-out. The powerful rhythm of the figures arranged diagonally on the white paper grasps attention and directs the eye to the text on top and bottom of the sheet. The form and rhythm of the clear-cut white block letters against dark colour strips are just as decisive components of the composition as are the figures almost wholly reduced to signs.

K. B.

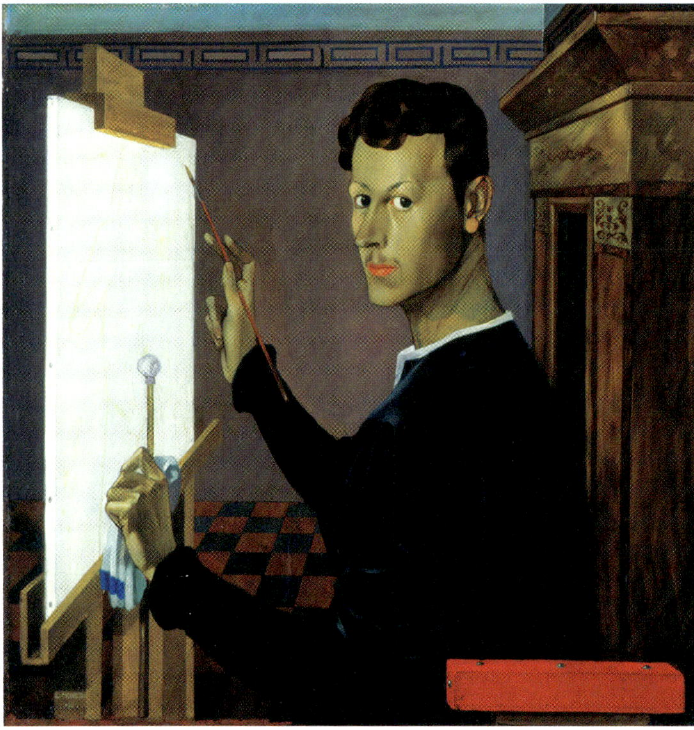

Jenő Medveczky
(1902–1969)
Self-portrait
1929
Oil on canvas, 80 × 80 cm
Inv. no.: 6347

In the late 1920s the Hungarian state founded the Rome scholarship with the intention of acquainting the supported young artists with the current Italian endeavours they deemed fit for emulation. Among the first scholarship holders was Jenő Medveczky, a painter of a neo-classical attitude, whose monumental nudes and portraits had displayed the influence of classical art before his stay in Rome. Painted under the spell of the Italian renaissance, this self-portrait of a devout mood adapts to an old picture type, that of the self-conscious painter at work who confronts his mirror image and poses for future spectators at the same time. The accurately set and meticulously painted sculpturesque half-figure of the artist is surrounded by the boxlike space of exaggerated perspective. The converging lines of the powerfully foreshortened motifs, the painting on the easel, the brown piece of furniture and the chessboard floor meet in the eyes, thus the painter's glance and the vanishing point of the central perspective determine the focus of the picture identically. The homogeneous empty surfaces of the composition are counterbalanced by drawn elements, the delicate lines of the face and hands, the pattern of the marquetry and the hardly visible outlines of the just begun female nude on the white canvas alleviate the strict geometry of verticals and horizontals.

A. Z.

Károly Patkó

(1895–1941)

Brick-factory

1929

Pencil, watercolour and tempera on paper

570 × 695 mm

Inv. no.: F.94.112

As one of the most widely acknowledged masters of the classicizing generation starting after World War I, Károly Patkó spent his year on scholarship at the Hungarian Academy in Rome in 1929–1931, in the company, among others, of Vilmos Aba-Novák and István Szőnyi. Similarly to his collegues, he was profoundly influenced by the ancient classical and early medieval remains as well as by the great renaissance masters, but in addition to the classics, he also got acquainted with contemporary Italian art. The three Italian years brought a turning point with a new attitude to colour, new technique and conception of form. Upon the impact of the light colours and airiness of the monumental fresco cycles of the trecento and quattrocento he was the first to change technique and start experimenting with tempera instead of oil, and also used more often the lighter watercolour technique producing brilliant colours. An important work of these years already painted in his studio in Rome is the Brick-factory. Under the bright blue sky the factory with the smokestack, the adjacent buildings and the staffage figures in the foreground frame the light-soaked middle area, the organizing force of a simultaneously static and dynamic composition. In addition to watercolours luxuriating in prismatic hues and saturated by light, the artist also used the tempera for the violet of the sea and the complementary orange and deep green hues of the foliage and soil the dull, light, opaque colours of which balance off the composition.

F. Zs.

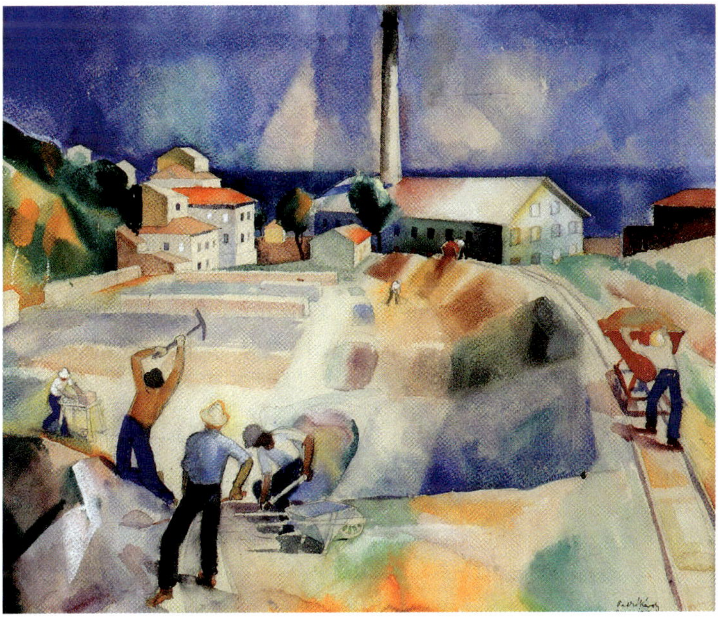

István Farkas
(1887–1944)
The Fool of Syracuse
1930
Tempera on paste-board, 80 × 99 cm
Inv. no.: 85.17 T

Strange figures populate the paintings of István Farkas who lived in Paris at the time of painting this picture. Lonely figures appear in the enigmatic, often depressing works. The fool of Syracuse is roaming in a distant Sicilian countryside. In the barren landscape there are hardly any motifs: the sketchy box of a little house, the ribbon of the road, the smoking flat-topped cone of the Etna in the distance. There are no trees or plants, the only living being is the strangely stiff dog "hitched" to the house by the thin white road. Owing to the dry incorporeal tempera technique the spatial relations are undefined in the picture, for lack of shadows the stepped zigzag of the coastline is not definite, the house tilting to one side appears to be floating in the air. Depth is suggested by the repeatedly appearing-disappearing road meandering into the distance; in the foreground it widens suddenly, running "under our feet": the spectator faces the titular fool along this road. The male figure appears to merge with the environment, the pale greenish yellow of his clothes does not stand out from the landscape, his beard repeats the ochre of the land, the white of his shoes and shirt echoes the road, his accented outline borrows its black from the sea. The gesture of his raised left hand is unintelligible, and we don't know what the splintery "wand" in his right hand is good for. His mysterious figure is the ill-boding herald of events still unpercievable for us.

A. Z.

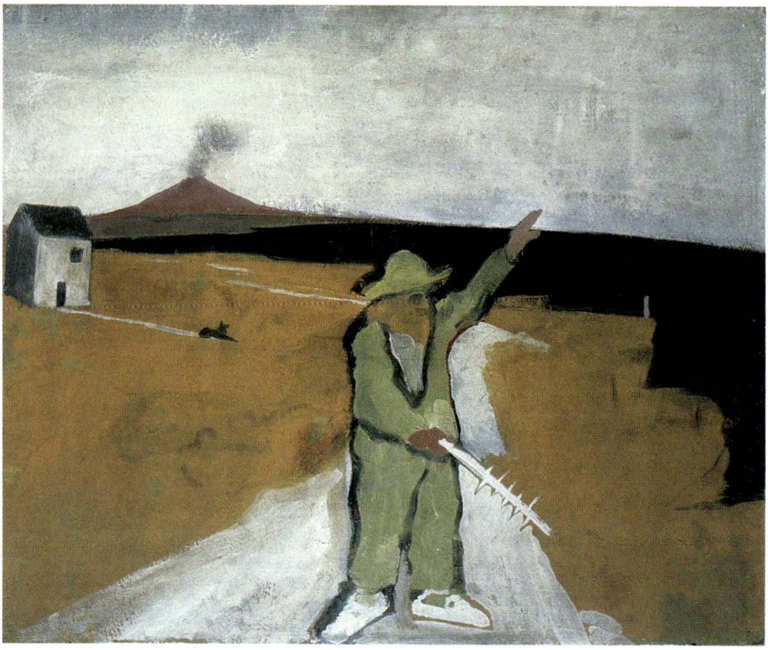

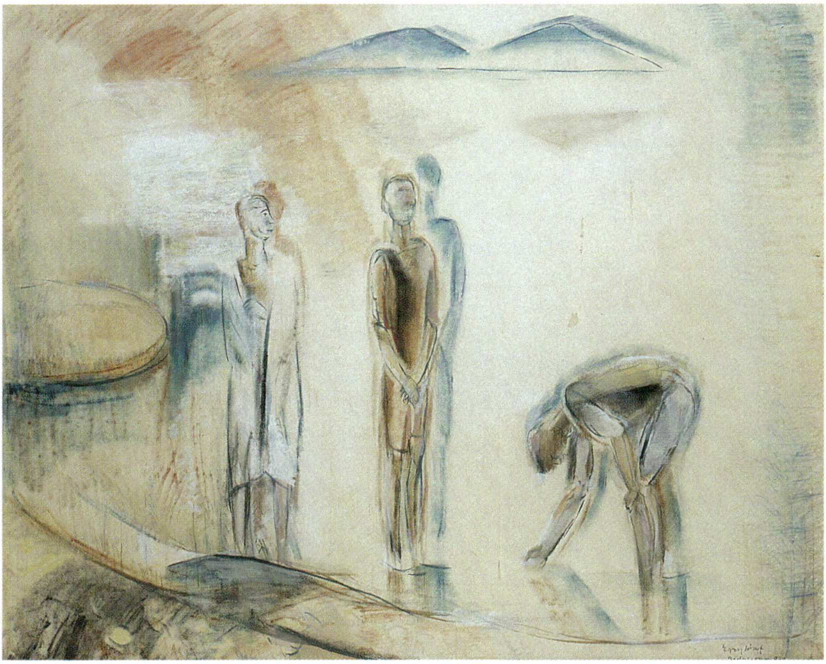

József Egry
(1883–1951)
Saint John the Baptist
1930
Oil, tempera on cardboard, 99.5 × 125.5 cm
Inv. no.: 64.54 T

Serving in the army József Egry was taken to the Balaton during World War I and after being discharged, he settled there for good. His main subjects became the lake, the surrounding landscape and the people living there. The Balaton is not always the venue of everyday scenes but often becomes the setting for events of another dimension: the fishermen, shepherds on the slopes of Badacsony are sometimes metamorphosed into figures in biblical scenes. Very few lines indicate the constituents of this composition: the double range of mountains on the other side and a thin strip of the shore on this side of the lake are indicated by a few arched brushstrokes. The jagged blurred outlines are coupled with vibrating translucent colour patches, in their smeared bands the misty air is vibrating above the surface of the water, but the white sheet remains blank in the radiant light over a large surface. In the all-pervading, all-dissolving radiance the mirage of the figures in the foreground are doubled, their "ghost images" repeating the two basic colours of the painting, blue and red. The figures are just faintly indicated, the features of Jesus in the middle and John bending down cannot be made out; the caricaturistic profile of the man standing on the left, however, carries the features of the painter. Instead of the descending dove frequently included in pictures on the theme, the double blue wings of distant hills hover above the figures standing in the water.

A. Z.

Hugó Scheiber
(1873–1950)
Fun-fair
Around 1932
Oil on cardboard, 66.5 × 100 cm
Inv. no.: 82.21 T

Hugó Scheiber spent his early youth among sideshows and circus tents; at the age of ten he was already working in the Prater of Vienna with his father, who was employed as sign-painter. He was both attracted and repelled by the bizarre world of clowns with white-painted faces, reckless acrobats, provocative equestriennes, by the swirl of the fun-fair. He admired the performers who acted out their stunts for life or death before the curious eyes of the public. In the centre of the fun-fair in the City Park of Budapest a merry-go-round is spinning, the faceless crowds of people—like a swarm of ants—waiting patiently for their turn. Upon the influence of Italian futurists, Scheiber presented a bird's-eye-view of the multitude around the carousel; from high up, everything appears smaller, more insignificant, helpless. We are presented the summer evening entertainment of town-dwellers shown as gesturing silhouettes or rod-figures condensed into a mass. The wheel turns round, and everyone will have their turn. The distant lights of the city and the outlines of tall buildings take shape against the blue of the darkening sky. The Italian futurists identified with the Hungarian painter's pictures, as they exceptionally allowed them to be shown together with theirs in their national exhibition of 1933 in Rome. Marinetti had two rooms emptied for Hugó Scheiber so that he could present his latest works in a separate showing.

M. G.

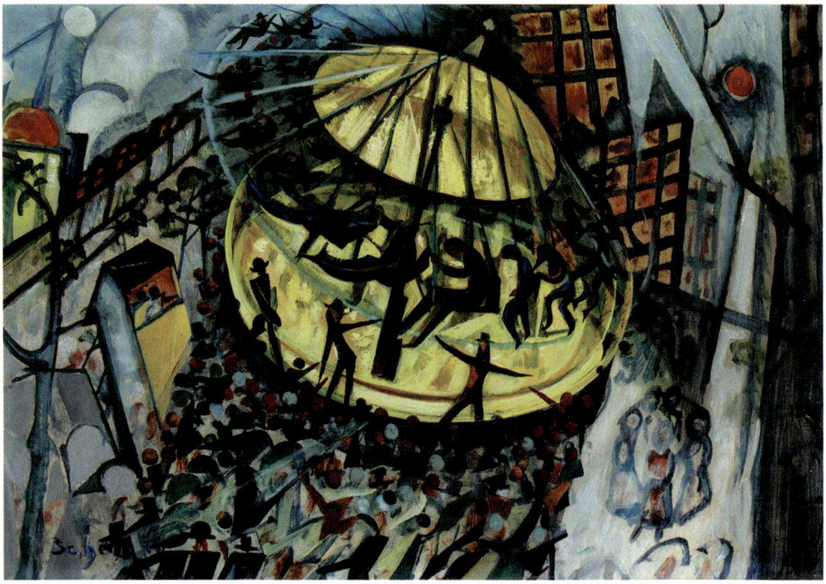

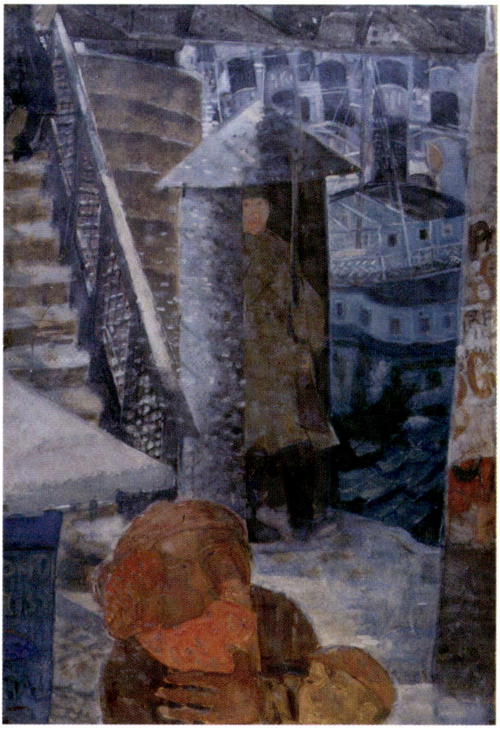

Gyula Derkovits
(1894–1934)
Bridge in Winter
1933
Tempera and pulverized silver on paper
119 × 83 cm
Inv. no.: FK 9982

Gyula Derkovits was a socially committed artist who passed judgment over the injustices of society in his paintings, sharing the life of the helpless masses. He depicted jobless proletarians, beggars, prostitutes facing the indifferent middle-class or the armed forces. He condensed the brutality of the clashes in street demonstrations with dramatic force. In his compositions, an important role is played by montaging, the tension created by forms incised into one another. The representation of space is always closely connected to the subject of the work. He packs the sight into a crammed space, placing monumental forms into the foreground that almost burst this setting. There is more concealed symbolism in Bridge in Winter, but the confrontation of opposites is also emphatic here. The little family is shivering with cold at the head of a bridge in the outskirts, next to the policeman on duty, the armed guard of the wharf appearing as the defender of power and property. The seeming tranquility is pregnant with tension. The gentle brown and pale red monumental figure of the mother protecting her children takes shape against the rigid silver-grey of the chilly winter town. The concise rendering of simplified forms transfigures into the exceptional moment of the revelation of truth via the subtle hazy transitions of pastel colours.

M. G.

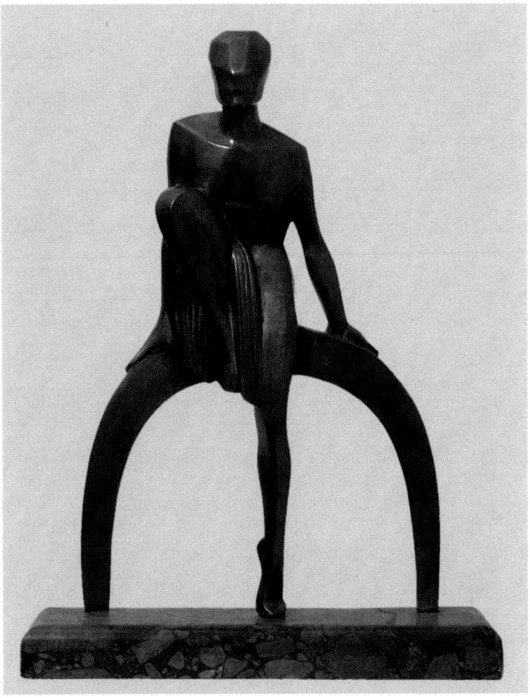

Elza Kövesházi Kalmár
(1876–1956)
Leaning Woman
1934
Brass, 30.5 × 8.5 × 39.5 cm
Inv. no.: 59.73-N

Elza Kalmár adopted the name Kövesházi in 1906. At first she learnt painting, then she started modelling in Munich in the summer of 1898. Her first statues of 1899 display the influence of Rodin. She lived in Florence in 1902–1903 and in 1905–1909, in Vienna in 1909–1912 and in Paris in 1912–1914. She was a nurse on the front during World War I and lived in Budapest later. Her oeuvre is characterized by a diversity of genres, materials and techniques. Her output includes paintings, lithographs, ceramics, designs in home decoration, as well as several wooden, bronze and brass small sculptures including her best works. Her sculpture was influenced equally by early renaissance small statues and Isadora Duncan and the dance art of the "essential theatre," an idea declared by Ödön Palasovszky. A major source of inspiration for her was movement, dance. Her sculpted works of the 1930s attest to the harmony of emotionally charged naturalism and the stylistic features of art nouveau and art deco. The graceful movement of this stylized female figure continues in the arched line of the architectural element. The function of the semicircular support is not so much statical as it enhances movement, dynamism with its trellised gentle form. The flashes of light on the surface of brass further intensify this effect. The female figure and the arched element are not separated, they constitute the sweeping decorative composition in close unity.

J. Sz.

Pál Pátzay

(1896–1979)

Danube Wind

1934

Bronze, 37.5 × 35 × 187 cm

Inv. no.: 77.63-N

Pál Pátzay was a pupil of Béla Radnai at the Academy of Fine Arts in 1912–1914, then he studied in the Nagybánya art colony. In the 1920s he joined the Gresham Circle, a group of artists intent on reviving the Nagybánya traditions and became one of its leading figures beside Aurél Bernáth and István Szőnyi. He enjoyed a Roman scholarship in 1928–30 and went on a study tour of France. After a brief period of trying out avant-garde possibilities, he took a stand by classicist modelling of a decorative effect, connected with the name of German Adolf Hildebrand, to which he adhered almost throughout his life. Originally Danube Wind was meant for a public space; it was first erected on the promenade by the Danube from where it was transferred to the precincts of Szabadság (today Dagály) bath in 1950 and from there to the National Gallery in 1977. Just like the rest of his public works made before 1945, this one is also characterized by freshness and openness. The dress of the young woman pressing against her body, the slight flutter of the skirt backward suggest a gentle waterside breeze. The somewhat idealized female figure standing on a quadratic base can be interpreted as the ideal projection of reality, but Pátzay also laid weight on keeping the anatomical authenticity of the figure. In 1994 the City government of Budapest had a copy made after the work in the Gallery to have it erected by the Danube, close to its original location.

J. Sz.

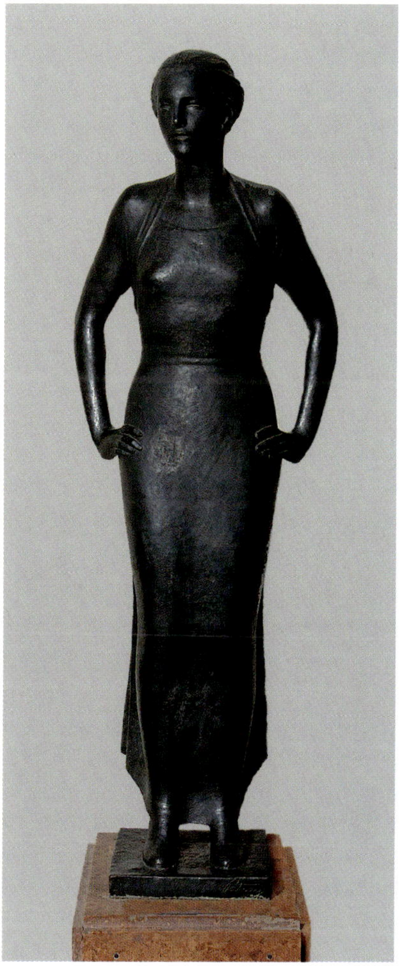

Vilmos Aba-Novák
(1894–1941)
The Fair at Csíkszereda
(Miercurea Ciuc), 1935
Tempera on panel, 78 × 95 cm
Inv. no.: FK 3287

The two years Vilmos Aba-Novák, the leader of the scholarship holders studying and working in Rome from the end of the 1920s, spent in Italy brought a radical turn. From the thick oil paint he switched over to the translucently light tempera technique, and his pictures began to be populated by the full-blooded and grotesque figures sometimes appearing in his previous works, too. The crammed world of the circus showmen depicted from the early 1930s led over to the lively and coarse figures of the market scenes built on the radiant contrasts of glaring, exuberant colours. The most characteristic range of Aba-Novák's output contains these rural genre scenes, which were inspired by his several visits to the Szolnok artists' colony and Transylvania. The instense colour surfaces applied with broad brushstokes side by side make up the composition, the ground showing through at several places. In the tempera paintings of a dry and thin surface effect the colours applied with casual virtuosity join one another as scraps with splintery edges, the finely drawn motifs not precisely fitting; like a variegated woven textile, the rapid linear drawing and colour patches coalesce into the endless swirl of caricaturistic figures of humans and animals.

A. Z.

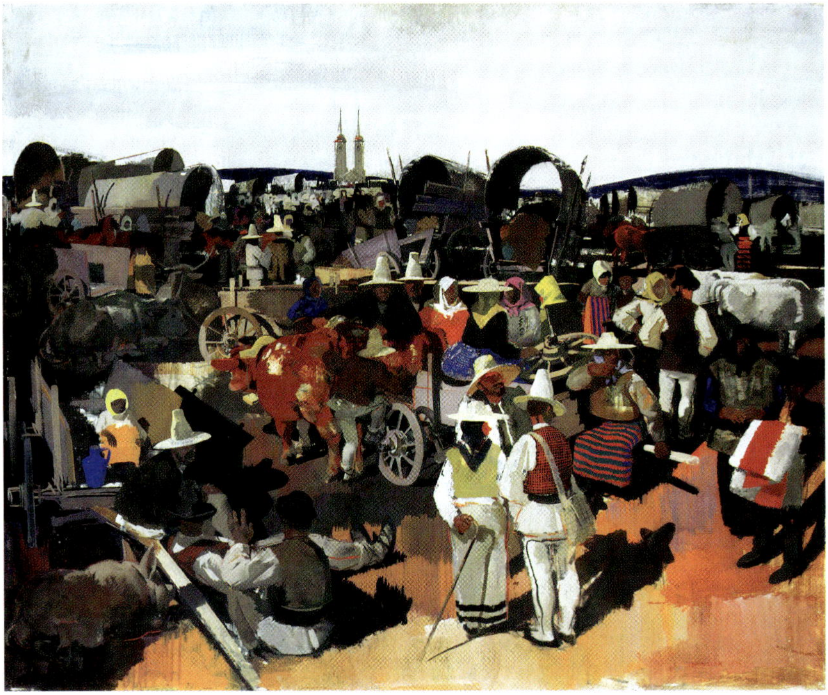

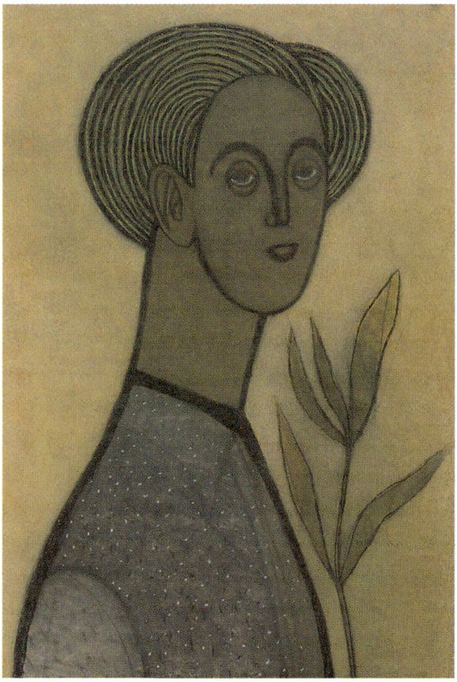

Lajos Vajda

(1908–1941)

Self-portrait with Lily

1936

Pastel on paper, 89 × 63.5 cm

Inv. no.: FK 8972

At the Academy of Fine Arts in Budapest Vajda was taught by István Csók, a professor responsive to the artistic experiments of the students, but from 1928 he joined the circle around Lajos Kassák's periodical Munka (Work). Another lifelong experience was his stay with his friend Dezső Korniss in Paris until 1934 where he got acquainted with the contemporary trends in art, the Russian avant-garde film and the ethnographic collections in museums. Back in Szentendre he and Korniss launched a program aiming to elaborate the elements of the town's most diverse cultural traditions including baroque and folk architectural details, Serbian, Jewish, Swabian religious symbols. The aim of the work defined by Vajda as elaboration of "constructive surrealistic thematics" was to synthesize the folklore forms evolving over centuries and the fresh avant-garde attitude. Through this synthesis they hoped to arrive at a new up-to-date pictorial version of the Bartókian model. One of the first crystallized examples of this process is Self-portrait with Lily, which unites the prophete-martyr attitude of the artistic self-portrait and the stylized forms of Orthodox icons emanating the presence of the divine spirit. The almost translucent composition built from carefully separated planes (dotting, hatching) is devoid of narrative elements, with the flower alone alluding to the mission of the artist—the creation of the harmony between transfigured man and the world —probably sensed to be beyond hope.

Gy. Sz.

Zoltán Borbereki Kovács
(1907–1992)
Cowherd with a Cow
1936
Bronze, 45 × 102 × 95 cm
Inv. no.: 56.399-N

Zoltán Borbereki Kovács studied painting at the Academy of Fine Arts from János Vaszary and István Csók between 1928 and 1933, and worked as the assistant of the latter. In 1933 he received a scholarship from the Italian state, in 1934–1935 he stayed at the Collegium Hungaricum on a scholarship. He didn't learn sculpture. He first visited the Szolnok art colony in 1933 and began to model sculptures there only to find it was his true medium. He laid the greatest stress on the composition of clear forms in his realist sculptures made in the thirties, too. His early sculptures were built of compact large blocks. At first he mainly worked in stone, changing over to bronze and wooden sculptures and reliefs in the second half of the decade. He modelled Hungarian types, to which Cowboy with a Cow also belongs. The closedness of the group of the drinking cow and the naked boy sitting on its back is slightly relieved by the boy's turn and glance to the side. The surface of the two figures can almost be designated with straight lines and planes, the whole unified sculpture being confinable to a geometric body. This enhances not only the rigidity but also the timelessness of the work. In this way, the actual genre scene mobilizes more general contents, making it similar to monuments, generating the feeling of universal permanence in place of the momentariness of the everyday scene.

J. Sz.

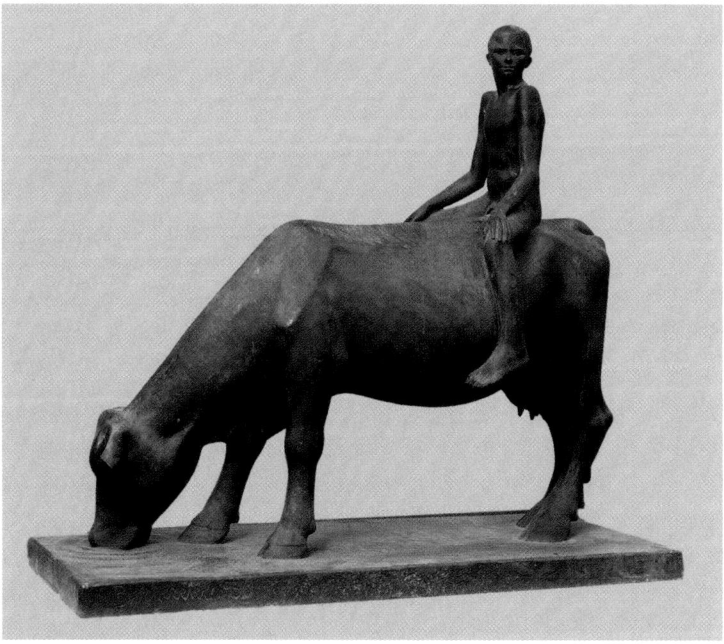

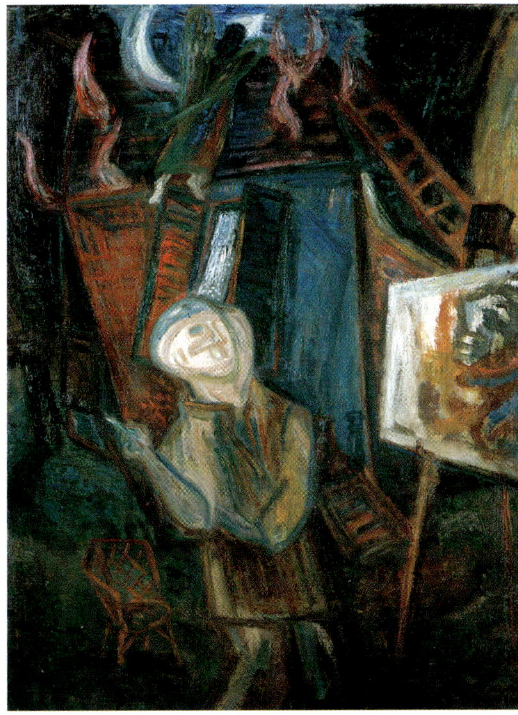

Imre Ámos

(1907–1944)

Painter in Front of a Burning House

1940

Oil on canvas, 90 × 69 cm

Inv. no.: 67.233 T

In Ámos' oeuvre the symbolic system fed by the Hassidic Jewish culture he had experienced in his childhood was charged with new meanings in the late 1930s. Behind this change the increasingly more menacing events of history can be traced. He was first drafted for forced labour service around that time. He described in his diary the circumstances of painting this picture, how he tried—like the painter in this work—not to take note of the catastrophe around him. The setting is Szentendre, the fairy-tale world of the narrow streets and staggering little houses of the little Danube-side town. The artist often appears in this idyllic setting, the symbolic motifs multiplying around his helpless figure. From under the roof of the house behind the painter working in the garden flames are darting up, but no one is fighting the fire from the ladder set against the wall, the winged angel with its back to the house is about to leave rather than help. The drama is suggested by the dark-toned colours, the suppressed contrast of reds, blues and greens. The petrified gesture of the deserted figure radiates helplessness, his masklike face turned upwards in a cramp shows incredulity. The pictures painted in the few years left of Ámos' life project in ever darker apocalyptic visions his presentiment of the indispensable perishing.

A. Z.

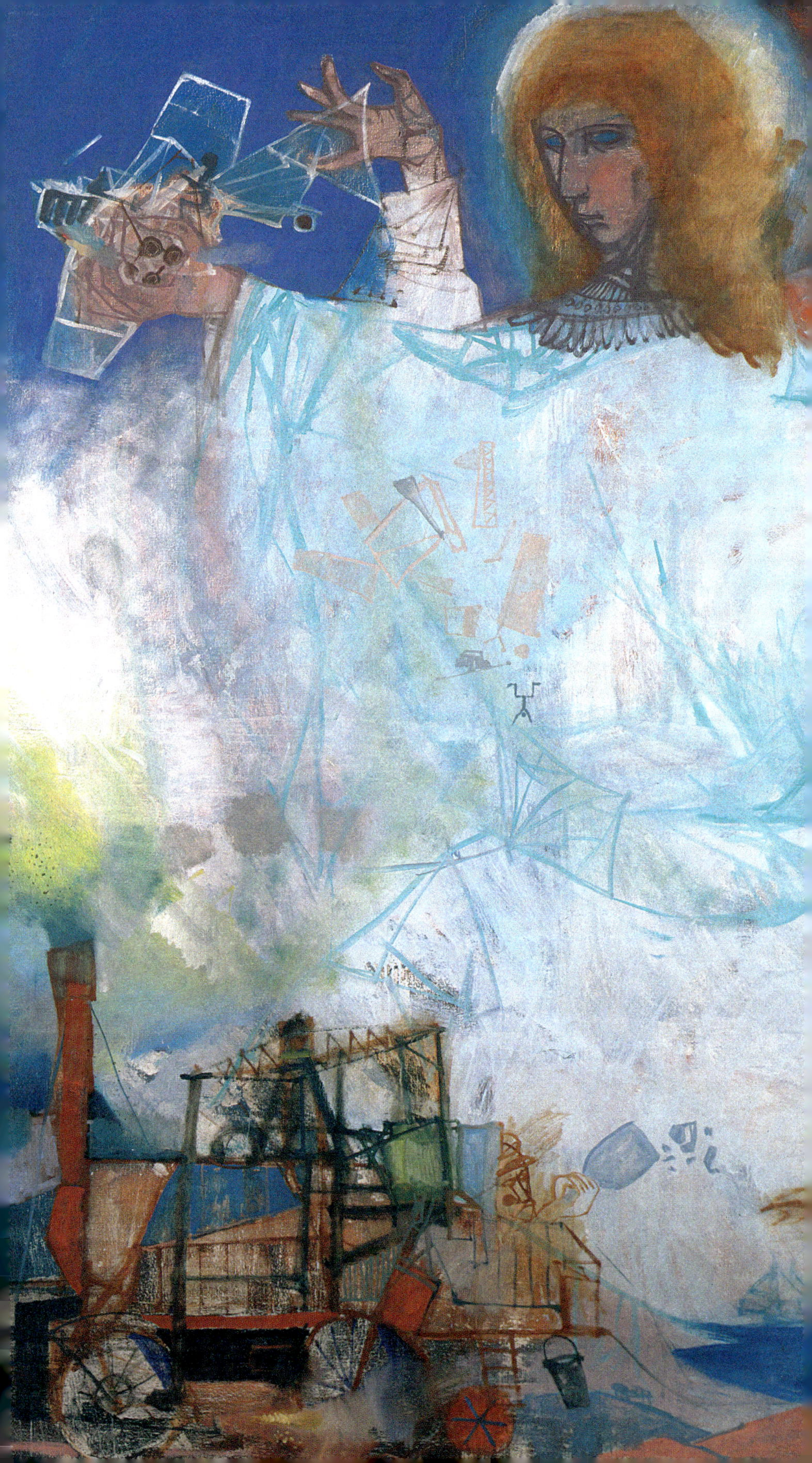

Contemporary Collection

Just like its legal predecessors, the Hungarian National Gallery has been regularly collecting contemporary art works since its foundation. Shortage of space in the building of the former Palace of Justice only allowed for the permanent display of pre-1945 art, therefore current art could only be encountered in temporary exhibitions. In addition to the ramifying traditional activities, the departments structured by art-work types could not cope with the novel tasks based on new networks of relations and requiring practically a new type of museological work. When the Hungarian National Gallery moved to the former royal palace in Buda Castle, adequate conditions arose to establish a separate department devoted to contemporary Hungarian art. In January 1974 the Department of Contemporary Hungarian Art was set up and entrusted with the creation of the collection as the background to a permanent exhibition of contemporary art. The works to be included were made after 1970 and owned by the institution since 1974, be they paintings, sculptures or prints and drawings. However, a dynamic collection enrichment did not tolerate the temporal boundaries. The incorporation of Béla Kondor's estate, the acquisition of a cross-section of Konecsni's oeuvre, of a selection of Lili Ország's and Menyhért Tóth's works all infringed the temporal limits only erected for practical considerations.

At the beginning, the enrichment was based on purchases by the Művészeti Alap (Art Foundation), a society of artists, and there was little possibility for the Gallery to do its own purchasing, or for donations. The system of state purchases gradually changed. At the end of the 1970s the professional staff of the museum were already allowed to make recommendations and later they were more and more involved in the work of the purchasing committees. The Art Department of the Ministry of Culture also promoted the growth of the collection by purchasing from studios. It was easier to access the earlier purchases of the ministry, and the considerably large collection given over by the ministry contained indispensable works not only of the art of the 1970s but also of the '60s, beside complementing the selections of some artists' works (Endre Bálint, Dezső Korniss, Erzsébet Schaár, Tibor Vilt) already represented in the Gallery.

Apart from the development of the collection, temporary exhibitions of various kinds afforded the public with a glimpse of the professional work of the Department. They included expositions of different artistic mediums such as the series of exhibitions of contemporary prints and drawings, retrospective exhibitions of great masters (Dezső Korniss, 1980; Béla Kondor 1984; Tibor Csiky, 1994) and of certain periods (Eclecticism, 1985; The Sixties, 1991). The collection was not only presented in the Gallery building but also in other Hungarian towns and at several places abroad. By lending several hundred works a year the department also helps the work of many other institutions.

The permanent exhibition of 20th-century art opened in the National Gallery in 1983 with the collaboration of the Contemporary Department. Its section showing post-1945 Hungarian art contains a considerable number of works collected by the department. Parallel with preparations for the permanent exhibition, the temporal limit of collecting was extended from our day back to 1945. As a result of the restructuring of the Gallery in the mid-1980s, the department became the Main Department of Contemporary Art, gradually taking over art works from the given period earlier kept by other departments. The collection of nearly 10,000 items served as the basis for the reorganization of the permanent exhibition of 20th century art in 2002.

István Dévényi

Tihamér Gyarmathy
(1915–2005)
Dynamic Composition
1946
Oil on canvas, 130 × 196 cm
Inv. no.: MM 82.247

Gyarmathy belonged to the second generation of Hungarian avant-garde. As a fresh graduate from the academy, he got acquainted with Piet Mondrian, André Breton, Jean Arp and Max Bill during his European study trip between 1937 and 1939. After the war he joined the so-called European School—a group of artists connected to European modernist trends, especially lyrical expressionism and surrealism—but in 1946 he left it and organized with art writer Ernő Kállai an artists' group called Gallery of the 4 Cardinal Points. Dynamic Composition of 1946 is a representative piece of this period. Its theme is the unity of the micro- and macrocosm, and its aim is to visualize the dynamic interrelation between space, time and movement. As Ernő Kállai put it, the work "...becomes the radiant mirror of the infinite and eternal organic existence in its incessant transformation of colour and form... Our eyes are lured into a spatial world in the intricate shafts of which life rampantly germinates and proliferates, pushing out thousands of roots."

I. D.

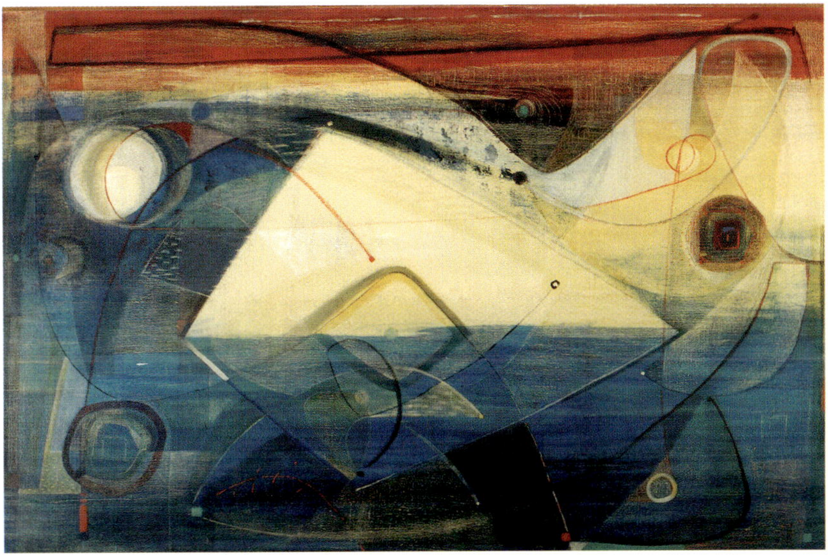

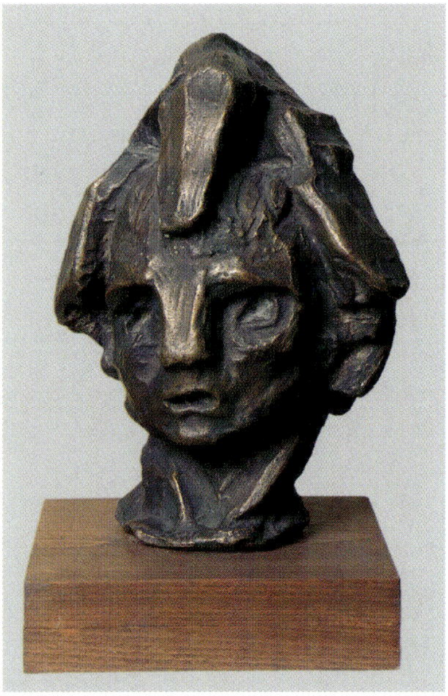

Tibor Vilt
(1905–1983)
Child's Head after the War
1946
Bronze, diam. 10 × 25 cm
Inv. no.: 66.39-N

The horrors of the war, the hopes inspired by peace and liberation, and the wish to rehabilitate the modernist trends mobilized several artists and critics already in the first days of 1945. After the termination of the war, the European School was founded on 18 October 1945, with Tibor Vilt as one of the founding members. The European School was not an avant-garde group or movement but a creative team bound by the "common experience and the jointly undertaken task." It was naturally the general ambition of artists to elaborate the monstrosities of the war, but this was increasingly characteristic as a programmatic task for the members of the European School.

Tibor Vilt's works are emblematic, exerting a dramatic effect with the simplest means of sculpture. Cut off drastically under the strong, muscular neck, the sculpture only shows the head and face of the little child, becoming a symbol of perishing already by its fragmentariness. Vilt enhanced the tragic message by distortion: the deep eye-pits, broad, flattened nose ridge, the matted tuft of hair with an uneven surface cover like a mask—and at the same time expose—the features of the child. The distortions of the child's face simultaneously allude to pain, dread, death and survival. The sculpture was created in the first bloom of Tibor Vilt's career, and fits into the set of expressive works begun in the second half of the 1930s, but it also expresses directly the everyday emotions of the artist.

J. Sz.

Béni Ferenczy

(1890–1967)

Boys at Play

1947

Bronze, 42 × 27 × 52.5 cm

Inv. no.: 50.763

Béni Ferenczy studied in Nagybánya, Florence and Munich in 1907–1910, then in Paris in 1912–1913. His masters included István Réti, Balthasar Schmidt, Émile-Antoine Bourdelle, Alexander Archipenko. After 1919 he lived abroad for two decades, mostly in Vienna and in 1932–1935 in Moscow. He returned home in 1938. In 1947–1948 he went on a study tour of Switzerland and Italy. In 1945–1950 he taught at the art academy in Budapest. In the 1950s he made a living by illustrating books. Despite the adverse social conditions and growing official requirements of communist cultural policy between 1950 and 1956, he progressed unwavering along the artistic course he set himself. A major work of this period is Boys at Play, a composition of two figures that he had matured in himself for nearly two decades. The evolution of the work can be traced back to his father Károly Ferenczy's painting Boys Throwing Pebbles of 1890 in a multitude of drawings, small-scale statuettes and medals. The two nude boys seemingly facing each other are not connected, their glances are directed elsewhere. The squatting figure is looking at the ground, the standing boy looks pensively past him. The real tie between them is playing, which is only alluded to by the title but not represented. He did not capture the typical self-forgetting moment of playing, as the two boys are engrossed in melancholic meditation, immersed in themselves. Instead of the movement of the figures, the difference in height caused by the different poses lends the statue its dynamism.

J. Sz.

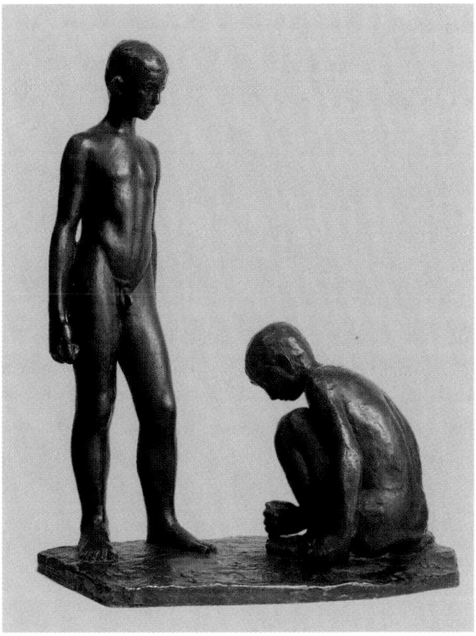

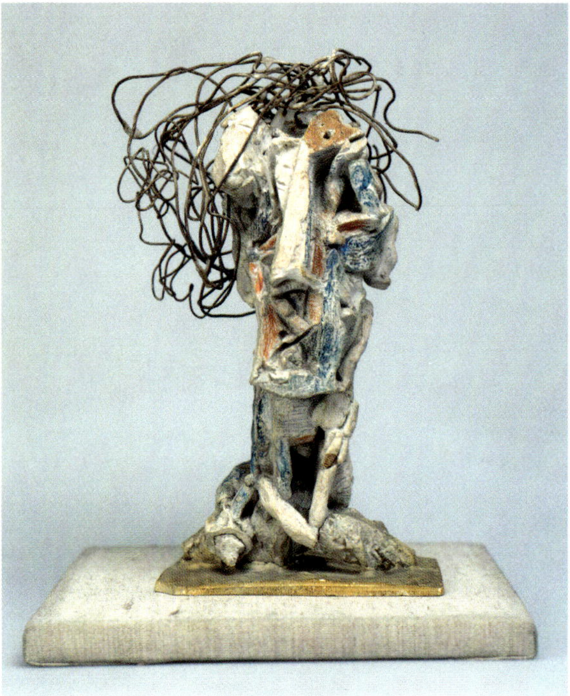

Tibor Vilt
(1905–1983)
Anatomy
1950
Coloured plaster, wire, height: 34 cm
Inv. no.: MM.83.285

Tibor Vilt tried to perpetuate the horrors of World War II, to set the upset world at rights in his small bronzes created with a claim to monumentalness. The more peaceful period after the war restored his playfulness, his flair for experimenting. He used all sorts of materials for his sculptures: plaster, wire, scraps of metal sheet, pieces of clay, turning these useless materials into meaningful form. "I always start out from the experience... The most important thing is the experience ... which may be a face, a movement... Sculptures? Maybe these sculptures are only the tools with which I carve and realize my new ideas." In Vilt's works the model gradually lost significance and his inquiry aimed at the depth beneath the surface. He was in search of the true self of man in his figures reduced to tense bronze sinews. In Anatomy, too, he descends into the depths of man. He exposes the real portrait: the blood circuits like "rose bushes", "carrying the eternal stream" (as the poet Attila József put it in his love poem Ode), the nerves, carrying ideas, the pulsaton of life. To quote Péter Kovács: "his art probed into the depth of the soul, at first with curiosity, prying open the secrets of loneliness, then it arrived at the experience and representation of merciless pain, before reaching a degree of reality when all you can do is acquiesce."

M. K.

Dezső Korniss
(1908–1984)
Plastic Calligraphy (Red)
1959
Oil on canvas, 60 × 200 cm
Inv. no.: MM.81.376

In the period between 1956 and 1962 Dezső Korniss painted expressive non-figurative works. These tachist calligraphies manifest the elementary outburst of the innermost emotional sphere. While in the action painting made with the dribbling technique of some other painters the endless possibilities of unrestrained self-expression predominate, Korniss' need to create signs render these compositions organized or constructed to some degree without any loss of the dramatism of psychic tension. Premeditation is especially obvious in the calligraphies made in 1959–1962. In the picture shown here, the plastic signs placed one after the other horizontally as in European writing on a homogeneous red plane emerge from a frieze-like band placed according to the rule of the golden section. The work is an early example of monochromous painting in Hungary.

I. D.

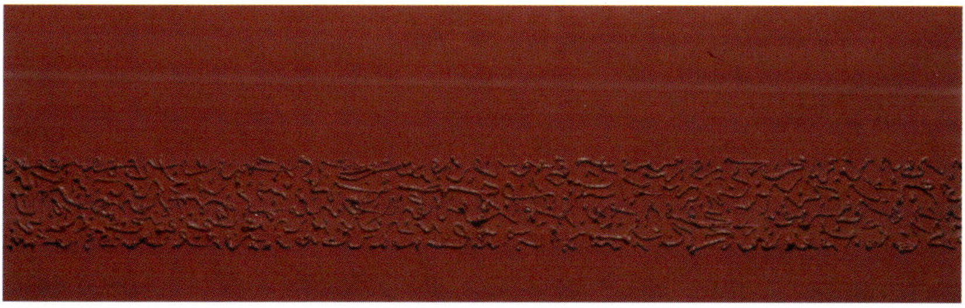

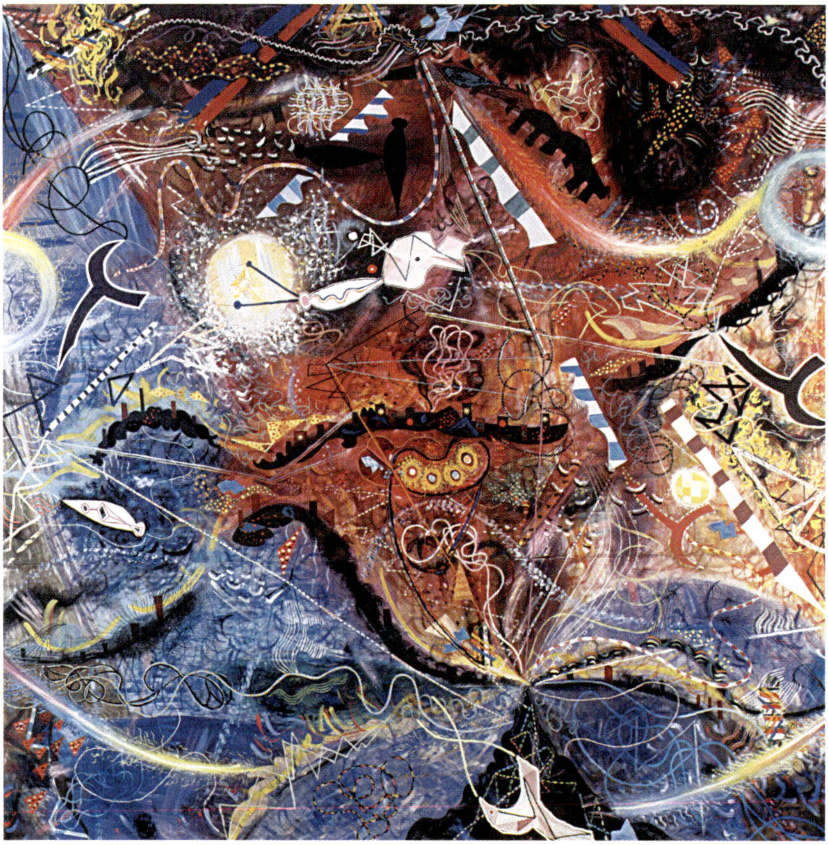

Tamás Lossonczy
(1904)
Great Purifying Storm
1961
Oil on canvas, 300 × 300 cm
Inv. no.: MM.89.23

Already in the early 1940s Ernő Kállai wrote in appreciative terms about the lyrical abstract and more powerful abstract-surrealistic compositions of Tamás Lossonczy. The term "bio-romanticism" coined by Kállai is most appropriate for Lossonczy's painting. Great Purifying Storm completed in 1961 is an elementary vision resolving the psychic tension of the artist who withdrew from public appearances for political reasons in the 1950s and also a synthesis of Lossonczy's worldview. This view of the world is close to that of the philosopher Béla Hamvas: "... as if mankind's experience collected over millennia were condensed into formations, and he had moulded the multitude of characteristic types from these thousand-year-old experiences of the soul. The type is not statuesque; quite contrarily, it appears to be a condensation of lines of forces." Though not exhibited before 1978, the painting became an emblematic work of the unfolding recovery of Hungarian art which began in the early 1960s.

I. D.

Endre Bálint
(1914–1986)
Grotesque Funeral
1962
Oil on canvas, 92 × 66 cm
Inv. no.: MM.82.131

Endre Bálint met and became close friends with Lajos Vajda in the second half of the 1930s, but he did not immerse in Vajda's constructive-surrealistic method before the fifties, adapting it gradually to his own ideas. He emigrated to France in 1957 where he made photomontages and illustrated the Jerusalem Bible, which brought him great success. In 1962 he returned to Hungary. His first work made at home—Grotesque Funeral—includes motifs also featuring in his Paris works: the full moon, the faceless black female figure, the cathedral. Things far removed from one another in time and place are represented in his pictures. This work is imbued with the memory of his father and his "frivolous" cemetery experience—he was a daywager as a young man at the same place where his father was buried.

I. D.

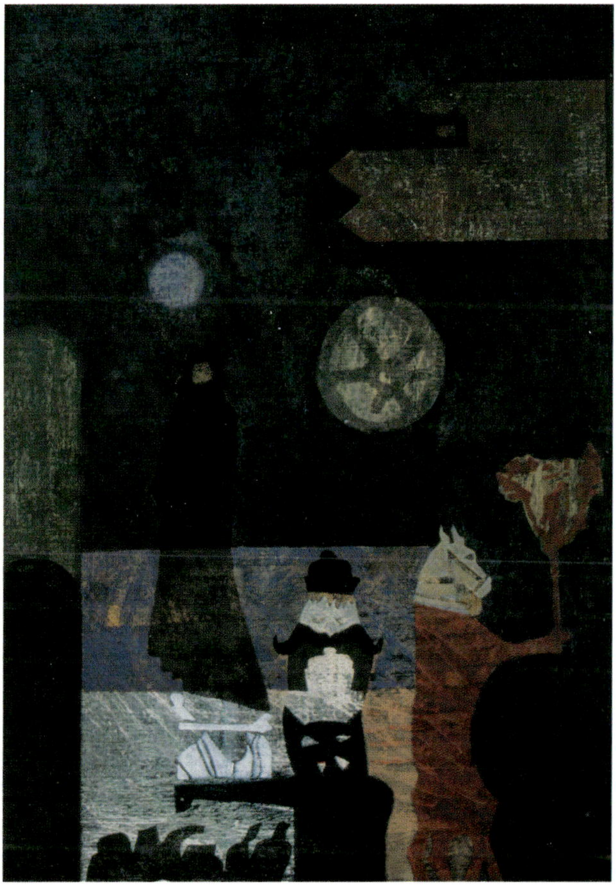

Tibor Csernus
(1927)
Modellers
1963
Oil on canvas, 140 × 182 cm
Inv. no.: MM.83.299

Using the system of means applied by Simon Hantai and Max Ernst, Tibor Csernus set a new course for the naturalist representation linked to the name of Aurél Bernáth. His pictures were created with a peculiar scraping technique, using tachistic and surrealistic elements, which drew a great following later. Art historian Géza Perneczky called the loose group surnaturalists. "Surnaturalism was [...] a sort of avant-gardization of sensation and pantheistically enlarged naturalism." Though this succinct statement applies to the group in its tendency, it must be noted that what preoccupied Csernus was not the compatibility of the avant-garde and naturalism but the question of the "possibility to represent existence"—to use Kokoschka's phrase—in the absurd set of sights deprived of their coordination. Painted in memory of the outstanding Hungarian aviatist György Endresz in 1963, the symbolism of Modellers interprets the predestined fate of artists, especially when the work is placed in the context of the works of the sixties devoted so often to the theme of flying.

I. D.

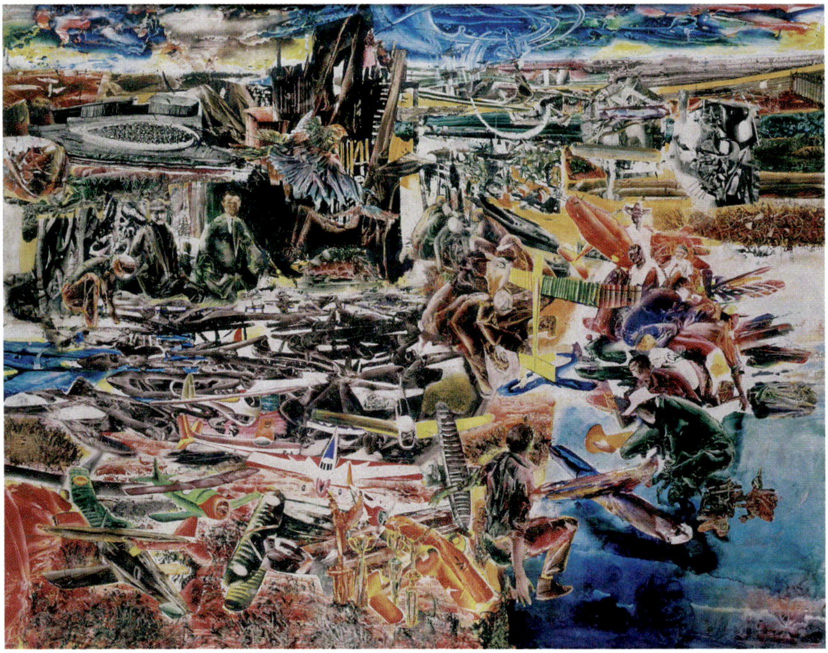

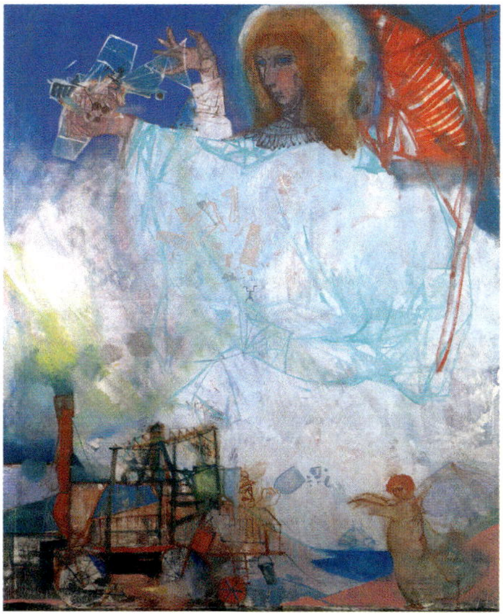

Béla Kondor

(1931–1972)

The Genius of Mechanical Flying

1964

Oil on canvas, 230 × 187 cm

Inv. no.: MM.77.186

"In Milan, passers-by stopped to stare in absorption at the life-sized poster of Kondor's Genius of Mechanical Flying. His works were revelatory in Lisbon, Madrid, Belgrade and Sweden, too," art historian Lajos Németh recalled the painter's reception abroad. The Milanese stopped long in front of the poster, presumably not only to see the miriad of finely elaborated details, but also captured by the polysemantic contents derived from Kondor's complex personality and so typical of his works. He walked along the endless axis of time, surfacing now in the world of the Bible, now in the Middle Ages as a sovereign participant, or again, in his own century symbolized by the aeroplane. The airplane defeats "Newton's faith", gravitation. The flight of the man-made machine is at the same time the flight of the human mind that triumphs over all retarding, shackling forces. Kondor's angels embody the creative human genius. The winged angels, airborn contraptions, flying freaks stand for the perennial opposition between the desire for flying and the dread of falling. The work can be regarded as a guide to technical history: the sail-boat, the puffing steam-engine appear and above the whitish-yellow smoke cloud of William Turner's Rain, Steam and Speed, man rises into a new dimension. The angel of human creativity lets the machine on its course with a tender finger movement, worried about its fate, anxious to know what it will develop into: the tool of progress or agression. In this ethereal setting the angel becomes the provident Creator in whose hand our future lies, just as the pioneers of flying in their rattling machines put their fate in his hands. They sometimes failed and sometimes triumphed, and thus mankind made its way from the first hesitant attempts to the stars very rapidly, just in the tragically short lifetime of Béla Kondor.

M. K.

Endre Tót
(1937)
Horizontal Picture II
1966
Mixed technique, paper, 55.7 × 147 cm
Inv. no.: MM.89.127

The "pressure for adaptation" characterizing the majority of the so-called Iparterv generation—a generation of avant-garde artists named after the venue of their first, influential exhibition in 1968—, the quickly changing, overlapping impacts after the information vacuum of the previous years were particularly typical of Endre Tót. The brief phase of "running amok towards up-to-dateness" lasting for hardly a decade and radically terminated in 1971 was an extremely fertile period divided into abstract expressionist, informel, pop art, geometic and analytic series telescoping into one another. Horizontal Picture II marks a turning point after the emotional tension and suffocating spaces of the "White pictures" and the depictions of states (of mind) in the Diary Sketches from Angyalföld. Giving vent to the instincts spontaneously and vehemently in painting was now paired with the need for order: parallel with the expanding colour range, more powerful painterly "imprinting" (broad brushwork, hatching, sprinkling), the picture structure was simplified. In Horizontal Picture II the red horizontal dividing line and the grill of the perpendicular red and white straight lines divide the picture space into smaller units in the lower row of which further numbered windows are opened. This system of coordinates puts a curb on the outpouring and fervour of emotions, yet it is still the expressive and subjective abstract pictorial language, forms and gestures created by the powerful thick brushprints that determine the basic impression. The nodes of the geometric structure are "fastened" by fragments of reality and typographic elements: newspaper cutouts enclosed and emphasized by brushstrokes and letter stencils as counterpoints or supplements to the painterly notes (from red and white chalk gestures to legible writing).

L. Sz.

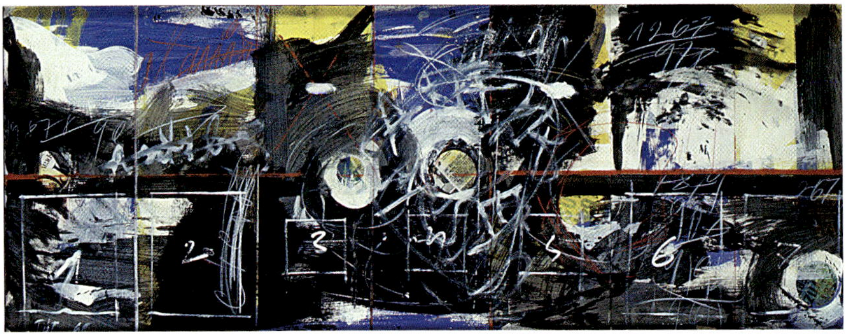

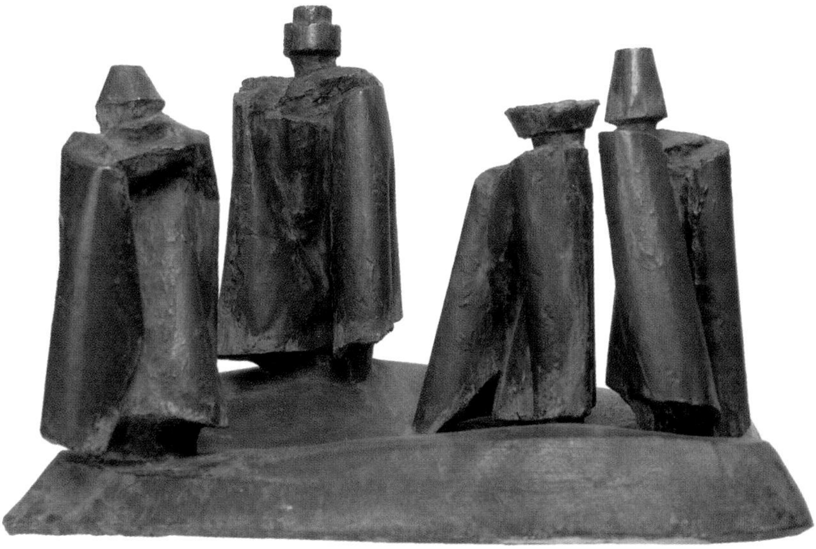

Tamás Vigh

(1926)

People of the Great Plain

1967

Bronze, height: 53 cm

Inv. no.: MM.82.90

"The Water Conservancy Board ... asked me to design the Vásárhelyi monument ... I thought the only befitting memorial to the immense earthwork of the regulation of the river Tisza was some earth sculpture. I had tumuli on my mind as the embodiment of the Great Plain... When however it turned out that my peasants were proclaiming their own greatness in their humanity, it immediately caused fierce opposition," Tamás Vigh wrote about the genesis of the small sculpture. The compositional layout for the monument of Pál Vásárhelyi—a 19th-century engineer who took an important part in the regulation of the Tisza river—was a masterpiece already as a design. After the rejection the artist cut it up (so it only survives in photos) and he cast the group of navvies into bronze for the small sculpture biennial in 1971. The small sculpture is a study for a detail of a larger work as its most important part carrying the core of the message. The composition is closed in form, the figures are blocklike, almost unarticulated, bordering on cubism. The external features—the fur cloak and horseherd's hat—are typical forms but beneath them a certain kind of human behaviour is suggested: the unshakable calm of herdsmen tending the flock, leaning on their sticks, the lankiness of the navvies, their hardiness withstanding the storms of nature. He depicts the people of the earth in both physiognomic and spiritual senses. That is how this taciturn group becomes a general phenomenon, a national ideal.

M. K.

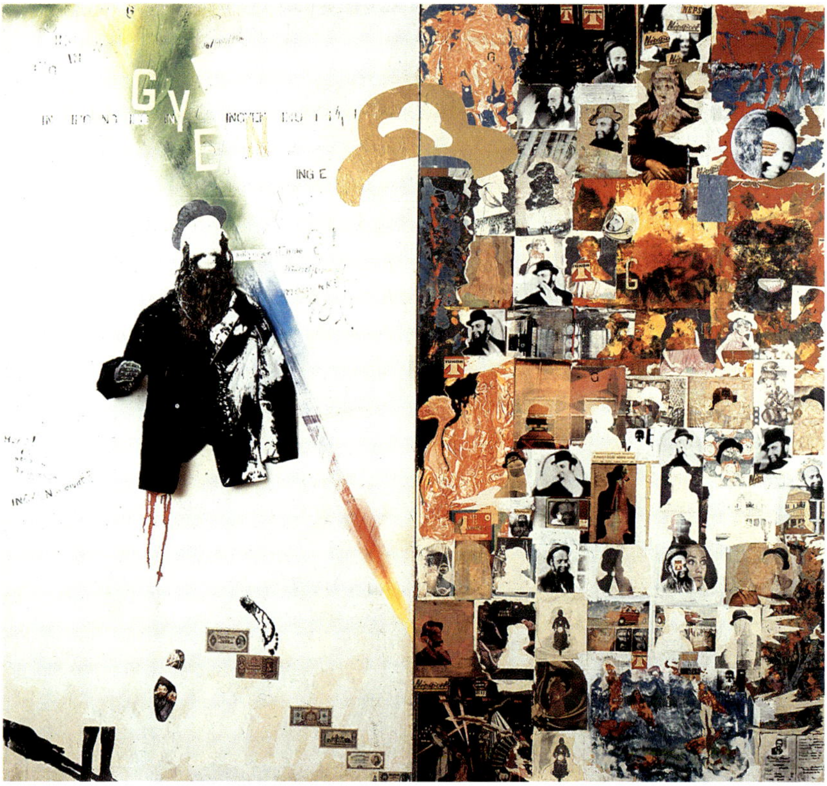

Sándor Altorjai
(1933–1979)
May I Sink Upwards
1967
Oil, mixed technique, fibrewood,
305 × 342 cm
Inv. no.: MM.82.354

Altorjai had already graduated as a pharmacist when he enrolled at the Academy of Fine Arts. After graduation he joined the "surnaturalists" for a short time. He made friends with Miklós Erdély and took part in various avant-garde events until 1968. May I Sink Upwards of 1967 is one of the major works of Hungarian pop art. The assemblage was created with Miklós Erdély's cooperation, the pasted photos were taken of him, and methodologically the work adheres to Erdély's thoughts exposed in his study entitled Hunger for Montage. The spaces of the two panels set side by side are on different scale, and they fit each other like two cuts of a film, so that the motifs appearing in both parts of the picture in different contexts can be cross-referential. The textual instruction and the operation of the movable parts invite the spectator to contribute to the realization of stage effects.

I. D.

György Jovánovics

(1939)

Man

1968

Plaster, textile, 180 cm

Inv. no.: MM.82.133

Jovánovics pursued parallel studies in sculpture and philosophy in Budapest, then he studied sculpture in Vienna and Paris. In the early 1980s he lived and worked in Berlin. From 1990 he has taught at the Hungarian Academy of Fine Arts (later university), led the master course, and been the president of the masters board. Jovánovics is an academic sculptor at the universal level of art, sculptor doctus in the literary and the figurative sense of the word. In the late 1960s he was one of the organizers of the avant-garde Iparterv exhibitions; Man was one of the three sculptures presented at the first Iparterv showing. The material of his sculptures is almost exclusively plaster from the early works onward. He has made plaster casts of human figures, draperies, and the interplay of the two. He was encouraged to use plaster by a decisive figure of American pop art, George Segal without becoming his epigon. Instead of Segal's dribbling method Jovánovics uses a smooth porcelaine-like surface. While Segal captures everyday life situations, Jovánovics tried to represent "inexplicable" man with his mysteriousness. The effect of ancient Egyptian relief sculpture can also be discerned in the mask-like face adorned with a pattern of lilies and in the frontal pose.

Zs. J.

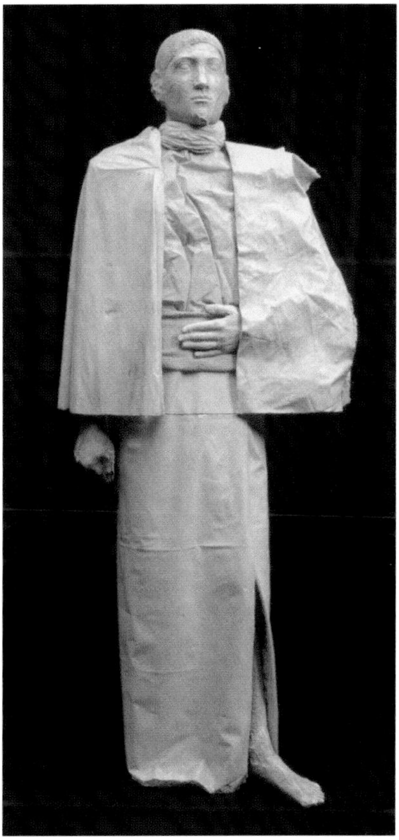

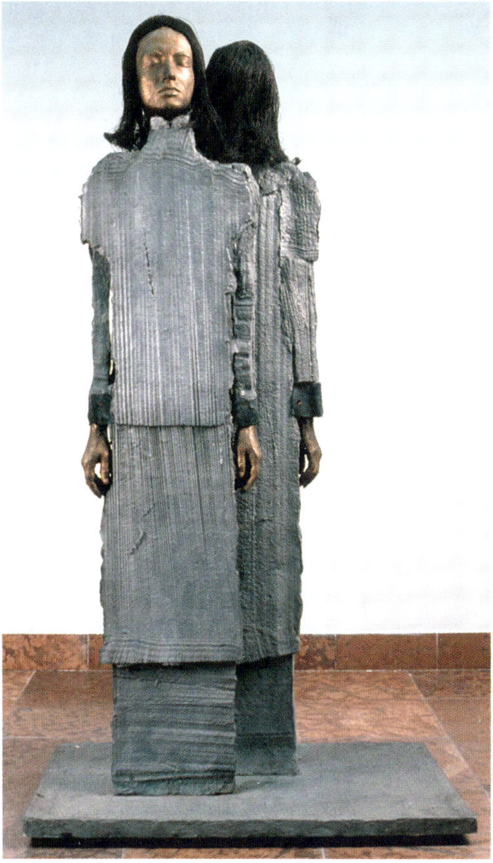

Erzsébet Schaár

(1908–1975)

Sisters

1968

Aluminium, lead, iron wire, 170 cm

Inv. no.: MM.76.56

After her Street of 1974 and Room of Mirrors (1975) in the 1980s some art critics subsumed Erzsébet Schaár in the category of pop art on account of her use of certain materials and tools. However, in view of the whole oeuvre the emphasis must be laid elsewhere. Inside and outside, the formal and thematic problem of reflection were already present in her small sculptures produced in the late 1940s. From the mid-1960s practically two-dimensional silhouette-like "asculptural" figures appeared in relation to architectonic elements. Schaár took an interest in styrofoam from 1966, and this material allowed her to work in life size. Sisters—the original of which was also styrofoam—was made in 1968. The elegiac tone and the different attitude to time separate this work from the contemporary sculptures produced using similar tools.

I. D.

Imre Bak
(1939)
Blue Frame
1968
Oil on canvas, 120 × 222 cm
Inv. no.: MM.87.65

Imre Bak belonged to the kernel of the Zugló Circle (a circle of artists keen on promoting abstract art which was repressed in Hungarian culture at that time); until 1964 his works displayed the imprint of the form-dissecting, analytic approach of lyrical abstraction represented by Jean Bazain and Alfred Manessier. During his West European study trip in 1965 he got acquainted with neo-geometric art and made friends with Karl Pfahler and Thomas Lenk. From then to 1970 his art was directly tied to the "hard edge". His program called for exactness, the consistent observation of structural purity by eliminating personal implications. In the highly dynamic composition of Blue Frame presented at the first Iparterv exhibition in 1968 sharply cut geometric shapes, intense colour effects and disciplined creative behaviour in keeping with the structuralist principle can be observed.

I. D.

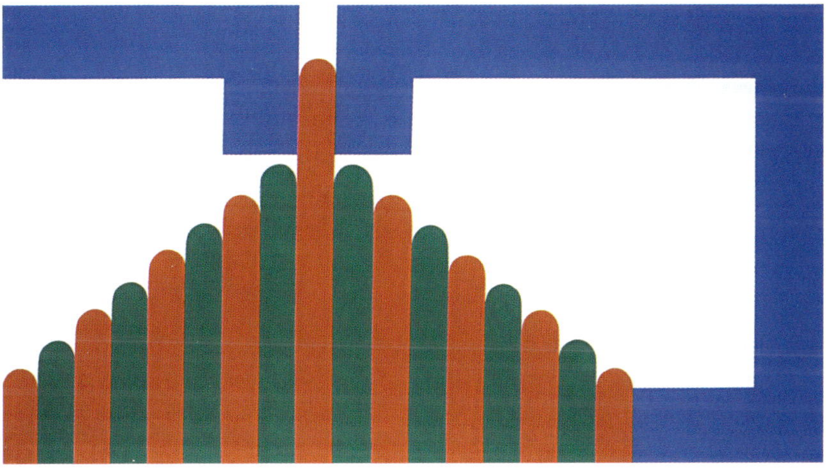

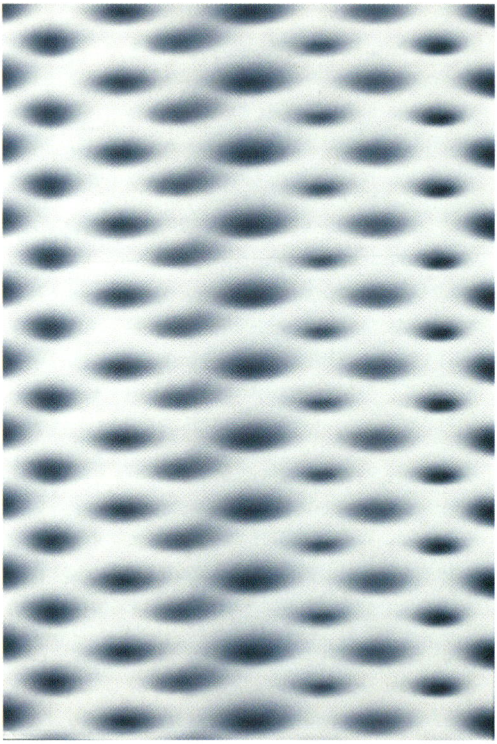

Tamás Hencze
(1938)
Dynamic Structure
1968
Oil on paper, 100 × 70 cm
Inv. no.: MM.90.114

In the second half of the 1960s Tamás Hencze used a new picture-creating technique (and tool): the paint roller. “I have been using a roller similar to that of wall painters and photographers for quite some time and exclusively. The progression of the roller provides a sort of continuity, which allows to create some specific rhythm in my pictures.” Unlike the brush, the roller applies the paint quickly and evenly, the paint can be distributed over the surface thinly and enables to produce extremely subtle tonal grades and transitions. But “the rhythm, clarity, elegance, aristocratic subtlety of his pictures devoid of any grain of uncertainty, however, could not be achieved by ‘technique’ alone,” art historian János Frank wrote. In the pictorial realm of Dynamic Structure the experience of space is decisive. The fine transitions of grey tones (as a result of the colour-blending effect of the roller) bring about an illusory, mystic space. The space arising from the monotonously repreated, blurred homogeneous discs covering the whole surface elicits the sense of infinite space, impersonal, cosmic silence. It is a cold, inpenetrable, empty space of undefinable material. This “optic screen” illumined by a mysterious light unwittingly generates the sensation of dynamic motion.

M. K.

Sándor Molnár
(1936)
Principle
1968
Oil and acrylic on canvas, lath, 98 × 134 cm
Inv. no.: MM.90.118

Parallel with his academic studies Sándor Molnár organized a group of avant-garde artists of the 1960s later called Zugló Circle. The point was to thrash out and test in practice the ideas of modern art theories. Visiting studios, they sought out contact with the members of older generations who had affiliations with the avant-garde and who were pushed to the periphery for their artistic attitude in the 1950s. In 1966 Sándor Molnár painted the Dragon Killer in which he summed up the possibilities of lyrical abstraction on the basis of French painting. Around that time individual courses began to be launched within the Zugló Circle. Sándor Molnár took a new direction with his series of "empty" pictures. Principle of 1968 is actually an object for meditation, the green colour creating the possibility for absorbed meditation, contemplation.

I. D.

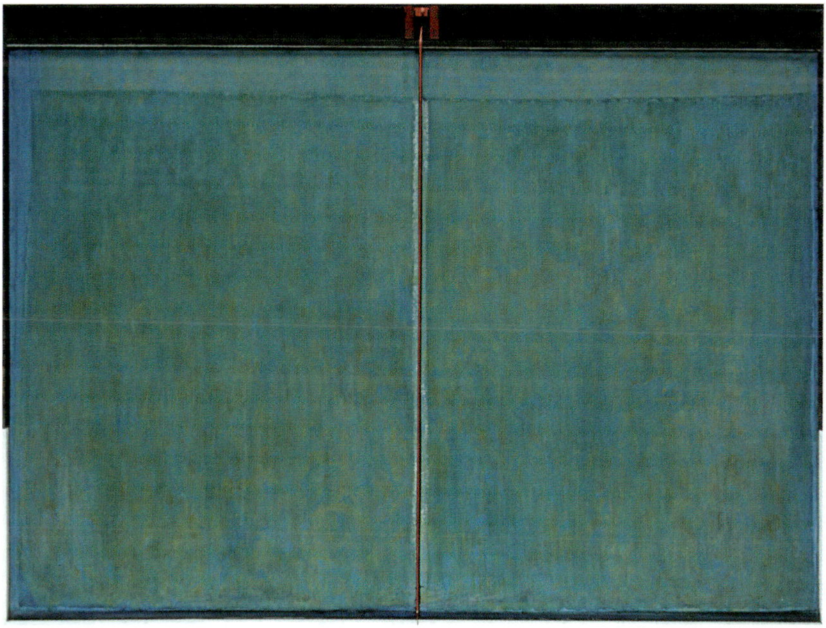

Ignác Kokas
(1926)
Around Man I
1969–1970
Oil on fibrewood, 134 × 258 cm
Inv.no.: MM.81.345

From the early 1960s Ignác Kokas gradually left behind his painterly, post-impressionist genre painting of a dramatic tone and progressed towards expressivity alloyed with surrealism. As for his themes, he turned from the topics of peasant life to more general questions such as loneliness, struggle and death. The vicinity of his native village, Ginza puszta provided the motifs. Kokas painted a row of paintings of the region assembled into a cycle. Returning to the venue of his childhood entailed introversion and soul-searching, resulting in the burst of emotional and moral problems to the surface. Sets of pictures speak about the inner struggle, loyalty and disloyalty (I'm Leaving the Village, Prodigal Son), the mission (Orpheus, The Stygmatized), and artistic responsibility a typical example of which is Around Man I painted in 1969–1970.

I. D.

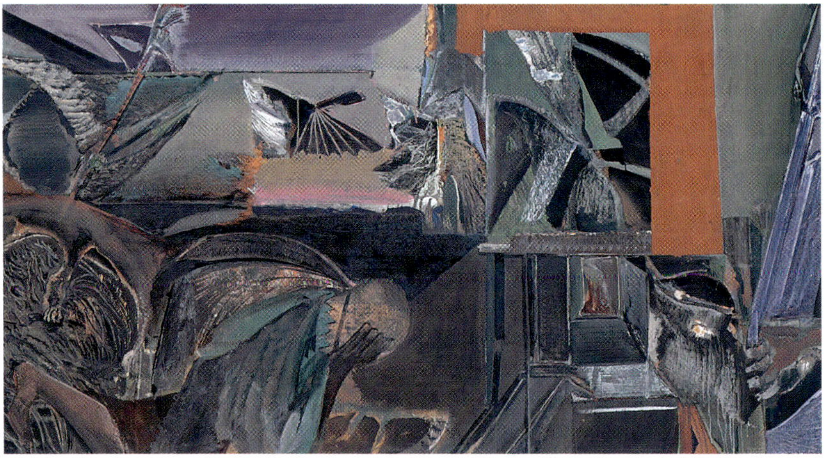

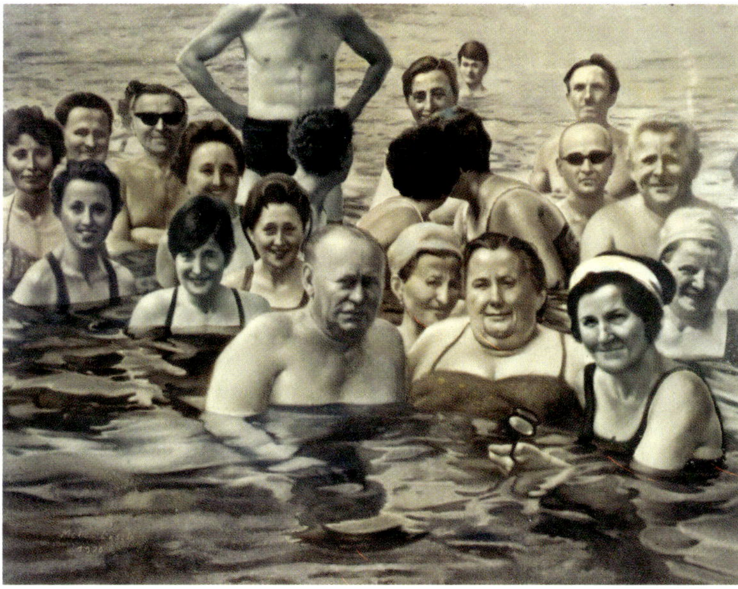

László Méhes

(1944)

Lukewarm Water I

1970

Oil on fibrewood, 60 × 80 cm

Inv. no.: MM.92.109

Already as a student Méhes developed his individual style combining surrealism and naturalism and joined the "surnaturalists" hallmarked by the name of Tibor Csernus. He took part in the Iparterv exhibitions in the late 1960s as a young graduate, and these events determined his subsequent alignments from pop art through concept art to hyperrealism and later to his floating canvases made with a special method. He renewed pop art's techniques of surface treatment and developed a new graphic procedure, monopoltype. He is the founder of one of the Hungarian branches of hyperrealism, photorealism. The series of Lukewarm Water was launched by his pencil drawing of 1969, Weekday, a peak of Hungarian hyperrealism. Méhes painted most pieces of the series in his new home in Paris. The basis of the classically elaborated paintings is a set of photos of an ad hoc group of people at a medicinal bath, on a trade union holiday. It is an examination of how people randomly assembled in lukewarm water behave. Méhes depicted the details impassionately, objectively, keeping a peculiar distance, which throws the banality of the situation into relief. "I am erecting a memorial to a moment of life," he noted later. Méhes created this series at the time of the international spread of hyperrealism and the emergence of the American photorealists, making a stir with his ironic and grotesque approach which is evident in the dual symbolism of the title as well: as László Beke put it, "you could not help interpreting it as hard criticism of the soft dictatorship."

Zs. J.

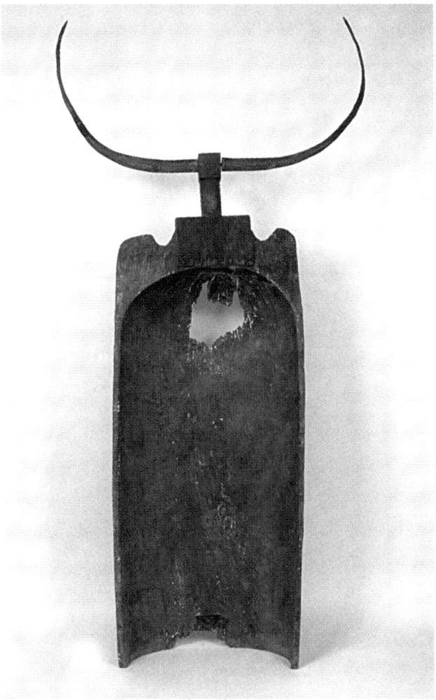

Géza Samu
(1947–1990)
Tub with Horns
1970–1971
Wood, 243 × 116 × 27 cm
Inv. no.: MM.89.16

"In the early 1970s my initially distinctly ethnographic inspiration based on pre-classical cultures was boosted by the start of a massive ethnographic movement but I tried to keep myself intact ... I learnt a lot of embryonic crafts from rush-work to wicker-work, which was sufficient to put me on my course ... I was also interested in the primitive crafts because what I learnt then I had already seen earlier: my grandfather was on good terms with nearly all the crafts: he wove baskets, did blacksmithing, carved wood, and when in arts and crafts camps I saw these crafts again, they resuscitated my memories." Géza Samu was a decisive figure of contemporary Hungarian sculpture in the 1970s–1980s. Similarly to rural people, he also noticed the poetry in the landscape and the objects, and he used the objects found in rural homes for his sculptures. But the objects are not real. There is only a single real object he used: a wooden tub he found in the loft. He used it for his Tub with Antlers of 1970. "I was hesitating whether to carve it or not. Then it appeared more practical, more tough to use it like that because it was more accurate. It refers more clearly to our material and spiritual legacy." Then he sawed the wooden tub and carved huge antlers to it, turning the old leaking utensil into an idol, a shaman of formidable power.

M. K.

Dóra Maurer
(1937)
V's May Day Demonstration on Artificial Ground (Private May Day Demonstration in an Artificial Field)
1971
Powdered paint, photo, paper, 69 × 88 cm
Inv. no.: MM.2001.18

The picture is a document of the conceptual period of an intricately ramifying œuvre (graphic art, painting, film) unfolding from the late 1960s. From picture multiplication, the "classic" graphic procedure Maurer changed over to the leaving of elementary signs. This is a special and at the same time archaic method: pedotype or sole-printing, a "flow print" realized as personal action. The work is the documentation of itself: it is the object, "subject" and proof of the action. The work consists of an about 1/4–1/3 section of a circle of footprints in lying rectangular format below which—like a predella—a sequence of black/white phase shots inform the spectator of the walking action in the studio, covering a whole circle. The footsteps treading one upon the other coalesce into a form closing in on itself—a circle—which is red, as befits Workers' Day, when great processions were held in Communist Hungary. The individual imprint is incorporated in the resultant visual sign which becomes unique via the incessant repetition. One cannot overlook what a verbal word-carpet is the "artificial ground" for the rite of the private procession: a crumpled glued issue of the official daily Népszabadság. On the trampled newspaper the circling is done with feet coloured by powdered paint of the most glaring colour: the motion can be continued till exhaustion but it leads nowhere, like a breather in a prison courtyard or the morning exercises in the army. Constraint and limitation: this—ironic and artistic— variant of physical exercise is—however indirectly—also the "imprint" of the mental context of the one-party-system, the life situation not devoid of some (social) critical weight.

L. Sz.

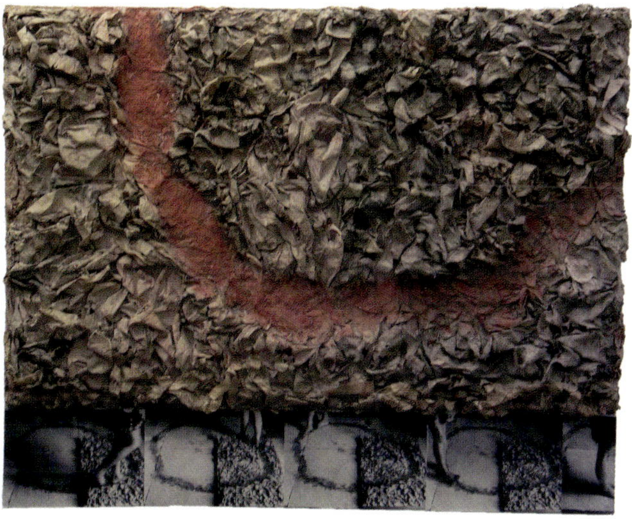

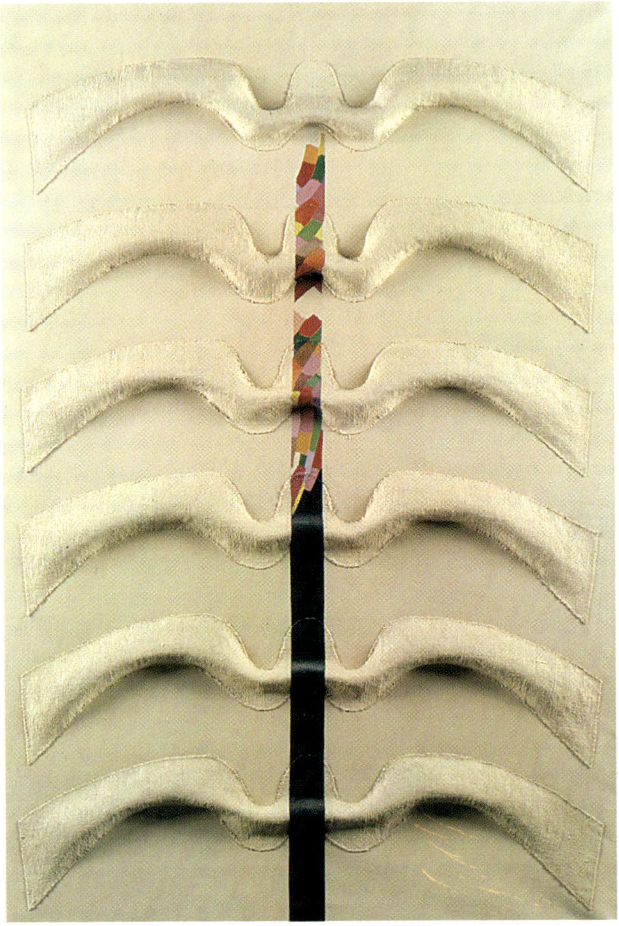

Ilona Keserü
(1933)
Villány II
1972
Oil on embossed canvas, 180 × 120 cm
Inv. no.: MM.87.171

From the 1960s Ilona Keserü painted works—in her definition: using the tools of abstract expressionism and gesture painting as the direct painterly manifestations of her states of mind and nerves—that have key significance in the evaluation of the period. In 1967 she discovered the heart-shaped gravestones in the cemetery at Balatonudvari, which remained the basic motifs—especially their closure—in her pictures for years. This simplified form is paired with a reduced but meaningful use of colours in Keserü's pictures painted in oil on embossed canvas. It all resulted in an organic network of relations tied to personal first-hand experience. This is well illustrated by Villány II painted in 1972.

I. D.

Ádám Kéri

(1944)

A Cannonball of 1848 in the Wall

1972–1973

Fibrewood, mixed technique, 104 × 122 cm

Inv. no.: MM.75.37

Kéri graduated from the painting course of the Hungarian Academy of Fine Arts and studied sculpture in Sweden; his early works are mainly objects. At the beginning of his career, he—like so many of his contemporaries—was influenced by the object culture of Pop. "I am looking for traces, signs found in reality—like a cannonball in the wall, bulletmarks on the walls of the Pest buildings, mars, electric boxes, distribution boxes, old letters, blurred writings, faded stamps, scribbling, stamp marks, crumpled letters, burnt paper, bullets, cartridge hulls, etc.—that carry certain human contents and may become symbols," he wrote about his life's work a few years ago in what may be his ars poetica. A Cannonball of 1848 in the Wall is a synthetic work of a new conception of objects starting out from the pop art of the early 1970s. He lifted a piece of a damaged wall from its natural setting and transferred it into another form of existence, a panel picture. He did not only create a new object but turned the war injury into a symbol: it reminds of the 1848 revolution in a period when it was not comme il faut to mention the anniversary, although it was not prohibited.

Zs. J.

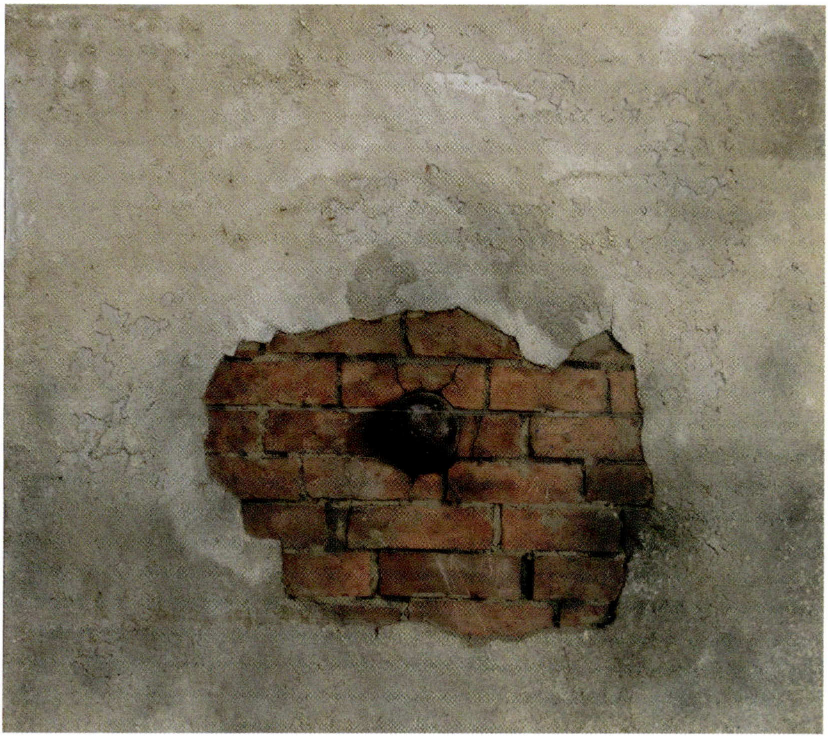

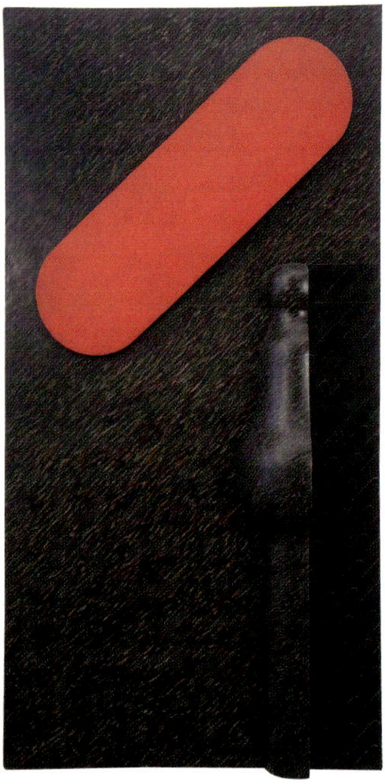

Pál Deim
(1932)
Sign II
1973
Oil on wood, 225 × 120 cm
Inv. no.: MM.79.60

In Deim's oeuvre sculpture did not entail a change in style but merely enriched the mode of expression. His reliefs and sculptures feed on the same elements as his pictures. Applying the forms cut out of wooden boards onto the paintings he did not only develop the effect of the grid into an exciting 3D experience but the rhythm of the cut-outs also animate the composition. The outline of the puppet suggests that rotated around its axis the shape of a human figure would emerge like a skittle-pin. The large tangible puppet of Sign II almost merges with the scratchily painted surface, only the play of light and shade turns it visible. With the colour combination of red and black, the work associates a looming great danger. The huge grid element hovering above the head of the puppet like Damocles' sword simultaneously alludes to the danger and the warning cry. The painting is depressing because the warning is in vain, the puppet-man is wholly helpless, defenceless, exposed, the only way to escape is hiding in or merging with the environment. The uncertain space caused by splintery hatching may perhaps hide it. In Pál Deim's art various media are not separated, their boundaries are blurred. Yet he had the greatest liking for sculpture: "We have the dual effect of painting and sculpture here. When you have a distinct plane on a plastic piece, you can turn it into loose, airy, transparent space with this relaxed painting. This impression is further enriched by the shadows cast by the convex forms that appear in this space. I was interested in this formal solution in these compositions."

M. K.

Imre Kocsis
(1940)
Suburb
1976
Oil on canvas, 106.5 × 161 cm
Inv. no.: MM.79.176

Soon after the beginning of his career Imre Kocsis became an outstanding representative of hyperrealist painting. He commemorated the city, the decaying tenement buildings in his works. "There was a time when I loved the city. (Today it depresses me.) It was an immense change in my lifestyle to move from Makó to Budapest as an adolescent. I liked the tattered city centre, the strange isolation of city life. It was close to me. I walked a lot after graduation, too, I knew all the buildings with passage-ways in them in the 6th, 7th districts. These shabby old tenement buildings did not change a bit over the decades. They had witnessed a lot, and I grew to be personally involved in them. That's what I wanted to elaborate. I only managed to when I was already looking at all this as an outsider." Imre Kocsis' own words also confirm that Attila József's "painful cry" is missing from his relation to the outskirts. He gives a detailed diagnosis of this wretched world through the eyes of an outsider. This is, however, a delusion because the use of hyperrealism in this context is itself an exclamation mark. He depicts with meticulous care all that is worthless, neglected, the litter, the simple lonely people living there who no one casts a glance at—there is bursting tension in the care devoted to carelessness.

M. K.

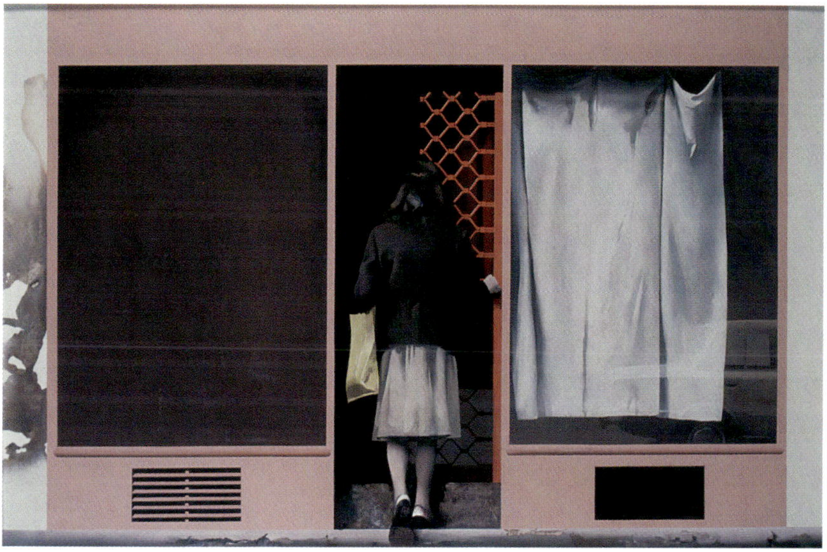

Tibor Hajas

(1946–1980)

Surface Torturing III (Fossils)

1978

Photo on wooden panel; photos:
24 × 30 cm, panel: 90 × 110 cm

Inv. no.: MM.90.5

He was a writer, poet, essayist and artist. The origin and exclusive "medium" of his performances, the main activity of his last years, was his own body. Art was a specific way of human cognition for the artist with an existential rather than aesthetic significance: the artist was the mediator of a force or message of a "different magnitude". His self-liquidation was a necessary "redemption trip", the archetypical experience of suffering, though doubtful as regards its outcome. "His physical presence exerts its effect in a sexual field, but the excitement he arouses is created by the appeal, the sex-appeal of death." "Illegal crossing of the dream-frontier": sacrifice, an example that cannot be followed. The physical, emotional and intellectual experiences of the performances are also elaborated by the "documentation" of a private rite series (photos by János Vető). Photo-woodoo, the magic doubling of the violation of one's own frontier even in the "public" actions and its "tools" (flash-light—burn scar, body painting): dual torturing of picture and body (emulsion laceration). The body petrified in the gestures and happenings of "self-erasure" is the "victim or creator of the events". It is the actor of prepared "fate xenoliths" cast into cold white or black space, naked. Here in a triptych composition: on the left wounded, with "charred" maimed legs; in the middle: his own shadow devours him like a black hole, he is standing, grabbing at his throat as if he were suffocating, his face a "glowing" hole; on the right: with a defensive, defeated gesture holding his head, while his back "is set on fire", his loins already scorched. The subtitles of further pieces in the series—Senses, Pompeii—generate the sequence of further associations: Hiroshima, Prague 1968, the Buddhist monk of the Vietnam war, the victims of a napalm bombing.

L. Sz.

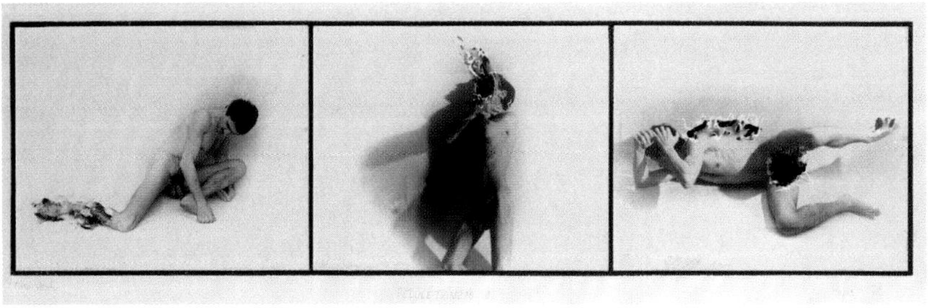

Gyula Pauer
(1941)
Maya
1978
Wood, silk, 203 cm
Inv. no.: MM.82.132

Maya is the "cultic object" and "demonstration aid" of Pauer's world explanation of PSEUDO ART elaborated for sculpture and extended to other media (painting, photo, theatre, performance). According to the levels and grades of manipulatedness and manipulability (sculpture → artist/art → existence → society → reality) PSEUDO interprets the expanding circles of the world. The endpoint of the logical road starting from art, from PSEUDO sculpture deceptively placing "the surface of another sculpture in front of the puritanic forms of a MINIMAL sculpture" is the recognition that the existential manipulation of sculpture (and art) refers to the general manipulation of life, of existence. Beside op art and minimal art, PSEUDO responded to the international trend of conceptual art with the "usual" Central European twist: the self-analysis of art unwittingly assumed a critical character on account of its social role. Maya is the only survivor of Pauer's work at the Sculptors' Symposium in Nagyatád in 1978 (Monument of the Tree, Pseudo Tree, Forest of Protest Signboards have perished). Her carved oakwood body bearing the light-and-shade copy of a young naked woman as a pseudo-glaze is the protagonist of the "ceremonies" of pseudo performances. The constantly "updated" mythology built around it including explanations, instructions of use and production, PR texts, free verse, photo documentation, chronological review also contains the accident of the "splitting" of the body as a "Maya experience" revealing that reality is appearance.

L. Sz.

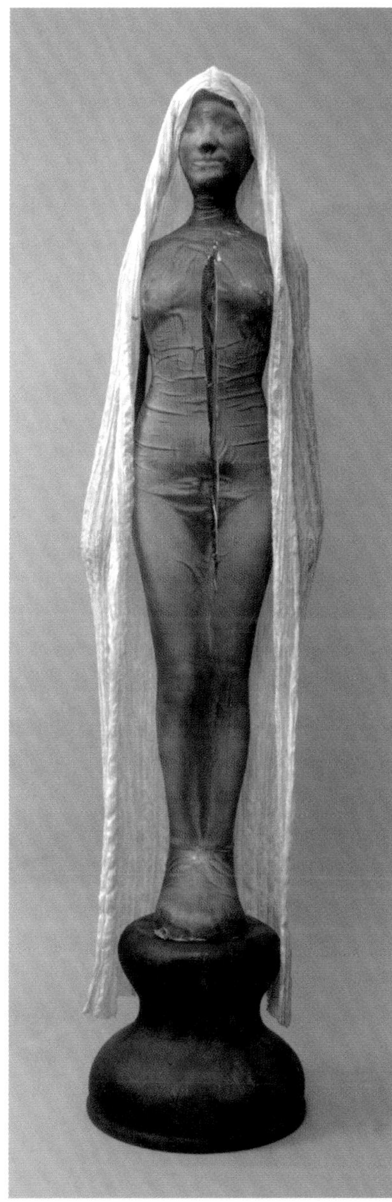

Menyhért Tóth
(1904–1980)
Providence
1979
Oil on canvas, 137 × 200 cm
Inv. no.: MM.81.181

Menyhért Tóth spoke often and gladly about his white period begun in the 1960s. In addition to formal, colour theoretical and technical aspects, his program also incorporated explanations of the world and attempts at defining his attitude to existence. In the first half of the decade he tried to interpret "totality" (white) pervading all phenomena of the world by starting out from white in the pictures and gradually adding various colours. This intention deepened in the works painted from the late '60s which coalesced into a tableau and a single "world-icon", so to speak. All this is summarized in his last finished work, Providence. By painting a composition on the grounded canvas with colour and then covering the whole with a richly textured white paint he achieved that the philosophical aura of the picture became physically perceptible via the radiation of reflected light. His aim was not to "depict" light but to visualize it, not to represent Providence but to reanimate the myth. In this way the whole became a magic object in its ambiguity and the artist became a magician like the cave painters who made the incarnation of their community's beliefs and desires possible.

I. D.

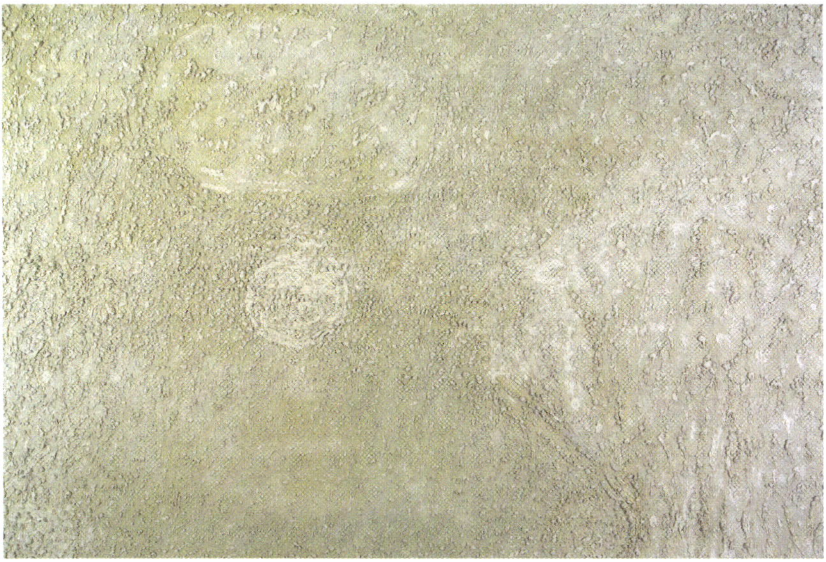

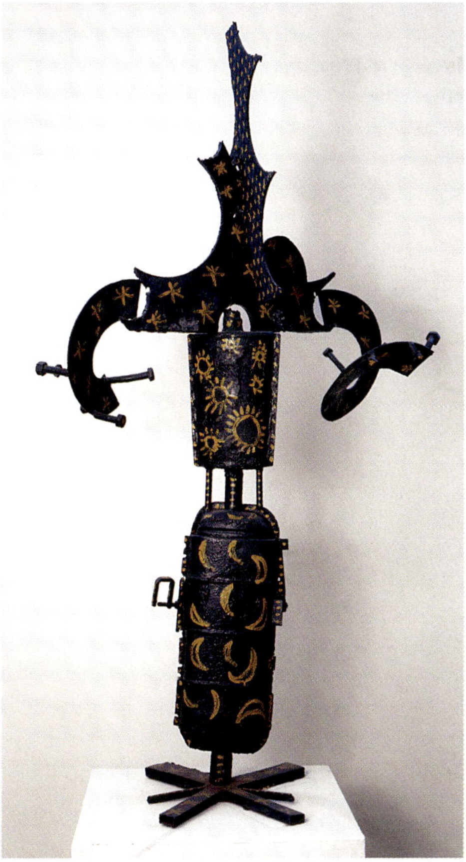

Ildikó Várnagy

(1944)

Queen of the Night

1980

Painted iron, 171.5 × 93 × 65 cm

Inv. no.: MM.87.174

In her works Ildikó Várnagy applied organic systems that are built on elementary comparisons and encompass an infinite number of things, preserving at the same time their specificity of being reducible to the basic formula. That is how the artist created the elements of "writing in space" without negating the criteria of sculpture. In her terracotta portraits she embarrasses both the model and the spectator by ironically confronting them with the inner traits instead of physiognomic similarities. Her idols and fetishes elicit associations with the magic deeds of primitive peoples without being archaized. This specially applies to works assembled from found objects such as the Queen of Night. The work, pieced together from car parts and iron waste, carries a typically 20th-century pathos-free worldview, the constituent elements also preserving their original character.

I. D.

István Harasztÿ
(1934)
Brain Cannon
1980–1981
Steel, bronze, copper and brass, plexi
230 × 250 × 70 cm
Inv. no.: MM.89.165

There are several Hungarians among the pioneers of kinetic sculpture, yet Harasztÿ did not follow in their wake. His course was determined by his creative attitude to contraptions already obvious in his childhood. Harasztÿ's mobiles do not reflect the realm of technology or the relationship between man and machine. True, his objects are run by the laws of mechanics and electronics, but this is only the foundation, the starting point from which the whole structure produces paradoxes of existential situations. Brain Cannon of 1980–1981 presents the absurd play of the political career stories of the that-time social system. The balls standing for functionaries are arranged in a hierarchy by size. The course they can cover is intricate but predetermined by the structure.

I. D.

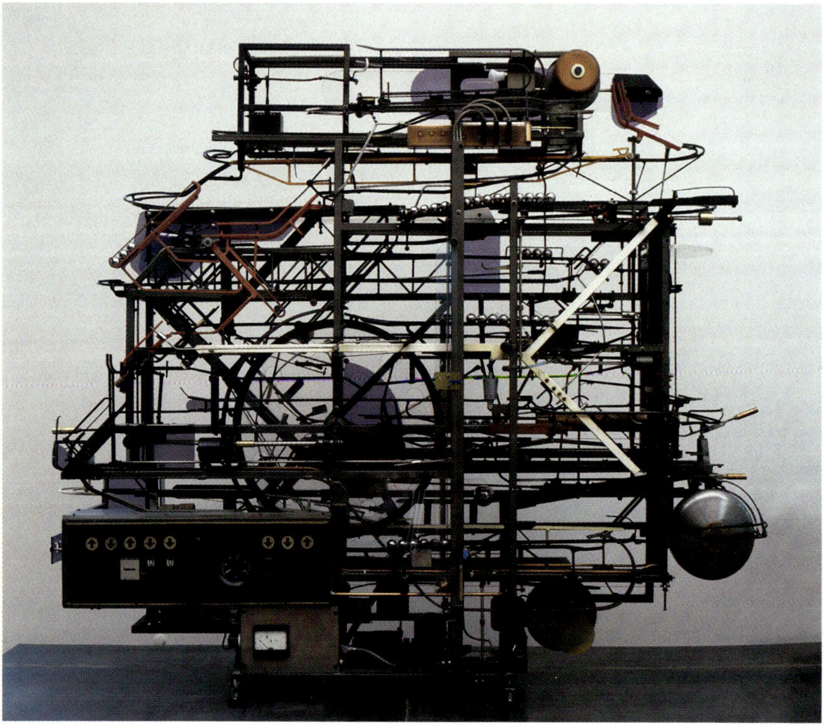

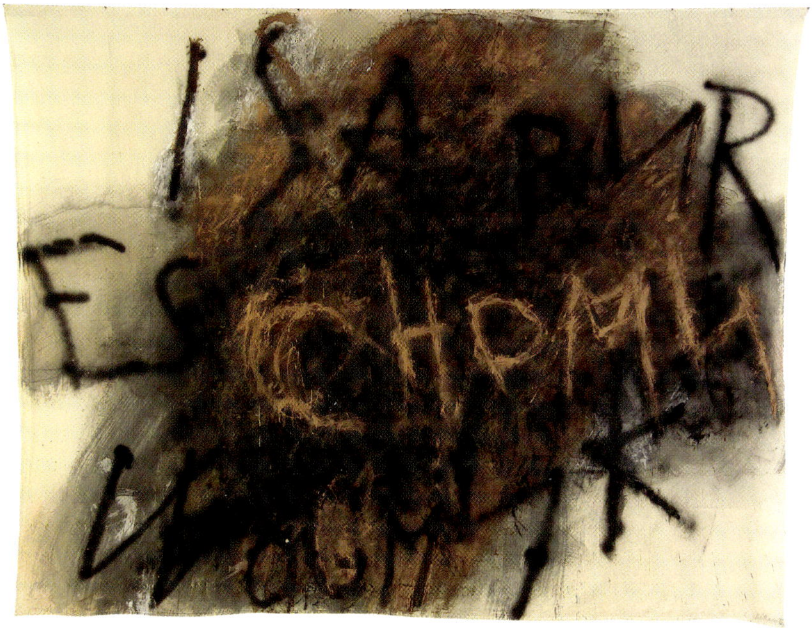

László Lakner

(1936)

Untitled

1981–1982

Acrylic and car varnish on canvas

232 × 316 cm

Inv. no.: MM.84.194

Lakner earned a name in the sixties with his pop art pictures. In the '70s he was attracted by hyperrealism, but he also made conceptual works. From the middle of the decade when he moved to West Berlin he took particular interest in written documents. During his study trip to New York in 1980 he got acquainted with the new tendencies of American painting and allowing more room for gestures he progressed towards expressionism, also influenced by graffiti. The work Untitled submitted for the exhibition "Homage to the Motherland" of Hungarian artists living abroad held in Műcsarnok (Palace of Art) in Budapest in 1982 was created by using the second line of the earliest Hungarian written text, the Funeral Oration (1192–1195). The lines, the black and bronze letters of which emerge from a tortured plane also weigh down on the spectator as a personal confession in addition to generating complex conceptual associations.

I. D.

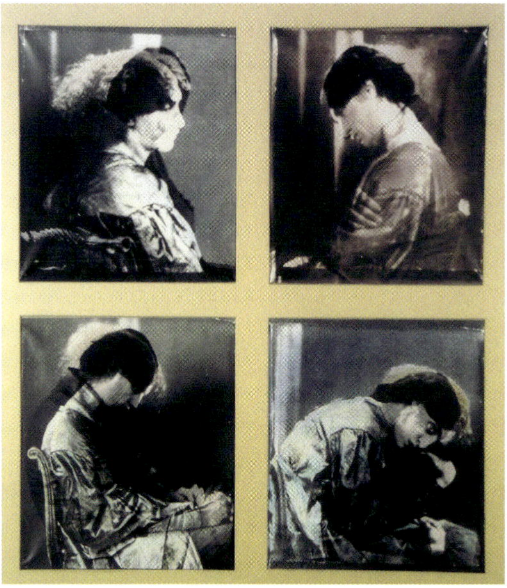

András Baranyay

(1938)

Self-portrait with Jane Morris I–IV

1982

Browned, coloured photo, paper

305 × 265 mm

Inv. no.:

Baranyay is one of the "neo-avant-garde" artists debuting in the exhibitions at the turn of the 1960s–1970s, a member of the so-called Iparterv generation. From the early '70s his oeuvre is predominated by photo-based works, and, importantly, by figurativity expressed in "classic genres" such as still-lifes, portraits. His portraits—most often of himself—show faces crabbed, developed or exposed one on top of the other, uncovered or hatched, "hiding" with the back to the spectator of sleeping. Jane Morris (1839–1914)—a pre-Raphaelite icon—was the "discovery" and model of Dante Gabriel Rossetti (1828–1882) and the wife and muse of painter, as well as poet, writer, designer and architect William Morris (1834–1896). She was photographed by John R. Parsons around 1865 in different poses as instructed by Rossetti. She was the protagonist of a strange and intense relationship of friend, lover, wife and model. The story was over a hundred years old when Baranyay stretched the circle in time and space: developing four photos of Jane Morris taken in a book onto his self-portrait quartet. Technical manipulation was followed by further—chemical and manual—manipulation: the discolouring of the photo and "redrawing" it in colour pencil. In the "end product" reminiscent of medium photos and aura pictures the simultaneous—or at least parallel—moments of two distant events are "montaged" into one, resulting in "contacting", in the confession of an attraction, an emotional "liaison" spanning ages.

L. Sz.

Imre Bukta

(1952)

Free Spraying at Dawn

1985

Wood, metal, plastic, painted installation

240 × 400 × 80 cm

Inv. no.: MM.91.24

In the 1970s avant-garde art took the last steps towards total freedom. It ensured shifts among the different media, abolished the rigid structure of genres, strove for unlimited use of tools and destroyed the borderline between art and non-art. For Imre Bukta this was a self-evident condition and he translated this experience in a creative manner. In his "agro art" works—including Free Spraying at Dawn (1985)—he reflected on the new value order of rural life built from banalities. His actions and installations using trivial materials (manure, waste, a thrown-away rusty hoe) are moments of a grotesque ritual of an ironic approach.

I. D.

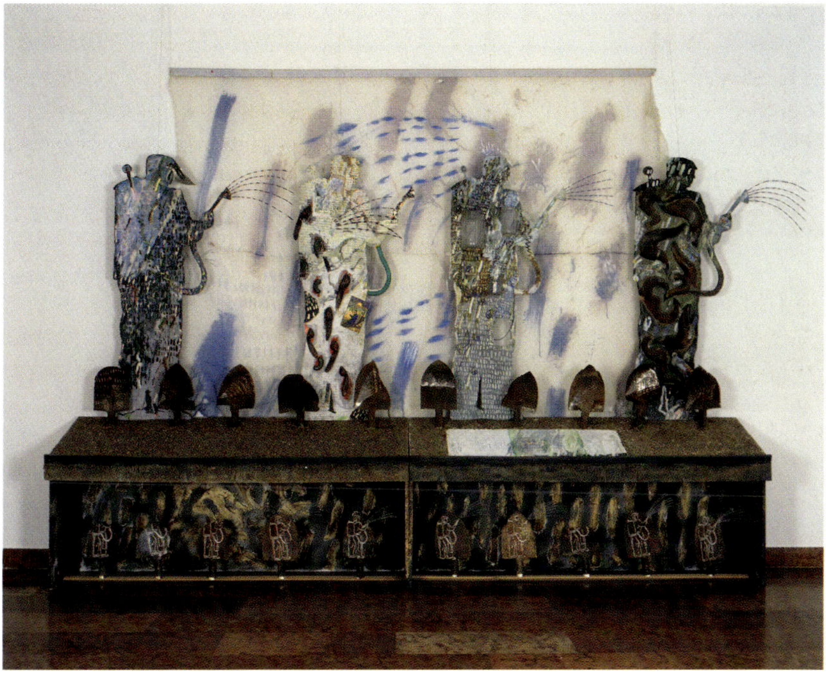

Miklós Erdély
(1928–1986)
√-1 (Square Root of Minus One)
1985
Oil, colour pencil on canvas, 147 × 195 cm
Inv. no.: MM.86.123

Miklós Erdély was the central figure of Hungarian neo-avant-garde who ensured his intellectual autonomy by keeping his status and circle of activities in constant motion and repeatedly questioning them. His integrative ability also manifest in a cross-tendencies approach (concept, minimal, fluxus, happening, etc.) generated the revision of established ways of expression and the opening of new lanes of association. Erdély's last great turn of direction, his painting "period" started at the turn of the 1970s and 1980s, reshuffled and reinterpreted his earlier activity and the spiritual-cultural context inspiring it. The conventional notions and symbols of philosophy, religion, mathematics, etc. appear as visual elements mobilizing painterly effects. √-1 is the enigmatic and emblematic key work of the period, the momentary diagnosis of our "world and fate". The main theme is Erdély's oft painted "identification mark" which—removed from reality—hoists the spectator beyond the original field of interpretation. The "signs", motifs sown amidst the painterly surfaces that are not "exact" in the least attract new semantic fields, becoming symbols of emotional relations and existential situations as a result of the "operations" applied as the compositional tool. This is illustrated by the negative gesture of turning it upside down and the qualifying gesture of endowing it with the minus sign, as well as by the confrontation with the mirror image or with absence. The oscillation of different meanings that mutually cancel out each other, their "communication" requires the active participation of the spectator: stepping back the eye corrects what needs correcting, stepping close, memory, fancy and the emotions eliminate the flaws.

L. Sz.

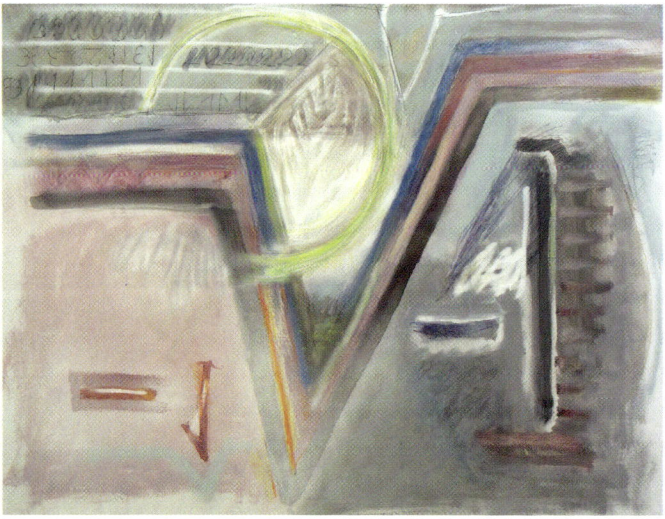

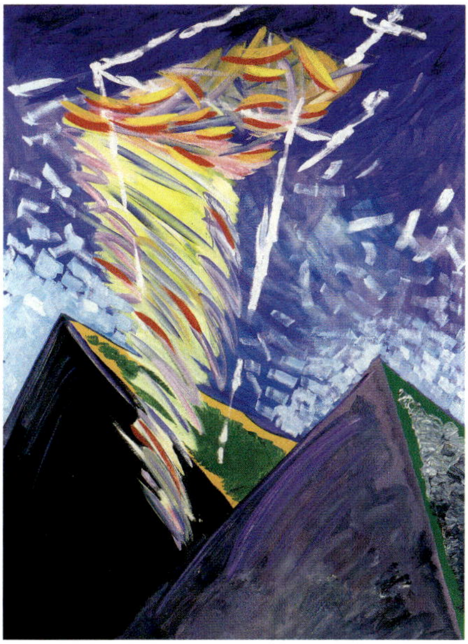

István Nádler
(1938)
Hommage à Malevics, July 7, 1985
1985
Oil on canvas, 201 × 149 cm
Inv. no.: MM.86.43

"Malevich belongs among the artists for whom the spirituality of geometry conveyed the complexity of knowledge. His art proceeded from the model to geometry and from there to a reinterpreted representation. He gathered the extremities of his abilities and created order in them," István Nádler said about his artist example. Malevich indeed decisively influenced Nádler's career; he has defined points of contact in their respective fates, but what has attracted him most was the sensitivity with which Malevich formulated his geometry. In his seven-piece series Hommage à Malevich he describes the process by which Malevich arrived from representation to abstract formulation. The first piece is filled with an atmospheric, sensitive landscape, in it appears the idea and then, resolute as it is, the ordering triangle claims its place in space. A system of relations evolves and harmony is created between the resultant space and the form. In the piece painted on July 7th the cubistic character is enhanced, light has an important role, and the idea, though present, is in the background. The form detaches itself from the symbolic sign; geometry and the painterly approach exist side by side in some relaxed state. In the rest of the series the geometric intention is stronger, the triangles become interrelated, light shapes the composition more powerfully and finally the white transcendental space appears. Nádler "re-creates the Malevichian form in a painterly manner, turning the transcendental signs of universal entity and abstract equilibrium radically personal and dramatic," Lóránd Hegyi writes. "This picture is about me, this form is my form," the painter sums up the personal inclination of his work.

M. K.

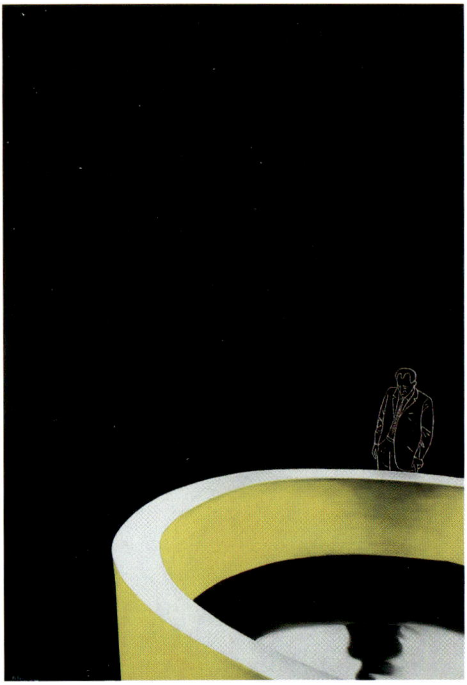

Fehér László

(1953)

Looking into the Well

1988

Oil on canvas, 250 × 180 cm

Inv. no.: MM.90.26

In László Fehér's oeuvre periods abounding in colour alternate with colour reduction. At the beginning of his career in the mid-1970s he debuted with photorealistic works—themselves a sort of social criticism—before his palette acquired colours and he painted pictures on themes determined by his family and religious affinities at first objectively and later more emotionally and expressively. 1988 marks a turn: his colour realm was reduced to three colours: yellow, black and white, his pictures featuring a single figure each, usually drawn with white outlines only. "I know I was in for something new and I could say more with these two colours, black and yellow, than with a lot of colours," he said about this period of a few years the products of which—rooted in the childhood and growing out of the family and private mythology but addressing universal existential problems—scored great international success at the Venice Biennale of 1990. Looking into the Well is among the first works of this period. The lonely transparent figure marked by the outline is dwarfed next to the yellow well-curb, almost lost in the enormous dark background. Like a frozen moment the composition alludes to the transiency of our presence in the relative eternity of the material and natural world. He also suggests the tense restlessness of the age (1988), the fear of the unexpected, the unknown, the incalculability of the future.

Zs. J.

Attila Mata
(1953)
Desire
1987
Wood, paint, 120 × 90 × 80 cm
Inv. no.: MM.88.62

From the mid-1980s to the second half of the '90s, Attila Mata, a member of the middle-generation of sculptors, focussed on stained-painted figural wooden sculptures. The treatment of colour, intimacy and degree of emotional charge, as well as the technique of free and self-governed use of tradition relate his works to the art concept of the new wave of painting in the '80s, new sensibility. His sculptures modelled with the chain saw do not hide the history of their assembling: the traces of jointing, fitting, additions enhace the brutal sensuality of the scabrous, splintery, rough surface. Colouring opens new spaces on the surface of the sculpture, or as contours it emphasizes, encloses some forms. The main asset of Mata's sculpture is the mutually complementary duality of deliberation and intuition: his emotion-laden constructions have an inner logic organized by emotions but capable of controlling the form. Desire is an excellent example: despite its wobbliness, twisted and anti-symmetrical character it is stability at its best. It is a body deconstructed by desire, a dissembled expressive body mass falling to cubistic forms: desire totem that instead of a single main view only has main views. The female figure "bounded" by red and dark lilac edge contours constructed in unity with the base is bent to form a bridge by two contrary motions. The endpoints are the sensuous mouth with smeared lipstick in the mask-like head turned back and at the opposite end the equally characteristic source of delight, the red gate of female genitals between the parting legs.

L. Sz.

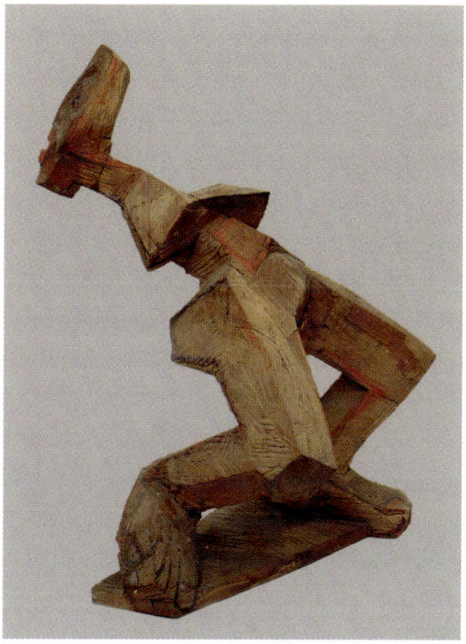

Gábor Roskó
(1958)
Let's See What's the News in the World
1989
Oil and acrylic on plywood, 153 × 153 cm
Inv. no.: MM.91.171

Gábor Roskó graduated from the Academy of Fine Arts as a graphic artist in 1980 but the boundaries of media do not hold him back: he is at home in painting and sculpture as well. His career began in the early '80s when Hungarian art was past the phase of its unfolding in the 1960s, past neo-avant-garde and various new tendencies of novel approach to objects. Roskó developed his peculiar, individual language on this foundation. He was attracted to Miklós Erdély's circle and the Indigó group led by him, but he did not belong to them. His art, independent of fashion, rejects labelling. Let's See What's New in the World was painted in 1989. As regards the technical solution, he reached back to Hungarian post-impressionist painting, the traditions of the Gresham circle. However, he populates this traditional realm of painting with strange figures and objects. Antropomorphic animals, objects with quite different functions from their original roles surround man who may be interpreted as the starting point or guiding principle in this enigmatic iconography. Roskó's creatures born of his singular mythology hold a distorting mirror to us, explosing our stumblings and mistakes. The paintings he created in that period are ironic stories, moral tales similar to Aesop's fables, gently mocking the "eternal human" without spoon-feeding the spectator.

Zs. J.

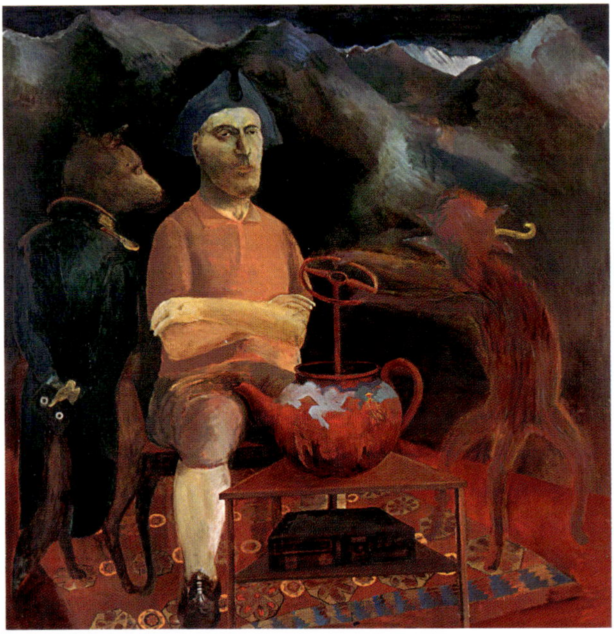

János Lóránt
(1938)
Butchers
1989
Oil on veneer, 148 × 151.5 cm
Inv. no.: MM.89.168

The artist has a highly singular tone. His formal idiom and painterly tools developed in the '60s when he moved to Salgótarján. He took an interest in the living conditions and work of miners. His pictures are laconic representations of run-down people with a hard life behind them, the landscape also contributing to the suggestion of intimate moments. His artistic approach resembles the realistic outlook of the then flourishing Vásárhely School centred around the artists' colony in Hódmezővásárhely, but his suggestive tools of expression also mark him off from it. His different periods are built upon one another, his visionary painting is always figural, concentrating on man and his activity, as well as his surroudings, but he conveys his message using the tools of abstraction. His Butchers was painted at the end of the 1980s. The tone is ironic, which is also confirmed by the syrupy colouring contradicting the theme. The picture is narrative like a genre-piece, the modelling of the markedly sketchy figures adopts the realistic manner of picture creation but the whole scene appears to take place in a surrealist space, in time out of joint, closer to the general, to the eternally human than to given reality. His typical block-like figures radiate a keen sense of character.

Zs. J.

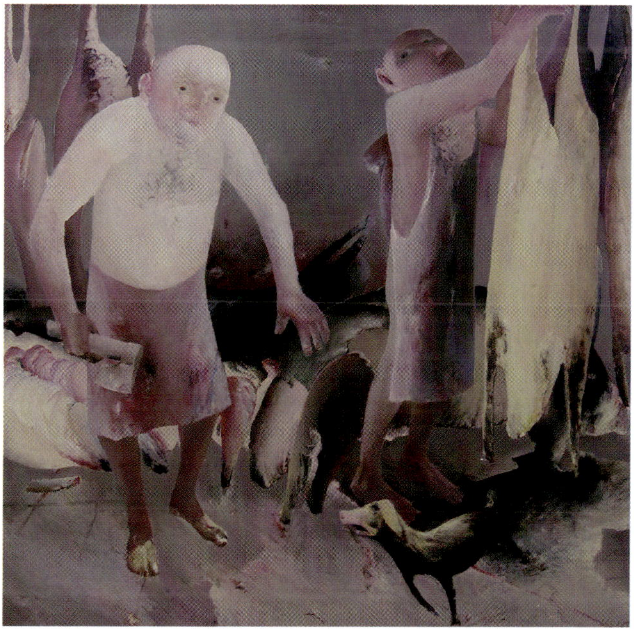

Péter Gémes

(1951–1996)

Predellum

1989

Photo, canvas, 100 × 240 cm

Inv. no.: MM.91.102

Péter Gémes used photography as a mediating agent, artificially creating pictures that he used as the bases which he further shaped by developing negative upon negative and staining them. The white scratches or grains often appearing in the pictures suggest planarity, providing the artist with the possibility of creating a painterly surface. He made long exposures, thus light dissolved the sharp outlines, bringing about apparently timeless blurred forms. Another painterly tool is the negative image, since the theme was far more important to him than the tiny details. He showed the layers with the visible edges of the celluloid. This together with the indication of perforation informs of the montage technique and allows a glimpse of the creative process.

This large work of 1989 alludes to the lower part of Gothic altarpieces, the praedella. In the elongated horizontal picture field the dead Christ was often depicted. Here the artist himself is lying on the bier—but his figure is bald and naked, that is, ageless and timeless. The evergreen plant meandering all along the body, the circle motif painted with light and the sign of the infinite refer to the immortality of the soul and to redemption. The model of the Greek galley on the central negative is the symbol of Charon's boat and indicates a turn in destiny, passage, the beginning of something new. As Zsolt Petrányi puts it: "Predellum is the artist's self-portrait, interpreting the mystery of acquiescence in death with a pictorial metaphor of shocking force."

M. K.

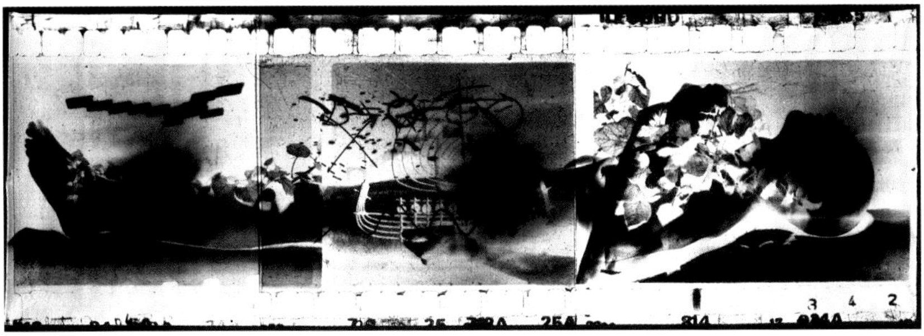

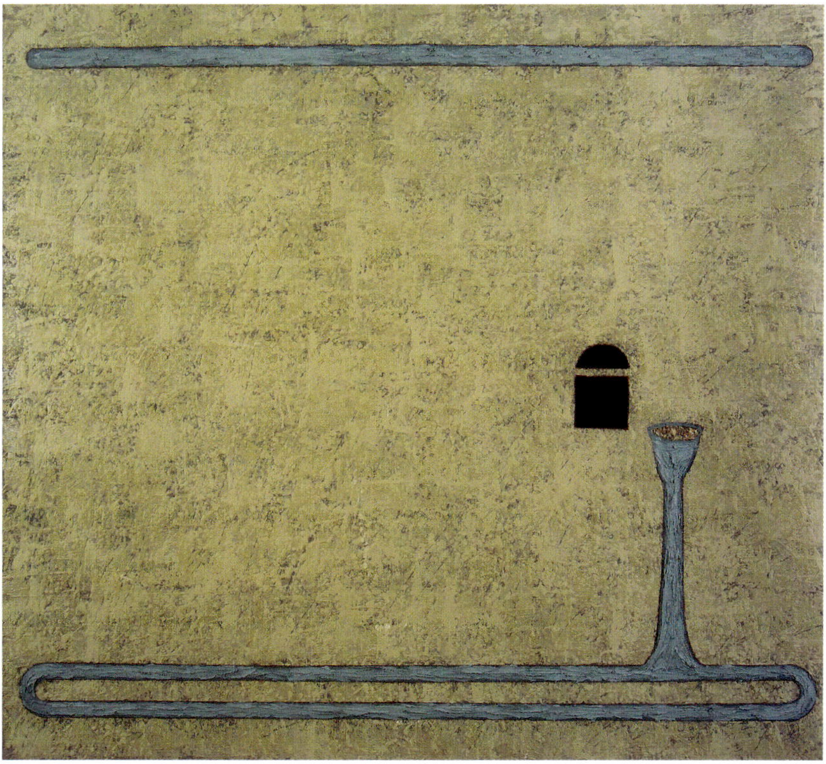

László Mulasics
(1954–2001)
In the Shade of Swords
1990
Oil on canvas, encaustic, 140 × 160 cm
Inv. no.: MM.93.50

Mulasics quickly rose to the vanguard of art. He was still a student when his monumental works of a dramatic tone were selected for the Eclecticism exhibition of Hungarian trans-avant-garde in 1985 and the curator Lóránd Hegyi regarded him as the most dynamic representative of new painting. From that year on he took part in the New Sensibility exhibitions monitoring the changes in Hungarian art of the '80s. At that time he still painted figural compositions with broad expressive gestures. By the end of the decade his art gradually changed, his figures disappeared and the picture surface became richly textured. His expressivity gave way to a meditative way of painting called "lyrical geometry" by János Frank. In the Shade of Swords painted in 1990 represents this type. He achieved the richness of the surface by reviving an ancient wax technique, encaustic, used by the Romans. The aim of the painter is to produce a perfect sight, that is, harmony. The motifs are apparently devoid of hidden messages beside the solemnity of the surface radiating timelessness.

Zs. J.

András Wahorn

(1953)

Running Boy with a Woman

1990

Oil on canvas, 160 × 200 cm

Inv. no.: MM.91.111

From 1972 to 1975 András Wahorn was active as a founding member of the Lajos Vajda Studio which promoted amateur artists in Szentendre. It was an alternative artistic association of self-taught artists which incorporated new impulses in addition to the Vajdaesque constructive surrealist tendencies up to the early '90s. Wahorn did not pursue academic studies of art but was active in various branches. He played music in the famous A. E. Bizottság (Albert Einstein Committee) band in the '80s, he took part in several actions and performances and achieved great successes as a film-maker. His early works were mainly drawings, but he used different ephemeral materials in his compositions, too. Running Boy with a Woman is a main work of the '90s. The theme—similarly to many other of his works—is the man–woman relationship without taboos, exposed with drastic forms and glaring colours. The provocative tone of his works is the concomitant to his flair for teasing the "decent" citizens or rather, the "comrades". "In my latest works the forms are utterly simplified... I draw a man and a woman, and that's all. With simple lines like graffiti or children's drawings... The only important point is to have it imply an unambiguous message," he commented on his paintings in the early '90s.

Zs. J.

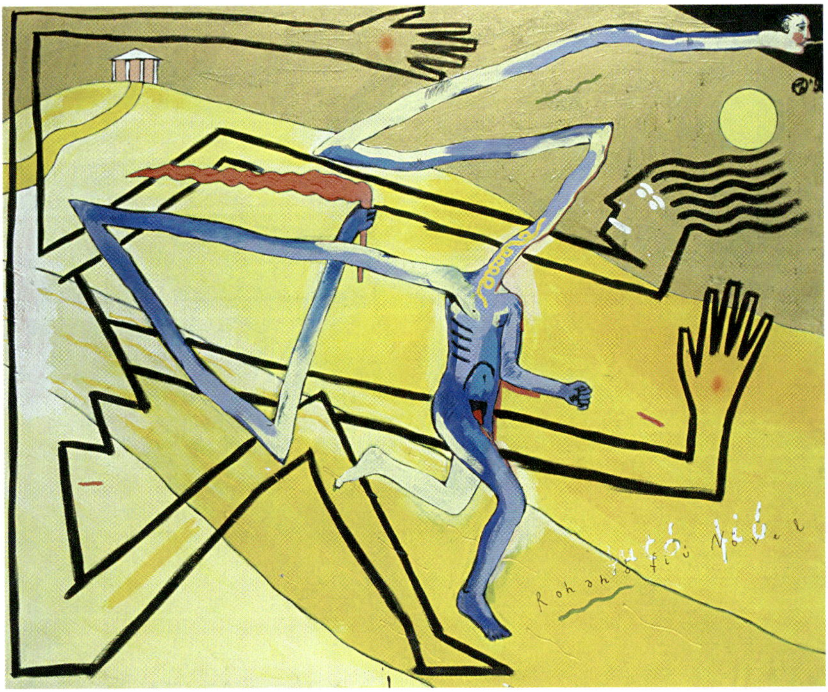

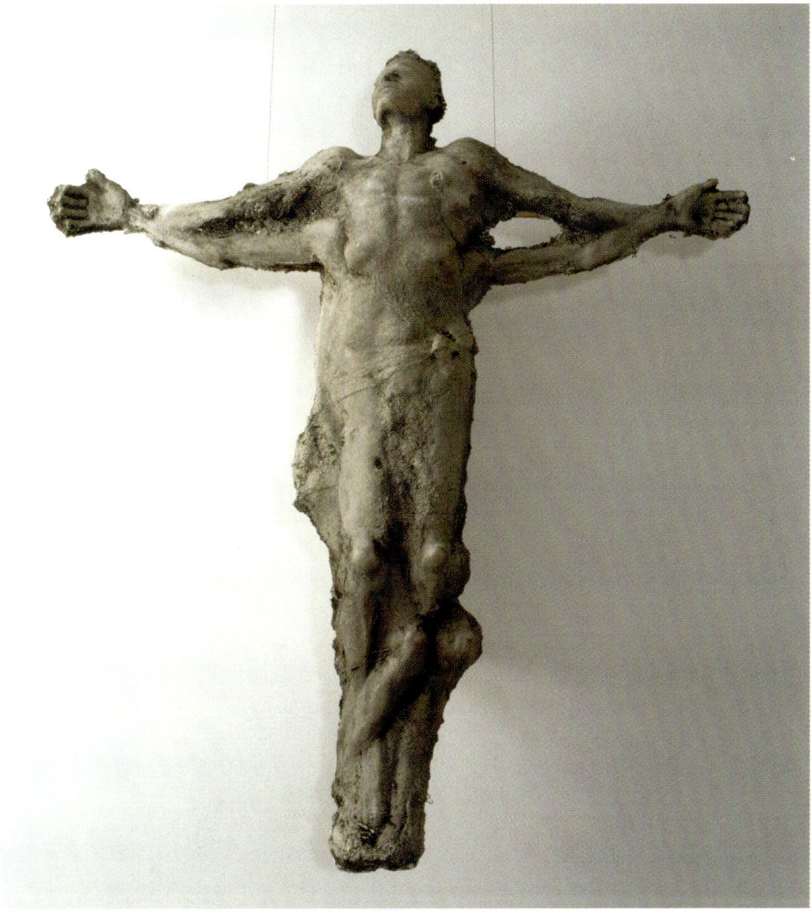

Zoltán Érmezei

(1955–1991)

Double Corpus

1990

Plaster, 200 cm

Inv. no.: MM.91.138

In line with the ideas of the conceptual range of radical avant-garde, Zoltán Érmezei formulated his art at a level where "life turned art... [and] where art was experienced as life". The consistency of work taught Érmezei that under the conditions of the merciless reality of being threatened in his personal physical existence by his illness, he could sublimate his experiences into art. With a ritual sequence of acts he repeated the pose of the crucified Christ. The meaning of the gesture was the adoption of Christ's example. Double Corpus is its documentation. The plaster cast of his own body fixed two phases of the happening which was no longer only personal: the work radiates the acceptance of the essence of human existence: action and passion, activity and suffering.

I. D.

Gábor Erdélyi

(1970)

Stream

1998

Oil and varnish on canvas, gabardine and silk, 137.5 × 238.5 cm

Inv. no.: MM.99.48

Erdélyi's pictures deliberately balanced on the verge of figurativity and abstraction with a reduced set of forms and colours are manifestations of a sophisticated and emotionally charged "sight painting" despite the seeming lack of a personal touch. His "sensual conceptualism" is characterized by the consistent mental and formal analysis of the painting as a pictorial object. What is a picture? What is a painting? What is the minimal gesture, shift in the picture surface that gives something extra to the apparently self-evident process of seeing? The motifs, ambiguous forms resembling optical delusions confuse and excite the eye, expanding the circle of possible associations. The painting also shown in the Hungarian pavilion at the 48th Venice Biennale is one of the synthesizing works of the late '90s. These pictures usually consist of the canvas with the—mostly—painted basic form as well as superposed translucent silk or satin layers also carrying "partial elements" of the composition, and the relaxed manner of painting is coupled with soft broken colours. In the case of Stream, reading the layers together produces "the" picture: the vertical stripes of the bottom canvas starting from the upper and lower picture edges "regulate" or enclose the chain of varnish spots in the top silk layer, snatching at the yellowish-green wave line undulating from one edge to the other on a broken olive green ground. The third "neutral" and homogeneous silk layer inserted between the pictorial elements "distributed"over the two mentioned layers further expands, deepens the space of the picture.

L. Sz.

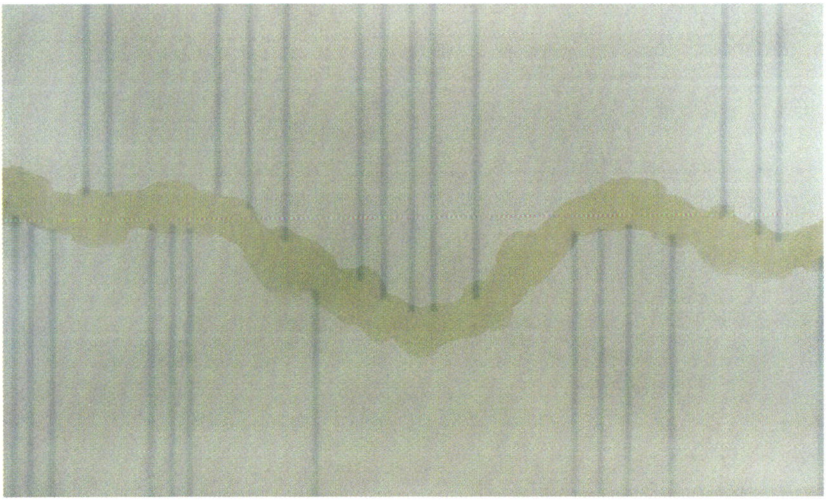

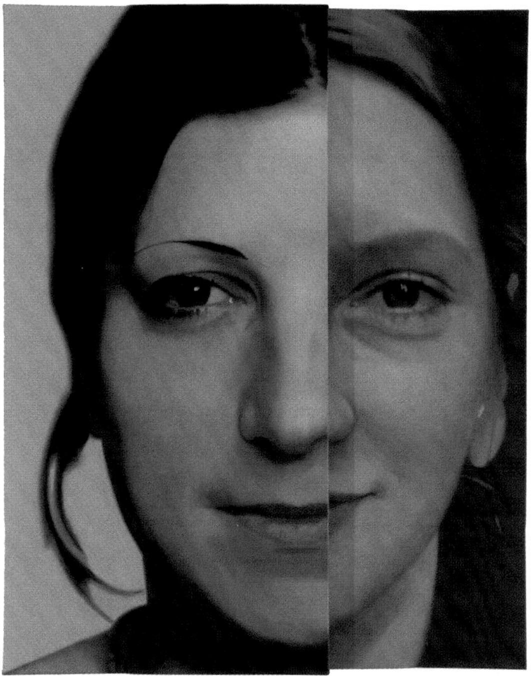

Ákos Birkás

(1941)

OT (3.9P-S) (Untitled)

1999

Oil on canvas, A: 179.8 × 90.1 cm, B:180.2 × 110.2 cm

Inv. no.: MM.2002.1

Birkás was intrigued by the portrait from the beginning: in the mid-'60s he started his career with expressive, at times grotesque portraits. In the '70s he did not remain intact from the influence of hyperrealism, just like the rest of Hungarian art. However, the face and the portrait played an important role in his art in those years as well. Since the 1980s his works have been built on a single basic motif, the oval or ellipse. His series of heads reached almost sacral depths in the simplification of form and colour scheme: he wished to convey an "image of universal man beyond personality". In the 1990s the anonymous heads gradually acquired distinct, realistic faces painted in light tones—two half-faces belonging to two different persons. OT (3.9P-S) – Untitled of 1999 belongs to the latter series. "The point is not so much to create one face from two different halves but to show a different person behind one of them. ... The question is where is the limit to our perception when we begin to see two different halves as one face ... What is important for me in this construction is that the break-line between the two halves cannot be eliminated, and so something remains wrong all the time, the tension cannot be relaxed. Something remains open," he wrote about his new portraits in 2001.

Zs. J.

Attila Szűcs
(1967)
Red Blindspot
1999
Oil on canvas, 120 × 150 cm
Inv. no.: MM.99.18

Attila Szűcs became a decisive figure in contemporary Hungarian painting by the end of the 1990s. In his works he leads "astray" the glance "trusting" in the classic genres (interior, landscape, genre-scene) by jolting the spectator out of the customary processes of picture creation and interpretation. He usually "recycles" elements of found photos, picture post-cards. The borrowed familiar places, situations torn from their time and setting generate moods and emotions. Szűcs appeals to imagination to fill the void created by the lack of causal connections: that is served by his "intentional lapses", the forms and formations in ambiguous and unusual positions. Such a formation is the red (blind) spot, which generates new paths of interpretation between the pictorial elements in ambiguous relationship with each other, while it exposes, in line with its physiological function. What is this floating red spot with its edge finished with the brush? A UFO? The mouth of a worm hole? Where did the two female figures come into this glacier tour of a strange atmosphere? The scale of the figures in the icy and snowy yet soft and gentle landscape resembling a model-train terrain covered with draperies is "just" a bit larger than expected so as to turn their status in the picture uncertain. They create a hazy aura around themselves and the reflexions of the hovering red spot add hues to their figures only. The light-and-shade relations are also problematic: neither the spot nor the figures cast shadows, which enhaces the feeling that they are "cast" into the picture. The peculiar, almost surrealistic mood of the painting mixes disillusion and melancholy—a blood-stain on the retina of the late 20th century.

L. Sz.

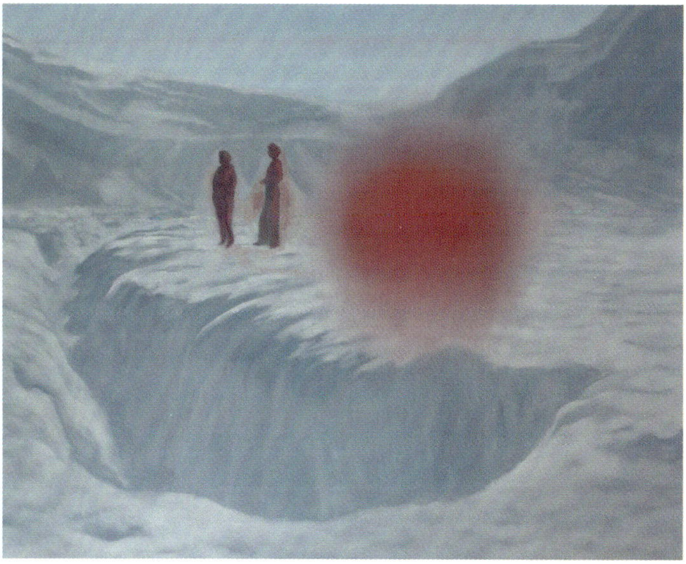

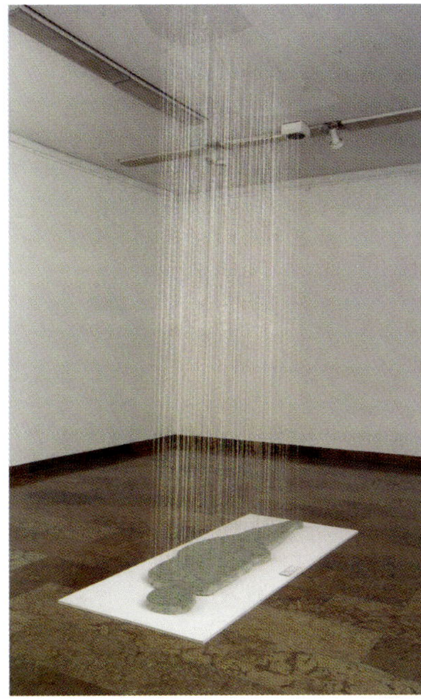

Mariann Imre
(1968)
Saint Cecilia
1997–2000
Concrete, thread, plastic, installation
Plexi: 0.5 × 200.5 × 80 cm,
sculpture: 5.5 × 108.5 × 60 cm
Inv. no.: MM.2000.15

A summary both of the post-conceptual wave culminating in the second half of the 1990s and of Mariann Imre's work so far, Saint Cecilia is an empathic, lyrical and emotionally surcharged reinterpretation of Stefano Maderno's (1576–1636) marble statue of the same title (1599, Rome, S. Cecilia in Trastevere): a memorial place modernized and "re-consecrated" by visualizing the psychological and celestial lines of forces, connections. The lower part is an "embroidered" concrete floor sculpture which unites the "characteristics" and "functions" of a gravestone set in the floor, a grave mound overgrown with grass and a carpet. The pattern spreading over the surface imitates organic ornaments: leaves are growing from the ramifying green tendrils. White threads are tied to the stitches of the "vegetation" and they connect the concrete silhouette of the model sculpture to its almost two-dimensional projection made of translucent plastic hovering under the ceiling. "The transparent structure" of the threads creates contact between the earthly and the heavenly spheres by creating a peculiar hybrid of the floor sculpture and the hanging piece. The knottings of the threads make out a third form, a spirit floating towards the transcendental world in the middle, at the height of the specatator. The contradictory characters of the applied everyday materials is metaphorically "charged" by subtle sensuality resolving the ambivalences, and by the power of the intimacy of "fiddling work" also associated with female roles.

L. Sz.

Index of Artists' Names

Aba-Novák, Vilmos 164
Alexy, Károly 66
Altorjai, Sándor 182
Ámos, Imre 167

Bak, Imre 185
Bálint, Endre 177
Barabás, Miklós 62, 70
Baranyay, András 202
Benczúr, Gyula 84, 104
Berény, Róbert 118, 153
Bernáth, Aurél 152
Birkás, Ákos 215
Bogdány, Jakab 41
Bokros Birman, Dezső 148
Borbereki Kovács, Zoltán 166
Borsos, József 65
Bortnyik, Sándor 151, 155
Brocky, Károly 68
Brodszky, Sándor 81
Bukta, Imre 203

Canzi, Ágost 72
Czigány, Dezső 124
Czóbel, Béla 119

Csernus, Tibor 178
Csók, István 95
Csontváry Kosztka Tivadar, 114, 116, 122

Dalmata, Giovanni 33
Deim, Pál 194
Derkovits, Gyula 142, 161
Donát, János 57
Donner, Georg Raphael 49
Dorffmaister, István 52
Dósa, Géza 80

Egry, József 159
Engel, József 89
Erdély, Miklós 204
Erdélyi, Gábor 214
Érmezei, Zoltán 213

Fadrusz, János 108
Faragó, Géza 127
Farkas, István 158
Fehér, László 206
Fényes, Adolf 117
Ferenczy, Béni 173
Ferenczy, István 58
Ferenczy, Károly 94, 111
Ferenczy, Noémi 146
Forray, Iván, count 63

Galimberti, Sándor 126
Gémes, Péter 210
Gulácsy, Lajos 109, 120

Gyarmathy, Tihamér 171

Hajas, Tibor 196
Harasztÿ, István 200
Hencze, Tamás 186
Hollósy, Simon 112

Imre, Mariann 217
Iványi Grünwald, Béla 113
Izsó, Miklós 76, 78

Jovánovics, György 183

Kádár, Béla 149
Kassák, Lajos 150
Kéri, Ádám 193
Kernstok, Károly 128
Keserü, Ilona 192
Kmetty, János 134
Kocsis, Imre 195
Kokas, Ignác 188

Kondor, Béla 179
Korniss, Dezső 175
Koszta, József 121
Kozina, Sándor 61
Körösfői-Kriesch, Aladár 132
Kövesházi Kalmár, Elza 162
Kracker, Johann Lucas 48

Lakner, László 201
Lesznai, Anna 133
Libay, Károly Lajos 69
Ligeti, Miklós 106, 110
Lóránt, János 209
Lossonczy, Tamás 176
Lotz, Károly 75, 102

Madarász, Viktor 71
Magyar-Mannheimer, Gusztáv 97
Mányoki, Ádám 42, 43
Márffy, Ödön 129
Markó, Károly the elder 59, 64, 67
Master M S 27
Mata, Attila 207
Mattis Teutsch, János 139
Maulbertsch, Franz Anton 44
Maurer, Dóra 191
Medgyessy, Ferenc 147
Mednyánszky, László 93, 96, 98, 135
Medveczky, Jenő 156
Méhes, László 189
Melegh, Gábor 60
Mészöly, Géza 87
Moholy-Nagy, László 141
Molnár, Farkas 145
Molnár, Sándor 187
Mulasics, László 211
Munkácsy, Mihály 83, 92

Nádler, István 205
Nagy, Sándor 130
Nemes Lampérth, József 137

Paál, László 79, 86
Patkó, Károly 157
Pátzay, Pál 163
Pauer, Gyula 197

Rippl-Rónai, József 99, 123
Róna, József 107
Roskó, Gábor 208

Samu, Géza 190
Schaár, Erzsébet 184
Schallhas, Karl Philipp 50
Scheiber, Hugó 160
Schletterer, Jakob Christoph 45
Stanetti, Dionysius Ignatius 47
Stock, Johann Martin 51
Straub, Philipp Jakob 46
Strobentz, Frigyes 125
Stróbl, Alajos 90, 101
Sustermans, Justus 37

Székely, Bertalan 73, 74, 85
Szinyei Merse, Pál 82, 88
Szobotka, Imre 136
Szőnyi, István 154
Szűcs, Attila 216

Thomas, Jan 38
Thorma, János 100
Tihanyi, Lajos 140, 144
Tót, Endre 180
Tóth, Menyhért 198

Uitz, Béla 143

Vajda, Lajos 165
Várnagy, Ildikó 199
Vaszary, János 105
Vedres, Márk 138
Vigh, Tamás 181
Vilt, Tibor 172, 174

Wahorn, András 212

Zala, György 91
Zanuoli, Ottavio 36
Zichy, Mihály 77
Ziffer, Sándor 131

Further Reading

The History of Art in Hungary

Radocsay, Dénes: Gothic Panel Painting in Hungary. Corvina, Budapest 1963.

Németh, Lajos: Modern Hungarian Art. Corvina, Budapest 1972.

Szabó, Júlia: Painting in Nineteenth Century Hungary. Corvina, Budapest 1988.

Barokk művészet Közép-Európában. Utak és találkozások / Baroque Art in Central Europe. Crossroads. Ed.: Galavics, Géza. Budapesti Történeti Múzeum, Budapest 1993.

Andrási, Gábor – Pataki, Gábor – Szücs, György – Zwickl, András: The History of Hungarian Art in the Twentieth Century. Corvina, Budapest 1999.

The Hungarian National Gallery and Its Collections

D. Fehér, Zsuzsa – Pogány, Ö. Gábor: Twentieth Century Hungarian Painting. A selection of paintings from the Hungarian National Gallery. Corvina, Budapest 1971.

Collections of the Hungarian National Gallery. Ed.: Solymár, István. Corvina, Budapest 1976.

The Hungarian National Gallery. The Old Collections. Ed.: Mojzer, Miklós. Corvina, Budapest 1984.

Hungarian Painting and Sculpture in the Nineteenth Century. Guide to the permanent exhibition at the Hungarian National Gallery. Ed.: Csorba, Géza. Budapest 1989.

The Hungarian National Gallery. Ed.: Szinyei Merse, Anna. Corvina, Budapest 1994.

The Collections of the Hungarian National Gallery. Eds.: Csorba, Géza – Szücs, György. Hungarian National Gallery, Budapest 2001.

Török, Gyöngyi: Gothic Panel Paintings and Wood Carvings in Hungary. Permanent Exhibition of the Hungarian National Gallery. Budapest 2005.

Modern magyar éremművészet I. 1896–1975 / Modern Hungarian Medals I. 1896–1975. From the collection of the Hungarian National Gallery. Compiled by L. Kovásznai, Viktória. Hungarian National Gallery, Budapest 1993.

Modern magyar éremművészet II. 1976–2000. / Modern Hungarian Medals II. 1976–2000. From the collection of the Hungarian National Gallery. Ed.: L. Kovásznai, Viktória. Hungarian National Gallery, Budapest 2004.

Exhibition Catalogues

Szinyei Merse Anna: Szinyei Merse Pál. [Pál Szinyei Merse] Magyar Nemzeti Galéria, Bp. 1990.

Hatvanas évek. Új törekvések a magyar képzőművészetben. [The Sixties. New Endeavours in Hungarian Art.] Ed.: Nagy, Ildikó. Képzőművészeti Kiadó – Magyar Nemzeti Galéria – Ludwig Múzeum, Budapest 1991. [with summary in English]

Id. Markó Károly (1791–1860). Written by Bajkay, Éva – Hessky, Orsolya – Szurcsikné Molnár, Erika. Magyar Nemzeti Galéria, Bp. 1991.

Pannonia Regia. Művészet a Dunántúlon 1000–1541. (Kunst und Architektur in Pannonien 1000–1541) Eds.: Mikó, Árpád – Takács, Imre. Magyar Nemzeti Galéria, Bp. 1994. [with summary in German]

Aranyérmek, ezüstkoszorúk. Művészkultusz és műpártolás Magyarországon a 19. században. (Goldmedaillen, Silberkränze. Künstlerkult und Mäzenatur im 19. Jahrhundert in Ungarn.) Ed.: Imre, Györgyi. Magyar Nemzeti Galéria, Bp. 1995. [with German translations]

Nagybánya művészete. Kiállítás a nagybányai művésztelep alapításának 100. évfordulója alkalmából (Die Kunst von Nagybánya. Ausstellung zur Hundertjahrfeier der Gründung der Künstlerkolonie von Nagybánya / The Art of Nagybánya. Centennial Exhibition in Commemoration of the Artists' Colony in Nagybánya.) Ed.: Imre, Györgyi. Hungarian National Gallery, Budapest 1996. [with summaries in English and German]

„Magnificat anima mea Dominum". M S mester Vizitáció-képe és egykori selmecbányai főoltára. (The Visitation by Master M S and His Former High Altar at Selmecbánya) Eds.: Mikó, Árpád – Poszler, Györgyi. Magyar Nemzeti Galéria, Bp. 1997. [with summaries in English]

Rippl-Rónai József gyűjteményes kiállítása (József Rippl-Rónai's Collected Works.) Eds.: Bernáth, Mária – Nagy, Ildikó. Hungarian National Gallery, Budapest 1998. [with summaries in English]

Modern magyar litográfia 1890–1930 (Modern Hungarian Lithography 1890–1930.) [Joint exhibition of the Hungarian National Gallery and the Miskolc Gallery] Ed.: Bajkay, Éva. Miskolci Galéria, Miskolc 1998. [with summary in English]

Székely Bertalan (1835–1910) kiállítása. (Exhibition of Bertalan Székely) Ed.: Nagy, Ildikó. Magyar Nemzeti Galéria, Bp. 1999. [with summaries in German]

Történelem–kép. Szemelvények múlt és művészet kapcsolatából Magyarországon. (Geschichte – Geschichtsbild. Die Beziehung von Vergangenheit und Kunst in Ungarn.) Eds.: Mikó, Árpád – Sinkó, Katalin. Magyar Nemzeti Galéria, Bp. 2000. [with summaries in German]

Árkádia tájain. Szőnyi István és köre 1918–1928 / In the Land of Arcadia. István Szőnyi and His Circle 1918–1928. Ed.: Zwickl, András. Magyar Nemzeti Galéria, Bp. 2001. [with English translations]

Mattis Teutsch and Der Blaue Reiter. [Joint exhibition of the Hungarian National Gallery, Haus der Kunst, München and MissionArt Gallery] MissionArt Gallery, Budapest – Miskolc 2001.

Zsákovics, Ferenc: A rézkarcoló nemzedék 1921–1929 (The Etching Generation 1921–1929) [Joint Exhibition of the Hungarian National Gallery and the Miskolc Gallery] Miskolci Galéria, Miskolc 2001. [with summary in English]

Jankovich Miklós (1772–1846) gyűjteményei [The Collections of Miklós Jankovich (1772–1846)] Ed.: Mikó, Árpád. Magyar Nemzeti Galéria, Budapest 2002.

Buzási, Enikő: Ádám Mányoki (1673–1757). Monographie und Œuvrekatalog. Ungarische Nationalgalerie, Budapest 2003.

Mednyánszky. Ed.: Markója, Csilla. Slovak National Gallery – Slovart Publishing Ltd., Bratislava 2004.

A modell. Női akt a 19. századi magyar művészetben / Female Nude Imagery in 19th-century Hungarian Art. Ed.: Imre, Györgyi. Magyar Nemzeti Galéria, Bp. 2004. [with English translations]

Modernizmusok. Európai grafika 1900–1930 / Modernismen. Graphik in Europa 1900–1930. Zeichnungen und Druckgraphik der Moderne aus der Graphischen Sammlungen der Staatsgalerie Stuttgart und der Ungarischen Nationalgalerie mit dem Beitrag der Graphischen Sammlung des Museums der Bildenden Künste in Budapest. Hrsg.: Bakos, Katalin – Róka, Enikő –Gauss, Ulrike. Ungarische Nationalgalerie – Staatsgalerie Stuttgart, s. l. 2004.

Munkácsy a nagyvilágban / Munkácsy in the World. Mihály Munkácsy's Works in Private and Public Collections at Home and Abroad. Ed.: Gosztonyi, Ferenc. Hungarian National Gallery – Szemimpex Kiadó, Budapest 2005.

A modern magyar fa- és linóleummetszés 1890–1950 [Modern Hungarian Wood- and Linocut]. [Joint exhibition of the Hungarian National Gallery and the Miskolc Gallery] Ed.: Róka, Enikő. Miskolci Galéria, Miskolc 2005.

Hungarian Fauves from Paris to Nagybánya 1904–1914. Eds.: Passuth, Krisztina – Szücs, György. Hungarian National Gallery, Budapest 2006.

Pre-press: HVG Press Kft.

Printed and bound by Alföldi Nyomda Zrt.
Responsible executive: director general Géza György